how the new apostolic reformation is
shaking up the church as we know it

This book belongs to the son of the King named Eric

churchquake!

C. PETERWAGNER

Regal

A Division of Gospel Light
Ventura, California, U.S.A.

Published by Regal Books
A Division of Gospel Light
Ventura, California, U.S.A.
Printed in U.S.A.

Cover Design by Kevin Keller
Interior Design by Carolyn Henderson
Edited by Virginia Woodard

Library of Congress Cataloging-in-Publication Data
Wagner, C. Peter.
    Churchquake!: the explosive dynamics of the new apostolic
revolution / C. Peter Wagner.
      p.   cm.
    ISBN 0-8307-1918-0 (pbk.)
    1. Independent churches—United States. 2. Church growth—United
States. 3. Independent churches. 4. Church growth. I. Title.
BR516.5.W34 1999
280—dc21
                                              98-53430
                                                CIP

2 3 4 5 6 7 8 9 10 11 12 13 14 15 / 05 04 03 02 01 00

Rights for publishing this book in other languages are contracted by Gospel Literature International (GLINT). GLINT also provides technical help for the adaptation, translation and publishing of Bible study resources and books in scores of languages worldwide. For further information, write to GLINT at P.O. Box 4060, Ontario, CA 91761-1003, U.S.A. You may also send e-mail to Glintint@aol.com, or visit their web site at www.glint.org

CONTENTS

CHAPTER ONE

The "Why" of New Wineskins

The greatest change in the way of doing church since the Protestant Reformation is taking place before our very eyes.

I have come to label this phenomenon the "New Apostolic Reformation" for reasons I will detail in the next chapter. However, I think it will be well to set forth as concise a definition of the New Apostolic Reformation as I can right at the outset. That way, readers will know up front exactly what we are discussing throughout the remainder of the book.

The New Apostolic Reformation is an extraordinary work of God at the close of the twentieth century, which is, to a significant extent, changing the shape of Protestant Christianity around the world. For almost 500 years Christian churches have largely functioned within traditional denominational structures of one kind or another. Particularly in the 1990s, but with roots going back for almost a century, new forms and operational procedures began to emerge in areas such as local church government, interchurch relationships, financing, evangelism, missions, prayer, leadership selection and training, the role of supernatural power, worship and other important aspects of church life. Some of these changes are being seen within denominations themselves, but for the most part they are taking the form of loosely structured apostolic networks. In virtually every region of the world, these new apostolic churches constitute the fastest growing segment of Christianity.

DYSFUNCTIONALISM IN THE PAST

A social activity or a social structure that begins to undermine the very social system in which it emerged is considered by behavioral and social scientists as dysfunctional. Books about cultural anthropology are replete with case studies of how the introduction of implements such as steel axes has caused radical disruption in whole societies. Or to bring it to more familiar turf, the books are yet to be written about how the introduction of the Internet is certain to change the fabric of our contemporary society.

The same thing has been happening to church structures. Structures that were originally developed to facilitate evangelism, Christian nurture, worship, social service and ministry in general are now considered by some as the *causes* of much inefficiency and ineffectiveness in these same areas. Dysfunctionalism has been setting in.

Among the first denominational leaders in the United States to observe and analyze this phenomenon is William M. Easum, whose ministry as senior pastor of Colonial Hills United Methodist Church in San Antonio, Texas, drew national attention because of its extraordinary membership growth and community outreach. Easum now directs a consultation firm called 21st Century Strategies, which regularly brings him in touch with large numbers of traditional churches across the spectrum. Two of his books, written to awaken traditional church leaders to the dysfunctionalism of many of their structures and activities, carry colorful titles: *Dancing with Dinosaurs* (Abingdon) and *Sacred Cows Make Gourmet Burgers* (Abingdon).

William Easum's dedication of *Dancing with Dinosaurs* is not only perceptive, but it is also rather touching. He dedicates the book as follows:

> *To the many faithful Christians*
> *who are wondering why ministries*
> *that once discipled people*
> *no longer work*

I say this is "touching" because many strong emotions are intertwined with what is happening in this contemporary change of the ways of doing church. The manners in which we relate to God and in which we encourage others to relate to God delve deeply into our inner persons. Most Christian leaders I know are indeed "faithful" in the sense that they love God and desire to please Him and obey Him in the best way possible. Those to whom Easum is writing, however, are increasingly frustrated and uncomfortable because they are realizing that what they have been trained to do is obviously not the best way possible to reach and minister to people in our day and age. Sadly, only a small percentage of them have the capacity to make the changes Easum and others are suggesting. The rest, in all probability, will not finish as well as they once had hoped they would.

EXPLOSIVE CHURCH GROWTH

For almost 30 years, I have carried the title "professor of church growth." I, therefore, became very interested when I began to realize that the new apostolic churches were the fastest growing group of churches on six continents. By saying this, I am not affirming they are the *largest* grouping of churches, although in some parts of the world, such as Africa, they undoubtedly are.

The fact is that it is difficult to count these churches, because they do not have a denominational headquarters to which they report annual statistics. Thus, statistical reports are not provided to editors of publications such as *The Yearbook of*

American and Canadian Churches (Abingdon). Some years ago, I undertook a research project to try to study the growth of independent charismatic churches in the United States, and I soon discovered that the word-of-mouth research trails I was uncovering were endless. John Vaughan of the International MegaChurch Research Center attempted a count of independent churches in general for *Churches and Church Membership in the United States: 1990*, and he discovered an estimate of 2 million adherents. Commenting on this, Kirk Hadaway and David Roozen assess the magnitude of what they consider to be Vaughan's *undercount*, and they estimate something between 3 and 3.5 million adherents in the United States.[1] I repeat, though, no one knows for sure.

My own observations lead me to conjecture that we have at least as many new apostolic congregations in the United States as Southern Baptist churches—around 40,000. I wouldn't be surprised if we actually discovered twice that many when all the facts become known. Therefore, I think it is not too far off to estimate 8 to 10 million adherents, more than double Hadaway and Roozen's estimate of some years ago, taking into consideration the high growth rate of the new apostolic movement.

The new apostolic growth is also reflected in the student enrollment at Fuller Theological Seminary, the interdenominational graduate school in which I have taught for more than a quarter of a century. For years, the denomination having the most students attend Fuller was the Presbyterian Church (U.S.A.). In 1994, however, that denomination was overtaken by students from new apostolic churches. From academic year 1994-1995 to academic year 1995-1996, the Presbyterian enrollment declined by 10 percent, whereas the new apostolic enrollment increased by 10 percent.

WHERE IS THE BLESSING OF GOD?

I first studied church growth under Donald McGavran, the father of the Church Growth Movement, back in 1967. He taught us that the best way to find out why some churches grow and some don't is to study growing churches. As I began to do that, I discovered that the essential methodology of church growth research can be boiled down to answering four crucial questions.

1. Why does the blessing of God rest where it does?
2. Because it is obvious that not all churches are equal, why is it that at certain times and in certain places some churches seem to be more blessed than others?
3. Can any pattern of divine blessing on churches be discerned?
4. If so, what are the salient characteristics of unusually blessed churches?

I am writing this book in an attempt to address these questions in our world today.

When I first began to apply this methodology 20 years ago, it was obvious that in Latin America, where I was working as a field missionary, the churches receiving the unusual blessing of God at that time were the Pentecostal churches. This was a bit embarrassing to me because I had gone on record as an anti-Pentecostal. Nevertheless, I swallowed my pride and began visiting and researching Pentecostal churches. I was amazed at what I found, and I reported it in my book *Look Out! The Pentecostals Are Coming!* (Creation House). Pentecostals led the way in worldwide church growth during the decades of the 1960s, 1970s and 1980s.

THREE SIGNIFICANT PHENOMENA

By the end of the 1980s, missiologists had begun to observe at least three interesting phenomena worldwide.

The first was the extraordinary growth of the African Independent Churches. This movement actually started soon after the turn of the century, when prominent African church leaders began to react strongly to what they perceived to be the cultural irrelevance of many forms and activities of the traditional mission churches. They began a process of radical contextualization, and the growth of African Independent Churches has far outstripped that of traditional Churches during our century. Granted, some of these churches are unacceptably syncretistic, but many are not.

There are now an estimated 16,000 independent *denominations* in South Africa alone, and many new denominations are initiated every day across the continent of Africa. It is largely because of the independent churches that Africa south of the Sahara is considerably more than 50 percent Christian today.

The second missiological phenomenon is the surprising emergence of the Chinese house churches, particularly since the end of the infamous Cultural Revolution in the 1970s. In spite of the often heavy hand of a Marxist government, outspokenly unfavorable to Christianity, China has been witnessing the most massive numbers of non-Christians voluntary turning to the Christian faith ever recorded in history. Estimates run up to 25,000 or 35,000 conversions a day. A figure of 100 million active Christians in China today is likely an undercount.

The third phenomenon is the mushrooming of what Mike Berg and Paul Pretiz call "Latin American grassroots churches."[2] Visit virtually any major metropolitan area in Latin America today and ask for the names of the largest, the second largest and the third largest churches of the city. You will generally find that at least two of them are pastored by individuals who had not been under the influence of a foreign missionary and who had not been trained either in mission schools in their own country or in seminaries or Bible schools abroad.

Awhile back, whenever I would visit a Latin American city, I would be greeted and hosted by foreign missionaries. This has no longer been the case for at least 15 years. The effective Christian leadership across the continent is now in the hands of culturally authentic Latin Americans who are leading the most significant churches and denominations.

As a professional missiologist, I was aware of these facts for some time, but they had not yet formed a pattern in my mind. I was also involved in researching the Pentecostal and charismatic churches in the United States for the *Dictionary of Pentecostal and Charismatic Movements* (Zondervan), and in that process I discovered that in our country the independent charismatic churches were the most rapidly growing segment of Christianity.

In 1993, a pattern of divine blessing (see question 3, in the previous list) began to be apparent to me. That was when I began my research on question 4, seeking to identify and describe the salient characteristics of what I began to call the New Apostolic Reformation.

TRADITIONAL DENOMINATIONS IN CRISIS

At the same time, the traditional denominations in the United States were in the midst of a crisis period. Almost as if in response to some unseen cue, Methodists, Lutherans, Episcopalians, Presbyterians and other "old-line" denominations (except for most Baptists) began losing members. The Episcopal Church, for example, dropped from 3.4 million in 1968 to 2.5 million in 1994. During that same time period, United Methodists decreased from 11.0 million to 8.6 million; Presbyterian Church (U.S.A.) from 4.2 million to 3.7 million; and United Church of Christ from 2.0 million to 1.5 million, just to name a few.

A Gallup survey showed that in 1974, old-line denominations included 51 percent of American adults, but that this number had dropped to 35 percent by 1994. At the same time, the "other Protestants" increased from 9 percent in 1974 to 24 percent in 1994.

The "other Protestants" include Pentecostals, but in the 1990s the growth rate of Pentecostals has also slowed down, although annual *losses* have not yet begun to appear as they have in the old-line denominations. Pentecostals topped the growth charts between 1950 and 1990, but no longer. For example, in the 1993-1995 Biennial Report of the Assemblies of God, General Secretary George Wood says, "The data indicate small growth in all our vital statistics."[3] The following are the recent decadal rates of the membership growth of the U.S. Assemblies of God:

- ◆ Decade of the 1970s — 65%
- ◆ Decade of the 1980s — 29%
- ◆ Decade of the 1990s — Projected as of 1996 at less than 5%[4]

Although Southern Baptists have continued to grow, the rate is not what it was in the 1960s and 1970s. Mark Shibley, a researcher, reports, "There is growing evidence that old-line evangelicals, like Southern Baptists, while still outperforming liberal Protestants in aggregate membership terms, are no longer the driving force behind the resurgence of born-again Christianity."[5] He sees the fastest growing churches within what he calls "new-style evangelicalism," of which he mentions the Vineyard as an example.

The National Association of Evangelicals, which rose to a position of considerable influence following Jimmy Carter's administration, represents the Assemblies of God as well as many of the other newer denominations. That influence, according to some observers, has now peaked and internal struggles are taking place.

I mention these facts because it could very well be that, in summary, the old-line denominations are losing their market share of the American public, so to speak. The newer denominations, including the Pentecostals, have flattened out; and an increasing share is being served, at least in part, by the heretofore semi-invisible New Apostolic Reformation.

WHAT ABOUT THE QUALITY?

Those who study and analyze church growth have had an ongoing discussion about the relationship between quantity and quality. Making a distinction between the two is legitimate, in my opinion. Rapid growth in churches can take place, of course, without ideal standards of godliness among the members. It is unrealistic, though, to separate the two as if they do not ordinarily go hand in hand. Some of the most vigorously growing churches have grown precisely because they are full of high-quality members. One study done by Win Arn quantified the level of love and care in each one of a significant sample of churches across denominational lines, and found that, by and large, the faster a church was growing the more love and care it exhibited.[6]

Almost invariably, when some attempt to polarize quantity and quality, arguing that large churches cannot also be high-quality churches, it turns out to be a thinly disguised cry of agony. For example, in 1995 Peter Jennings of the ABC television network did a television special about America's megachurches called "In the Name of God." One of the featured churches was Willow Creek Community Church in South Barrington, Illinois, pastored by Bill Hybels. An older mainline magazine, which does not need to be identified, ran an editorial criticizing the production.

The editor said, "As one who still hews to the traditional, I confess to some discomfort not just with Willow Creek but with the way the megachurch phenomenon has been picked up by secular journalists like Jennings, who argues that the churches he examines are the new 'mainstream' of American Christianity. To be honest, I feel not only discomfort but more than a little jealousy. Willow Creek gets lots of ink and airtime while old-style mainstream churches go about their business largely outside media scrutiny."

The editorial goes on to contrast the ministry of Bill Hybels and that of John Wesley. "Wesley," it argues, "didn't give his fol-

lowers what they wanted; he gave them what he felt command-
ed to preach." The implication: Wesley was much more faithful
to God than is Bill Hybels, and his churches were, therefore, of
a higher quality.

This attempt to polarize Wesley and Hybels says more about
the editorial writer than about either of those leaders. It is the
groan of a loser—the agony of defeat. In reality, Wesley and
Hybels were cut out of the same piece of cloth. John Wesley was
the Bill Hybels of his day. The coal miners in England got what
they wanted, namely, an answer to the meaning of life. That is
exactly what the members of Willow Creek get, and it is the
principal reason they come back week after week. In both cases,
the meaning of life is discovered in a personal, life-changing
relationship to Jesus Christ.

BRINGING IT ALL TOGETHER

Through the years, my most creative research has come in sea-
sons. The decade of the 1970s focused on the *technical* side of
church growth. I organized courses and wrote books about such
things as the vital signs of healthy churches, church pathology,
institutional factors, contextual factors, church planting, the
ministry of the Body through spiritual gifts and pastoral
leadership.

During the 1980s, my focus shifted to the *spiritual* side of
church growth, teaching courses and writing books about
power evangelism, divine healing, demonic deliverance and the
like. More recently, prayer and spiritual warfare have headed
my research agenda, including some new areas such as strate-
gic-level spiritual warfare, spiritual mapping, identificational
repentance and prayer evangelism.

Not long ago, after having completed 15 years of teaching
the book of Acts, I wrote a three-volume commentary on Acts.
The reason I wrote it was that I believed the classical commentaries on Acts were deficient in their understanding of power

ministries and missiology. This was serious in light of the consensus that Acts 1:8 provides the outline for the whole book: "You shall receive power when the Holy Spirit has come upon you; and you shall be witnesses to Me in Jerusalem, and in all Judea and Samaria, and to the end of the earth." The two components of this verse, and the whole book, are power ministries and missiology, carrying the gospel cross-culturally. My commentary highlights these two factors more than most commentaries do.

I have mentioned this background to say that as I have been studying the churches of the New Apostolic Reformation very carefully, I must confess they appear to be the nearest thing to applying the principles of the book of Acts I have yet seen in any grouping of churches. As a whole, they understand and apply both the technical aspects of church growth and the spiritual aspects of church growth in a remarkable way. Getting to know these churches in various parts of the world has excited me more than anything since beginning my research on the Pentecostals more than 30 years ago.

THE CONSTANT NEED FOR NEW WINESKINS

For 2,000 years, Jesus has been building His Church, just as He announced He would when He was here on earth (see Matt. 16:18). Through the ages, the Church has grown and expanded across the continents. Century after century, however, the Church grew in a variety of ways. It grew one way in New Testament times and another way in the Roman Empire before Constantine. It grew another way in the Roman Empire after Constantine, another way in the Middle Ages and another way at the time of the Protestant Reformation. Then it grew another way during the era of European colonization, another way in post-World War II and another way in our own times.

Church history could be sliced even thinner than that, and growth variables for each period could be enumerated. One of the constants, though, was that as each change appeared on the horizon of history, a new wineskin was required to contain the new wine of the Holy Spirit.

Jesus spoke of the subject of new wineskins when John the Baptist was having some trouble understanding the transition from the old, which he represented, to the new, which Jesus represented. Jesus said, "[People do not] put new wine into old wineskins, or else the wineskins break, the wine is spilled, and the wineskins are ruined. But they put new wine into new wineskins, and both are preserved" (Matt. 9:17).

This book is about one of those new wineskins God is providing for another crucial hinge of church history.

THE OLD WAGNER WINESKIN

I have been aware of this new wineskin for only five years. During my nearly 45 years of ordained ministry, however, I have developed considerable awareness of and involvement in the old wineskin. I served as a missionary to Bolivia for 16 years under two mission agencies that belong to the the the Interdenominational Foreign Missions Association (I.F.M.A.). This is an outspokenly noncharismatic association of traditionally oriented missions. My ordination is under the Conservative Congregational Christian Conference. We Congregationalists came over on the *Mayflower*!

The church I belonged to for more than a quarter of a century is Lake Avenue Congregational Church in Pasadena, California. It is a remarkable church—the only local church I know of that has celebrated its one-hundredth anniversary and that has grown during each one of the 10 decades of its history! Boasting 5,000 members, it is one of the largest churches in the nation, but it has been and still is very traditional. Even those who have been attending its contemporary service for more than five years seem reluctant to lift their hands over their shoulders during worship.

The Wagner Wineskin, so to speak, was formed, more than anything else, by Fuller Theological Seminary. I received a degree from Fuller in the 1950s, another degree in the 1960s, and I have taught on the faculty during the 1970s, the 1980s and the 1990s. Fuller Seminary is very traditional. It was founded in 1947 for the explicit purpose of serving the mainline denominations in the United States, and it has operated within that context ever since.

I say all this to make it clear that by highlighting these non-traditional churches in this book, at times using undisguised enthusiasm, I am not promoting my own cause. Like many who are reading this book, I am a novice in the things of the New Apostolic Reformation, and desire to learn all I can from this obvious contemporary moving of the hand of God.

LIVING ON THE THRESHOLD

We live in a threshold time of history. As I have said, this is the day of the most radical change in the way of doing church since the Protestant Reformation. Argentine Pablo Deiros, one of Latin America's foremost church historians, addresses the new apostolic phenomenon and says, "These churches, taken as a group, exhibit (especially in our decade) an extremely radical change within Latin American Protestant Christianity. In some aspects, these changes in the life and ministry of the Christian church are more significant than anything we have seen since the days of the Protestant Reformation."[7]

This is not only a radical change, but the change is also coming more rapidly than many think. We live in a time when both the *degree* of cultural changes, and the *rate* of cultural changes, are accelerating alarmingly. George Barna says, "There is a great deal of disagreement among sociologists, but they agree that change is happening faster today than ever before. Our culture is reinventing itself every 3 to 5 years. We are having new patterns of behavior 2 or 3 times per decade.

We must be innovative in the church."[8]

Here is an important question: How many church leaders today are prepared to cross this threshold? Are we ready to hear what the Spirit is saying today? The Bible says, "He who has an ear, let him hear what the Spirit says to the churches" (Rev. 2:11).

WHAT TO KEEP AND WHAT TO CHANGE

Many of the characteristics of traditional Christianity are not being changed. For one thing, the bedrock theology of the Protestant Reformation is not up for revision. New apostolic leaders are not questioning justification by faith or the priesthood of all believers or the authority of Scripture. The Apostles' Creed maintains its high profile as an acceptable summary of the doctrinal foundations of the Christian faith. New apostolic churches continue to celebrate Christmas and Easter. For the most part, they worship on Sunday. They build church buildings and hold wedding ceremonies in their churches. The churches have pastors, children's programs, youth departments, ushers, holy communion, women's ministries, church suppers and nurseries.

Donald Miller says,
"If Christianity is going to survive,
it must continually reinvent itself."

Many other things are being changed, though. In fact, it could be argued that many things *must* be changed. Donald Miller, author of *Reinventing American Protestantism*, says, "If Christianity is going to survive, it must continually reinvent itself, adapting its message to the members of each generation, along with their culture and the geographical setting."[9]

Predictably, the well-known dynamics of diffusion of innovation theory will operate and sort out who will adopt the new wineskins of the New Apostolic Reformation and who will choose to stay with the old ones. Innovators introduce new ideas into social networks. Those who first accept them are called "early adopters." Others come in as "middle adopters," still others eventually as "late adopters," and those who never accept the innovation are "nonadopters." There was a great deal of controversy, for example, when the "horseless carriage" was first introduced into American society. Not all were ready to switch at first, but eventually most Americans did, and now just about everyone uses automobiles. The Amish, however, are an example of nonadopters.

As I write this, we are well into the early adoption phase of the New Apostolic Reformation, when we can expect fairly strong objections from traditionalists who are threatened by these changes. The major opposition, undoubtedly, will come from denominational executives, but it will not last forever.

THE PLIGHT OF THE DENOMINATIONS

For 400 years, denominations have constituted the principal traditional model for Protestant Christianity. The church structures in which most of us were raised assumed the validity of denominations without question.

Granted, our denominations were not always called denominations. Most of our Protestant church traditions go back to the European Reformation, characterized by state churches such as Lutherans or Reformed or Anglicans or Presbyterians. So-called "free churches" did emerge, but they were politically inferior and they did not receive state support. However, when European state churches sent missionaries abroad, outside the boundaries of the "state," they sooner or later found themselves in one of many kinds of Protestant churches in the receiving nation, and they began to take on the characteristics of denominations. The colonization and Christianization of America is an outstanding example.

As I have mentioned earlier, 1965 was a year when American mainline denominations entered into crisis. For the first time in their history, they found themselves in serious and sustained membership decline. Then 25 or 30 years later, even the newer denominations have begun to confront growth obstacles they had not previously experienced.

Denominational leaders began asking themselves, "Why?" The best explanation the power structure could think of a couple of decades ago was that the declines must be attributed to *contextual factors*. The reason for this was obvious. They did not want to take the blame. The next generation of leaders, however, began suggesting that the crisis might more accurately be attributed to *institutional factors* for equally obvious reasons. They wanted to place the blame on poor decisions of the past generation of leaders.

Let me explain the difference between contextual and institutional factors.

CONTEXTUAL FACTORS
VERSUS INSTITUTIONAL FACTORS

Church growth researchers agree that accurate analyses of either growth or decline of churches must take into consideration both contextual and institutional factors. *Contextual factors* are those sociological factors the church cannot control. Certain changes in the social, political, educational, economic, cultural, international and scientific environment occur that can either enhance or retard church growth. The church leadership can do nothing about it. On the other hand, *institutional factors* can be preserved or changed by decisions the church leadership makes both on the local church and on the denominational levels.

Both contextual and institutional factors can unfold in either the local sphere or the national sphere, so we look at four sets of factors: local contextual, national contextual, local institutional and national institutional.

This terminology was developed by a consortium of 30 denominational executives, church statisticians and consultants that met under a Lily Endowment grant in 1976, 1977 and 1978 under the mandate to address the alarming decline in mainline churches since 1965. I was privileged to be one of them. The chief product of this consortium was a book titled *Understanding Church Growth and Decline 1950-1978*. Of the 30 comprising the consortium, 28 of them attributed the decline chiefly to *contextual* factors. Only two, Dean Kelley and I, thought the main cause might have been *institutional* factors.

Dean Hoge and David Roozen, the general editors of the book developed from the consortium, say, "We should note that people hold different views about the relative importance of the four sets of factors. For example, Wagner stated in Chapter 12 that local institutional factors are more important than local contextual factors, basing his view on his experience. Also, Kelley's influential theories of church growth and decline are based almost entirely on the scrutiny of institutional factors (both national and local), with the implication that contextual factors are much less important. It seems to us that *action-oriented church analysts and consultants* tend to estimate the weight of local institutional factors more highly than the best research would warrant" (emphasis mine).[10]

In his recent book focusing on "the suicide of liberal Christianity," Thomas Reeves throws some light on the underlying desire of denominational leaders to attribute church membership decline to contextual factors. He says, "Observers see the mainline churches as mere victims, casualties of such modern phenomena as urbanism, industrialism, rising educational levels, prosperity, social mobility, the changing nature of the family and so on."[11] In other words, it is not their fault!

The consortium finished its work in 1978, when the decline had been going on for 13 years. It did nothing to change the trend, however. Now conclusions of researchers are beginning to change.

Sixteen years later, John Ellas remarks, "*Understanding Church*

Growth and Decline 1950-1978 left in people's minds the feeling of a cloud of contextual determinism floating overhead. Their conclusion seemed to discount Kelley's thesis handily, minimize the validity of research from the church growth movement, and remove any potential guilt for nongrowing churches and denominations. Their conclusion, unfortunately, left many readers with the empty feeling of a helpless pawn. In other words, churches are at the mercy of society and their communities and there is little anyone can do about it."[12]

TAKING ANOTHER LOOK

Interestingly enough, some of the principal advocates of contextual factors in the 1970s are now taking another look at the importance of institutional factors in the 1990s. David Roozen recently teamed with Kirk Hadaway, another member of the consortium, to produce a book titled *Church and Denominational Growth*. In it, Michael Donahue and Peter Benson share some research that leads them to conclude: "The results...indicated several things. Chief among them is that growth is largely in the hands of the congregation."[13] In other words, *institutional* factors are determinative.

In the same book, Daniel Olson, a sociology professor at Indiana University, concludes: "Churches that want to grow can grow or at least slow their declines. This is the most important finding from among the program variables, and one of the most important findings in this study. This longtime assertion of church growth advocates (e.g. Wagner's *Your Church Can Grow: Seven Vital Signs of a Healthy Church*) appears to receive strong confirmation even among these mostly declining mainline congregations."[14] Needless to say, this was a highly encouraging affirmation.

If institutional factors are now acknowledged as crucial, what are some of the more significant institutional factors that have produced the necessity for new wineskins in the 1990s?

SEVEN INSTITUTIONAL FACTORS
THAT HAVE CAUSED AND PERPETUATED
DENOMINATIONAL DECLINE

1. DENIAL

Many denominational leaders have refused to admit they have a problem. The milder form of this denial is indifference, but the extreme form is the contention that church decline is a blessing of God. No one has expressed this more clearly than Richard Hudnut, who is a Presbyterian pastor, in his book *Church Growth Is Not the Point*.

In his book, Hudnut says, "It is a tough time for the American church. In many quarters membership is down. Attendance is down. But church growth is not the point. The point is whether the church is being true to the gospel. And, in city after city and town after town, it is. Indeed *because* it is being faithful it is often *losing* members. The 'deadwood' is gone. The 'faithful remnant' remains. The church is lean and stripped for action in the '70s....People are leaving the church. It could not be a better sign."[15]

Hudnut thought the church was "stripped for action" in the 1970s. However, the Presbyterian Church (U.S.A.) has continued to lose members annually ever since. This would not have been necessary if appropriate action had been taken by denominational executives. This problem has been vividly described by Thomas Reeves, an insider. He says, "For one thing, as we have seen, many liberal Protestants, especially at the leadership levels of the mainline churches, are pleased with the current situation. They are proud of their conduct, see themselves in the vanguard of even new and more progressive change, and are convinced that membership declines are dropping off and may even have been beneficial."[16]

2. LIBERALISM

Church growth studies have largely bypassed the subject of liberal versus evangelical theology. Because virtually all church growth advocates have held a strongly conservative evangelical theology that is biblical, the curious absence of this discussion can undoubtedly be attributed more to indifference than to conviction.

The theological conviction has been quite vocal, however, among Southern Baptists, the major mainline denominational exception to the declines experienced since 1965. Fearful of beginning to lose members, as they were observing in the other mainline American denominations, evangelical Southern Baptists launched a sustained power play against liberals (who termed themselves "moderates"). After 15 years, they won ongoing control of their major institutions. It would be hard to deny that conservative, biblical theology has played a significant role in the continued growth of America's largest denomination.

Dean Hoge, Benton Johnson and Donald Luidens, researchers who have roots in the mainline denominations, carefully studied the religious habits of mainline baby boomers. Their conclusion is significant, in my opinion: "Our findings show that belief is the single best predictor of church participation, but it is orthodox Christian belief, and not the tenets of lay liberalism, that impels people to be involved in church."[17] Southern Baptists could have told them that long ago.

3. INFLATED TOLERANCE

Liberal theological presuppositions lead to the notion that there is no such thing as absolute truth. All sincere beliefs have their own validity, integrity and truth. Therefore, one would not live or die for truth. Political correctness is a supreme value, and strictness about matters of truth are often perceived to conflict with loving our neighbor as we should. If it ever came down to a choice between truth and tolerance, a large number of our mainline denominational leaders would choose tolerance.

Kirk Hadaway and David Roozen recently did an analysis of trends, markets, denominational influences and directions for the future in mainline denominations. One of their observations was this: "The fear of intolerance and imposition is so great that Americans rarely talk to one another about religious issues, beliefs, and questions. This fear extends to discourse in mainstream churches....The values of religious tolerance and theological openness are paramount within the mainstream. Greater effort is made to communicate our acceptance of diverse views than to communicate what we do, in fact, believe about God."[18] Tolerance is a virtue, but *inflated* tolerance can dilute truth and weaken churches.

Tolerance is a virtue, but inflated tolerance can dilute truth and weaken churches.

---

4. MISPLACED PRIORITIES

Ever since the Lausanne Congress on World Evangelization in Switzerland in 1974, a consensus among evangelicals has been that our mission to the world involves two mandates: the *cultural mandate* (social ministries) and the *evangelistic mandate* (soul-saving ministries). The Lausanne Covenant also states, "In the church's mission of sacrificial service, evangelism is primary" (Article 6). This prioritizes evangelism without neglecting ministries of mercy or compassion.

In the 1960s, the mainline denominations began to change their priorities. This was because of their responding to the major social disruptions in our nation highlighted by the civil rights upheavals, the Vietnam War, the hippie movement and the erosion of Judeo-Christian moral standards. At the time, the mainline denominations, through the National Council of Churches, carried the most influential religious voice in America.

In a short period of time, the cultural mandate became supreme and the mainline churches believed it was more important to improve society than to win the lost for Christ. Partially as a result of this shift in priorities (despite energetic denials on the part of denominational leadership), the mainline denomi-nations began to decline in 1965. Again, the Southern Baptists were the exception. They continued to prioritize the evangelis-tic mandate, and they continued to grow vigorously.

The study by Hadaway and Roozen, which I cited in the last point, addresses this point also. They conclude: "People expect churches to be *religious* institutions, not social-service organiza-tions or social clubs."[19]

In contrast, Hadaway and Roozen found that the evangeli-cal churches, which were still growing, also did social work, but without shifting priorities. They say, "Many evangelical denom-inations increased emphasis on social-justice concerns. Nevertheless, these denominations never had a complete reori-entation of their priorities. Traditional evangelism and new church development efforts continued to receive the lion's share of denominational mission funds."[20]

5. AVERSION TO EVANGELISM

During the 1970s, I frequently conducted church growth sem-inars for mainline denominational groups. On many occasions, my hosts would speak to me before I started and say words to the effect: "You would do well not to use the word 'evangelism' in your teaching. In our denomination it is a turnoff."

After this happened a few times, it began to occur to me that no matter what I taught, these churches were not likely to grow. My concern increased when I discovered that some were considering my position as "conversionist," which to them was a pejorative term. They considered preaching the gospel as a kind of proselytism, which certainly could offend the personal dignity of unbelievers. I haven't been invited to do another one of those seminars for quite a while.

I thought perhaps I was missing something. It is not sur-prising, then, that conclusions reached by Hadaway and Roozen were reassuring to me personally. They say, "We must realize that few mainstream churches will ever be aggressively evangel-istic in the manner encouraged by most books on church growth. Based on poll data, mainstream members and marginal members, though they may desire intimacy with an immanent God, generally do not believe that an individual must 'accept Christ as their personal Savior' in order to avoid going to hell....Mainstream Christians may invite their friends to church, visit prospects, and even talk to others about their faith, but they won't do evangelism. In other words, they will not try to *convert* anyone."[21]

6. SUSPICION OF GROWTH

Denominational leaders seem to have a lurking assumption that high quality churches are not expected to grow. Therefore, if churches do show unusual growth, something must be wrong with them.

I will never forget that back in the days when denominations were inviting me to conduct church growth seminars, I ministered to leaders of the Reformed Church in America in New York state. At the time, I was also teaching three or four times a year on the faculty of Robert Schuller's Institute for Church Leadership in Garden Grove, California. The institutes were drawing huge numbers of pastors from across the nation because Schuller's church, now called the Crystal Cathedral, was one of the largest churches in the United States and certainly the largest church in his denomination, the Reformed Church in America. I was shocked when in my preseminar briefing in New York, my hosts advised me that I would do well not to mention Robert Schuller's name during my sessions.

They wanted me to teach church growth, but I was not to use the fastest growing church their own denomination had ever experienced as a role model. Why? Because of the deep-seated suspicion of growth among the denominational executives.

7. DISTRUST OF CHARISMATIC LEADERSHIP

Among many denominational executives, as well as among some seminary professors I know, the word "entrepreneur" is used almost as a cuss word. Trust is essentially in the leadership of consensus groups rather than in individuals. The pastor is not supposed to be the leader of the local church, but rather an implementer of the leadership of the elected board or of the congregation. Denominational decisions, whether on the regional level or on the national level, are made by officially constituted committees, and denominational executives are expected to carry out the desires of the policy-making group.[22]

Hadaway and Roozen say, "Mainstream church leaders are not charismatic figures, by and large. They are persons with integrity, but they are more comfortable with consensus-building than at exercising visionary leadership."[23] This is so dramatically at opposite poles from the New Apostolic Reformation that I will discuss it in detail in a chapter about pastors and in another chapter about apostles.

THE FUTURE OF DENOMINATIONS

In August 1994, The Leadership Network held a summit meeting entitled "The Future of Denominations." A prominent figure at the summit was Lyle Schaller, highly regarded as the dean of American church consultants and one who characterizes himself as a loyal denominationalist (United Methodist).

Is there a future for denominations?
Lyle Schaller has said they must be
"willing and able to adapt to a new era."

In the report of the meeting, Schaller said, "Is there a future for denominations? That would be determined almost entirely by the *denominations*." The key to it, Schaller adds, is that they must be "willing and able to adapt to a new era."[24] To put it in other terms, what Lyle Schaller is saying is that *institutional* factors will be crucial to denominational influence and survival. By extension, it is now more than obvious that institutional factors were also the principal cause of their decline.

What are the characteristics of the "new era" to which Schaller is referring? For one thing, denominations will certainly have to learn how to attract baby boomers. To do so, radical changes will have to be made. Donald Miller's research revealed, "[Baby boomers] don't like bureaucratic structure, and the mainline churches are monuments of rites and organizational rules."[25]

In his book *The New Reformation*, Lyle Schaller addresses these concerns and says, "*I am not proposing that the substance of the gospel be changed. I am proposing that we need to radically change the way we package and proclaim the substance of the gospel.* Making a few adjustments here and there will not help. If we simply do better what we presently are doing in our old wine vats, we will continue to be irrelevant and, in time, extinct."[26]

Schaller also discusses the subject of new versus old wineskins, and asks, "Should the old wineskins be cleansed and patched to carry the gospel of Jesus Christ to new generations in a new social context? Or should that investment of time, commitment and energy be made in new wineskins?"[27] Later on he answers his question by saying, "If a new reformation is well underway, it will be more productive to invest in new wineskins, rather than to patch the old ones. This is an urgent, and perhaps even a life-and-death, issue for several denominational systems."[28]

WHO WILL BE FILLING THE NEW WINESKINS?

New wineskins are inevitable for the twenty-first century; but who will be filling them with new wine? I think we can expect they will be filled from at least three sources:

1. The churches that are already doing it will continue to fill the new wineskins. They are the new apostolic churches. The subtitle of Lyle Schaller's book *The New Reformation* is: *Tomorrow Arrived Yesterday.* Schaller admits he was blindsided by what I call the New Apostolic Reformation, but he clearly realizes it is molding the shape of our ecclesiastical future.

2. Virtually every mainline denomination has some innovative congregations that I consider new apostolic congregations. They are not always admired and affirmed by denominational bureaucrats or by other more traditional pastors. It might turn out that some entire denominations will reengineer themselves and adopt apostolic characteristics. It is reported that the Assemblies of God in Australia have done that very thing, and I will explain the details in chapter 6. Denominational new wineskins are, therefore, a distinct possibility.

3. New church networking paradigms are emerging that will be fulfilling many of the functions we have usually attributed to denominations. This will happen on three levels:

A. INTRADENOMINATIONAL NETWORKS. Hadaway and Roozen say, "As we see it, the pastors, local church leaders, and seminarians who will form the leadership core of a denominational revitalization movement will begin as an informal collection of individuals who share a common understanding of the flaws of the current system, but a deep commitment to the heritage it represents."[29] The key players in this process are frequently the megachurch pastors of the denomination. Predictably, activities of this sort are not usually endorsed by the entrenched leaders.

B. INTERDENOMINATIONAL NETWORKS. Lyle Schaller says, "From the perspective of the twenty-first century, perhaps the central point in this chapter is the shift in identification of the partners for interchurch cooperation. In the first five or six decades of the twentieth century, the initiators and the key players were denominations and denominational officials. During the last two decades of the century, that has shifted to pastors and congregational leaders with an especially highly visible role for the senior pastors of large congregations."[30]

C. EXTRADENOMINATIONAL NETWORKS. These groupings of churches are forming on a territorial basis, particularly in cities. Some are identifying the "anchor churches" of a city and developing ways and means for the pastors of those churches to network together for the benefit of the whole city. In many cases the personal relationships, the mutual accountability and the camaraderie among pastors of a city across denominational lines far surpasses their sense of loyalty to fellow pastors of their own denominations who live in different locations.

Kent Hunter of the Church Growth Center in Corunna, Indiana, has identified a cohort of pastors whom he calls "post-denominational wanna-bes." Some of them remain in their denominations, but they have divorced their own churches and ministries from any significant participation in officially sanctioned denominational programs, unless a certain program happens to appeal to them. Others are proactively looking for a way out of their denominations and seeking new ways of affiliating their church with other churches of a like mind. These are the most likely candidates for either creating new networks and associations or joining existing ones.[31]

Notes

1. C. Kirk Hadaway and David A. Roozen, *Rerouting the Protestant Mainstream* (Nashville: Abingdon Press, 1995), p. 33.
2. See Mike Berg and Paul Pretiz, *Spontaneous Combustion: Grass-Roots Christianity, Latin American Style* (Pasadena, Calif.: William Carey Library, 1996).
3. George O. Wood, "The General Secretary's Report," The General Council of the Assemblies of God 1993-1995 Biennial Report, p. 8.
4. Taken from data presented in a brochure published by Assemblies of God headquarters, Springfield, Missouri: "Statistics on the Assemblies of God (USA) 1997."
5. Mark A. Shibley, *Resurgent Evangelicalism in the United States* (Columbia, S.C.: University of South Carolina Press, 1996), pp. 108, 109.
6. See Win Arn, Carroll Nyquist and Charles Arn, *Who Cares About Love?* (Pasadena, Calif.: Church Growth Press, 1986).

7. Pablo Deiros, *Protestantismo en América Latina* (Nashville: Editorial Caribe, 1997), p. 49 (translation mine).

8. George Barna, "Current Trends Impacting Ministry," an unpublished seminar handout written January 25, 1996, p. 1.

9. Donald E. Miller, *Reinventing American Protestantism* (Berkeley, Calif.: University of California Press, 1997), p. 18.

10. Dean R. Hoge and David A. Roozen, "Some Sociological Conclusions About Church Trends," *Understanding Church Growth and Decline 1950-1978*, Dean R. Hoge and David A. Roozen, eds. (New York: The Pilgrim Press, 1979), p. 327.

11. Thomas C. Reeves, *The Empty Church: The Suicide of Liberal Christianity* (New York: The Free Press, 1996), p. 31.

12. John Ellas, *Clear Choices for Churches* (Houston, Tex.: Center for Church Growth, 1994), p. 6.

13. Michael J. Donahue and Peter L. Benson, "Belief Style, Congregational Climate, and Program Quality," *Church and Denominational Growth: What Does (and Does Not) Cause Growth and Decline*, David A. Roozen and C. Kirk Hadaway, eds. (Nashville: Abingdon Press, 1993), p. 231.

14. Daniel V. A. Olson, "Congregational Growth and Decline in Indiana Among Five Mainline Denominations," Roozen and Hadaway, eds., *Church and Denominational Growth*, p. 219.

15. Richard Hudnut, *Church Growth Is Not the Point* (New York: HarperCollins, 1975), pp. ix, xi.

16. Reeves, *The Empty Church*, p. 200.

17. Dean R. Hoge, Benton Johnson and Donald A. Luidens, *Vanishing Boundaries: The Religion of Mainline Protestant Baby Boomers* (Louisville, Ky.: Westminster/John Knox Press, 1994), p. 185.

18. Hadaway and Roozen, *Rerouting the Protestant Mainstream*, pp. 76, 77.

19. Ibid., p. 76.

20. Ibid., p. 100.

21. Ibid., pp. 79, 80.

22. Ibid., p. 61.

23. Ibid., p. 118.

24. Lyle E. Schaller, Leadership Network, *Forum Files* (November 1994), p. 1.

25. Miller, *Reinventing American Protestantism*, p. 17.

26. Lyle E. Schaller, *The New Reformation* (Nashville: Abingdon Press, 1995), p. 14.

27. Ibid., p. 17.

28. Ibid., p. 53.

29. Hadaway and Roozen, *Rerouting the Protestant Mainstream*, p. 19.

30. Lyle E. Schaller, *21 Bridges to the 21st Century* (Nashville: Abingdon Press, 1994), p. 137.

31. See Kent Hunter, "The coming of the post-denominational age," *The Church Doctor Report* (Winter, 1997), p. 1.

CHAPTER TWO

Protestantism's
New Look

This is clearly a day calling for new wineskins. The old wineskins may last for generations, but they will no longer be on the cutting edge of the expansion of the kingdom of God. The new wine of the Holy Spirit requires reengineered vessels.

To go back to the list of church growth research questions— yes, a distinct pattern of the blessing of God on certain churches has become quite evident in the 1990s. What, then, are the distinguishing characteristics of these churches? Before we look at these specific characteristics we would first do well to understand, as thoroughly as possible, the generic and specific names of the movement as well as to gain an overall picture of the size and scope of these new wineskins.

THE GENERIC NAME:
THE NEW APOSTOLIC REFORMATION

When I began researching the Pentecostal movement back in the late 1960s, the churches I was studying had a generic name. Both insiders and outsiders had embraced the designation "Pentecostal," and no further discussion was necessary. When I titled my book *Look Out! The Pentecostals Are Coming*, everybody knew who I was talking about.

This time we are facing a different situation. The shape of

this current movement had become clear to many observers.
Some saw it long before I did. It took me until 1993 to realize
there was an unusual pattern of divine blessing on certain
churches in our times. However, the movement had no general
name. I had been noticing that when I would ask my Fuller
Seminary students to introduce themselves to each other at the
beginning of each course, the Baptists, Lutherans,
Presbyterians, Nazarenes and Assemblies of God were comfortable sharing their identities, but not so my students from these
newer groups. They would typically hesitate and mumble at
that point, at times attempting a bit of humor to cover up their
identity insecurities.

Some of the subdivisions had names, which I mentioned in
the last chapter, such as African Independent Churches,
Chinese house churches, American independent charismatics
and Latin American grassroots churches, but no name was used
to identify the global movement as a whole. Obviously, a term—
a neologism—was needed.

Where do such terms originate? Sometimes they originate
from insiders such as "The Church of the Nazarene," "The
Congregational Church," "The Disciples of Christ" or "The
Salvation Army." Sometimes, however, terms generated by out-
siders are the ones that stick, such as the name "Christians" in
New Testament times. More recent examples include
"Methodists," "Lutherans" and "Quakers."

Probably for every outside name that sticks, 10 do not.
"Holy Rollers," for example, never stuck as a term for
Pentecostals. Who constitutes the jury to make the decision?
Only history. If the name works, it is used. If not, it is discard-
ed to oblivion.

As I explained in the last chapter, I came to this movement
as a distinct outsider. I needed a term, though, to describe it
because I was organizing a new course on the subject at Fuller
Seminary, and courses need names. The name I finally chose is
the "New Apostolic Reformation." Will it stick? History will
tell. Meanwhile, I have begun teaching the course.

WHY "APOSTOLIC"?

The first time I saw the term "apostolic" used in this context was in an issue of *NetFax* published by the Leadership Network of Tyler, Texas, on September 4, 1995. It spoke of "The New Apostolic Paradigm." I filed it only because I was experimenting with another name at the time. At about the same time, I had come into contact with Ed Delph of Phoenix, Arizona, who was pastor of Hosanna Christian Fellowship and who had started an organization called N.A.T.I.O.N.S. (Networking Apostolic Thrust Internationally or Nationally). I heard Ed calling the churches with which he was relating "apostolic churches."

One of the reasons I hesitated using Ed's term was that one overtone of "apostolic" was that the New Testament gift and office of apostle might be active in some churches today. A large number of these new churches would have gladly affirmed that. I thought, however, that, at the same time, it might have excluded many significant churches of that nature such as Bill Hybels's Willow Creek Community Church, Rick Warren's Saddleback Valley Community Church, Walt Kallestad's Community Church of Joy, John Ed Mathison's Frazier Memorial United Methodist Church and many others.

I continued to believe I shouldn't use "apostolic" until the day, in early 1996, I received a prepublication copy of George Hunter's book, *Church for the Unchurched* (Abingdon). In that book, Hunter, much to my delight, had written about those very churches and labeled them "apostolic congregations." I called my friend George on the phone, thanked him for doing this fine study, and told him that now that I had the *imprimatur* of the dean of the E. Stanley Jones School of World Mission and Evangelism at Asbury Theological Seminary, I had decided to use the term as well!

WHY "REFORMATION"?

A month or so before receiving Hunter's book, I had read Lyle Schaller's book *The New Reformation* (Abingdon). In it, Schaller describes what he thought were the four major failures of his otherwise brilliant and distinguished career as a parish consultant.

The most serious of the four failures, Schaller says, could be attributed to "a combination of (a) age, (b) thirty-five years invested in consultation with congregations, (c) personal bias as a denominationalist, (d) excessive optimism about the usefulness of old wineskins, and (e) a natural tendency to study the trees rather than to see the forest." What was his failure? He confesses: "I was focusing on the renewal of the old, and failed to see that a new reformation in American Christianity was well underway."[1]

Lyle Schaller's arresting subtitle, as I have mentioned, is: *Tomorrow Arrived Yesterday*!

More than anything else, this helped me decide to use the word "reformation." I was reassured when Donald Miller said in a later book, "I believe we are witnessing a second reformation that is transforming the way Christianity will be experienced in the new millennium."[2] The first reformation is considered the Protestant Reformation of the sixteenth century. As I have mentioned previously, we are now witnessing the most radical change in world Christianity since then, and I would not be surprised if the degree of current changes turned out to be at least as radical as those of the Protestant Reformation.

The current reformation is not so much a reformation of faith, *but a reformation of* practice.

The radical change in the sixteenth century was largely theological. The current reformation is not so much a reformation of *faith* (the essential theological principles of the Reformation are intact), but a reformation of *practice*. A major difference was that the sixteenth century reformation came in reaction to a corrupt and apostate church.

This current reformation is not so much against corruption

and apostasy as it is against irrelevance. It is true that important changes in practice did come about in the centuries following Martin Luther and John Calvin, but for the most part they came relatively slowly because in those days culture changed gradually. Given the accelerated rate of culture change we now see in our generation, it might be expected that changes in church life will also be more rapid and, therefore, more radical.

WHY "NEW"?

"New" modifies both "apostolic" and "reformation." I have just explained why the "reformation" is being seen as new. How about "apostolic"?

It could be argued, although it should not be overstressed, that what is taking place today is a new reflection of the apostolic nature of the first three centuries of the Church. The *NetFax* of September 4, 1995, to which I referred, hints that such might be the case because it divides the scope of church history into "The Apostolic Paradigm" (first to third centuries), "The Christendom Paradigm" (fourth to mid-twentieth centuries) and "The New Apostolic Paradigm" (late twentieth to twenty-first centuries).

During the era of the Christendom Paradigm, however, several churches adopted the designation "apostolic." I will provide more detail about this later, but at the moment the Roman Catholic Church and the Church of England (Episcopalians) are familiar examples. The adjective "new" is also intended to distinguish what is happening today from such older movements, which might be seen as "old" apostolic movements.

I want to be clear that it is not my role to dictate to others what name they should use for this movement. I am using "New Apostolic Reformation" for my courses and my books, but it remains to be seen what the ongoing name will be. Meanwhile, let's look at some other options.

Alternate Names

Since beginning this research, I have examined and rejected more than 60 possible names. For most of them, such as "Sprouting Churches," "Budding Churches" or "Blooming Churches," the decision not to use the suggested names was easy. Others definitely had some merit and were worth considering. I am going to name and make brief comments about eight of them because each of the comments will reveal important insights about the nature of these new apostolic churches.

1. Postdenominational Churches

I am listing this first because I actually used and promoted this name in 1994 and 1995. My first attempt at an article on the subject was published in *Ministries Today* (July/August 1994) as "Those Amazing Postdenominational Churches." The name has several good qualities, not the least of which is that it is historically accurate. In fact, the two historians on our Fuller School of World Mission faculty, Paul Pierson and Pablo Deiros, insist that we should continue to use it. I see their point, and for some months I defended it strongly; but I eventually lost the battle for the term for two reasons.

First, the term did not embrace (without lengthy and clumsy explanations) the new apostolic congregations *within* denominations. In a luncheon meeting, Jack Hayford, pastor of the 9,000-member Foursquare church, The Church On The Way, in Van Nuys, California, was very confrontive when I described my choice of the word "postdenominational" church. He challenged me directly, in the presence of a half-dozen other leaders. He thought the term *excluded* pastors like him. Although I argued my point, he could not understand how his church, loyal to his denomination, could be categorized in such a way.

Second, the word "postdenominational" actually sounded *pejorative* to many of my denominational executive friends. At first I thought we could agree to disagree, but it turned out to

be much more serious than that. After receiving strongly word-
ed letters from two friends (both Fuller alumni), George Wood,
general secretary of the Assemblies of God, and David Rambo,
president of the Christian and Missionary Alliance, I began to
realize I was in danger of introducing a divisive term into the
Body of Christ, which I had no desire to do. I then scrapped the
term, and wrote apologies to George Wood, David Rambo, Jack
Hayford and others.

2. INDEPENDENT CHURCHES

Many denominational executives would love to call these
churches "independent" churches. They are, in fact, more independent than many other churches, particularly those new
apostolic churches within the denominations. I have already
mentioned how the executives of the Reformed Church in
America could hardly cope with the Crystal Cathedral back in
the 1970s.

Ironically, new apostolic leaders consider the term "independent" as pejorative. They do not consider themselves "Lone
Rangers," functionally disconnected from the Body of Christ.
They consider themselves, rather, as *interdependent*. I first heard
this from Ed Delph in 1995, when he said in a meeting,
"Churches must give up their 'declaration of independence' and
make a 'declaration of interdependence.'" No new apostolic
leader I have met would disagree.

A notable exception to this nomenclature concern are the
African Independent Churches (AIC). They are interdependent
as well, but AIC has now become a technical term to distinguish
these churches from the traditional mission churches, and
most church leaders and scholars on both sides continue to
find it a useful distinction.

3. CHARISMATIC CHURCHES

It is a fact that most new apostolic churches are what traditionalists like me would characterize as "charismatic." In some parts
of the world, this could be up to nearly 100 percent. I do not

have empirical data for the United States, but my observation is that some 80 percent of the new apostolic congregations in this country are charismatic and some 20 percent are noncharismatic. Notable examples of the latter are the Crystal Cathedral, Willow Creek Community Church and Community Church of Joy.

Few of the denominational new apostolic pastors, however, would typify themselves as "cessationists," arguing that certain of the spiritual gifts went out of use in the Church after the close of the Apostolic Age. At the same time, they would not embrace the term "charismatic."

Furthermore, it is my opinion that the adjective "charismatic" has a half-life of some three to five years. It was an important term in the 1970s when charismatics had an inferiority complex and were struggling for identity. This is no longer the case. Certain aspects of the charismatic lifestyle are filtering into traditional churches in an increasingly remarkable way. Barriers are coming down.

In response to this, for example, the Charismatic Fellowship of Asia, led by prominent new apostolic leaders such as Joseph Wongsak of Thailand, Eddie Villanueva of the Philippines and Dexter Low of Malaysia, has changed its name to "Christ for Asia." The official announcement of the change states: "CFA hopes to foster unity in the Body of Christ through significant leaders coming together in a relational way. It has worked well for the initial group of leaders with a charismatic/Pentecostal belief, but the council now seeks to embrace the larger Body of Christ, seeing charismatic/Pentecostal delineations as merely past usefulness."[3]

It should also be noted that in certain parts of the world, the term "charismatic" is especially problematic. In Latin America, for example, the adjective "charismatic" has been applied mostly to Catholics, but rarely to Protestants. This is changing, but it still confuses many. In Australia, "charismatics" can refer to some who may speak in tongues, but who do not necessarily hold evangelical views of biblical authority, the deity of Christ, the virgin birth, the Resurrection and other biblical doctrines.

Therefore, many Australian evangelicals prefer "Pentecostal" to "charismatic."

4. RESTORATION CHURCHES

Some new apostolic leaders, who have roots in the Latter Rain Movement, which emerged after World War II, like to refer to their churches as "restoration" churches. The implication is that they are restoring true biblical Christianity for the first time since New Testament days.

On a broader scale, however, most church leaders today would associate the term "Restoration Movement" with the innovations initiated in frontier Presbyterianism by Barton Stone in the Cane Ridge revival and Alexander Campbell in western Pennsylvania in the early 1800s. Current denominations such as Disciples of Christ, Christian Churches and Churches of Christ trace their origins to this Restoration Movement, and church historians would regard them as the original owners of the brand name, so to speak.

5. GRASSROOTS CHURCHES

This is a good term coined by Mike Berg and Paul Pretiz for their book *Spontaneous Combustion: Grass-Roots Christianity, Latin American Style* (William Carey Library). It could be particularly useful for indigenous Third World churches that have sprung up on what used to be the "mission field." It might not be so useful, though, for new apostolic churches in the traditional Western missionary-sending nations. Ironically, it is almost impossible to translate the term into Spanish or Portuguese.

6. NEO-DENOMINATIONAL CHURCHES

Dan Simpson of the Fuller Seminary Office of Continuing Education makes a case for calling these churches "neo-denominational." He argues, "What if we were to define a denomination as a *movement, fellowship, association, network,* or *family of like-minded, like-faithed churches?* Then we could understand this new movement, not as a rejection of denominations, but as an endorsement of them! Neo-denominationalism is an embracing of the concepts that have made denominations a central part of Christianity for centuries: strength in numbers, power in cooperation, edification in fellowship, safety in accountability, effectiveness in synergy, and fruitfulness in relationship."[4] Good point!

7. NEW-PARADIGM CHURCHES

Donald Miller of the University of Southern California conducted an intensive three-year research project of selected new apostolic churches. His book *Reinventing American Protestantism* (University of California Press) is the first book-length study of such churches. The term he selected is "new-paradigm churches." Miller says, "A subtle revolution is transforming the face of Protestantism. While many mainline denominational churches are losing members, overall church attendance in North America is not declining. A new style of Christianity is dawning in America, and to some extent worldwide. These 'new-paradigm churches,' as I call them, are changing the way Christianity looks and is experienced."[5]

8. THE NEXT CHURCH

In 1996, *Atlantic Monthly* carried a fascinating article by Charles Trueheart, titled "The Next Church." It was significant that such a respected secular publication, highly regarded for responsible journalism, would also show interest in this new phenomenon. Here is how Trueheart begins:

> No spires. No crosses. No robes. No clerical collars. No hard pews. No kneelers. No biblical gobbledygook. No prayerly rote. No fire, no brimstone. No pipe organs. No dreary eighteenth-century hymns. No forced solemnity. No Sunday finery. No collection plates.
>
> The list has asterisks and exceptions, but its meaning is clear. Centuries of European tradition and

Christian habit are deliberately being abandoned, clearing the way for new, contemporary forms of worship and belonging. The Next Church, as the independent and entrepreneurial congregations that are adopting these new forms might collectively be called, is drawing lots of people.[6]

"APOSTOLIC" IS NOT A NEW TRADEMARK

As I have said, one of the reasons I use "new" to modify "apostolic" is to distinguish these churches from others that have used the term "apostolic" through the years. Some theologians actually define the true Church as "one, holy, catholic and apostolic." The official name of the Catholic church, for example, is "The Holy Catholic Apostolic and Roman Church."

In the early nineteenth century, a movement called "The New Apostolic Church" started in England, led by Edward Irving and others, but it subsequently grew more in Germany than in the U.K. Frederick Burklin says, "Ultimately, twelve men were declared to be apostles and were solemnly ordained to that ministry on July 14, 1835, in London. The aim of these prophets and apostles was to unite the divided church according to the pattern established by Paul in the New Testament."[7] The church observes a fairly orthodox doctrine, but tends to keep its distance from the rest of the Body of Christ. The group has about 500,000 adherents, mostly in Germany.

A strong denomination in Australia and New Zealand is The Apostolic Church, which started almost 100 years ago as a product of the Welsh Revival. Friends such as Don Lake and Rex Meehan tell me the New Zealand Apostolic Church has been among the fastest growing denominations in New Zealand for some time.

The Azusa Street Revival started in 1906 in the Azusa Street Mission in Los Angeles, the real name of which was "Apostolic Faith Gospel Mission." This derived from the movement started by Charles Parham in Topeka, Kansas, in 1901, which he called the Apostolic Faith Movement.

Among the African Independent Churches, the word "apostolic" appears many times in the names of the various groups. In all probability, most of these African churches could best be considered a part of the *new* apostolic reformation, rather than the *old* apostolic churches. After describing them, Harvey Cox says, "At present rates of growth, by the year 2000 these churches will include more members in Africa than either the Roman Catholic Church or all the Protestant denominations put together."[8]

The Yearbook of American and Canadian Churches (Abingdon) lists nine current denominations that use the word "apostolic" in their official title. A sampling of names: Apostolic Overcoming Holy Church of God, Inc.; National Organization of the New Apostolic Church of North America; Apostolic Christian Churches of America; Church of Our Lord Jesus Christ of the Apostolic Faith, Inc.; Apostolic Catholic Assyrian Church.

THREE IMPORTANT NUANCES OF "APOSTOLIC"

One of the questions I am most frequently asked is the meaning I am giving to the term "apostolic." In my mind, there are three important nuances of the term, all of which apply to the New Apostolic Reformation.

1. NEW TESTAMENT CHRISTIANITY

Speaking of "apostolic Christianity" brings to our minds the days of the 12 apostles. For example, the reformers of the sixteenth century used "apostolic" to distance themselves from the Roman Catholic Church and to affirm their doctrine of *sola scriptura*, meaning that the Bible, written or authorized by the 12 apostles, was our only, final authority for faith and practice.

Early Pentecostals used "apostolic" to describe what they

considered to be a restoration of the apostolic faith after Christianity presumably had abandoned it for 1,800 years. Some of them might have carried this too far, and they have been criticized for it. Charles Nienkirchen says, "Pentecostals, who were concerned to restore the supernatural powers of their first-century apostolic predecessors, tended to collapse history into an apostolic age then, and its full restoration now. It made for ahistoricism, exclusivism, and sectarianism."[9]

I have noticed some of this ahistoric restorationism among current new apostolic leaders, but not what I judge to be a significant amount. Even so, my observation is that collectively these new apostolic churches more closely reflect New Testament style than do our more traditional churches. For the most part, the New Testament principles are skillfully contextualized into contemporary culture.

Apostolic churches, by nature, give a high priority to reaching out effectively to the unchurched.

---

2. PRIORITY OUTREACH TO PRE-CHRISTIAN POPULATIONS

The root meaning of the Greek *apóstolos* is one who is sent out with a commission. Apostolic churches, by nature, give a high priority to reaching out effectively to the unchurched. This is what George Hunter had in mind when he chose to label certain churches "apostolic congregations."

Hunter elaborates on this by saying the following:

> I delineate the distinctiveness of "apostolic congregations" along lines like these: (1) Their main business, often the obsession, is to reach and disciple lost people; (2) Like the ancient apostles and the churches they planted, they study, profile, and target a distinct, largely-undiscipled population, not merely lost individuals; (3) To reach that population, they adapt their music, language, liturgy, leadership style, etc., to fit

the culture of the target population; (4) They have a distinct (apostolic) vision of what people, as disciples, can become; and (5) They are driven to experience, and they do experience, substantial conversion growth from the world.[10]

3. THE GIFT AND OFFICE OF APOSTLE

Recognizing the New Testament office of apostle as alive and well in churches today is the biggest leap with which many readers of this book will be confronted. Of all the differences between new apostolic churches and traditional Protestant churches, this, I believe, is the most radical. I will not say much more here, but I will develop the subject in detail in chapter 5, "Five Crucial Questions About Apostolic Ministry."

INFINITE CREATIVITY: NAMES OF CHURCHES AND NETWORKS

The rule for naming local churches and apostolic networks appears to be *infinite creativity*! I was in the Philippines for a spiritual warfare conference in 1994 sponsored by Jesus Is Lord Church. About 1,000 leaders attended, representing 63 churches or denominations. When they gave me a copy of the list of 63, I was amazed. Only 4 of them were names the average Christian would recognize.

Here is a small sample of the other names: Charity and Faith, Christ the Living Stone, Flock of God, House of Praise and Worship, Jesus Conquers, Jesus the Bread of Life, Lord of Glory, Psalms of God, Salt and Light, Voice of the Lord. When I commented on this, I was told that another Philippine church that was not present was called The Warm Body of Jesus Church!

Check some of the names in the United States: Vineyard Christian Fellowship (founded by John Wimber), Cathedral of Faith (Kenny Foreman), Springs Harvest Fellowship (Dutch Sheets), Brooklyn Tabernacle (Jim Cymbala), Community

Church of Joy (Walt Kallestad) and Crystal Cathedral (Robert Schuller).

In England, you will find Icthus (Roger Forster), Pioneer (Gerald Coates), Kingdom Faith Church (Colin Urquhart). In Germany, you will find the Christian Church of Cologne (Terry Jones); in Kenya, The Prayer Cave (Thomas Muthee); in Nigeria, Deeper Life Bible Church (William Kumuyi) and He's Alive Chapel (Austin Ukachi). In Thailand, you will find Hope of Bangkok (Joseph Wongsak); in Malaysia, Latter Rain Church (Dexter Low). In Brazil, The New Birth Church (Esteban Hernandez); in Guatemala, El Shaddai Church (Harold Caballeros); and in Colombia, The International Charismatic Mission (Cesar Castellanos).

WHAT IS THE SIZE OF THIS MOVEMENT?

In the last chapter, I explained how difficult it is to make an exact count of the New Apostolic Reformation. At the moment, it is only semivisible. What we are able to observe may well be only the tip of the iceberg. Back in 1996, David Barrett, editor of the *World Christian Encyclopedia*, told me he had 1,000 apostolic networks on his database and he would estimate at that point considerably more than 100 million new apostolic adherents worldwide. He later wrote and said, "Every time I do an approximate statistical count of this movement it seems bigger and bigger. We are sure to be startled out of our wits over the next few months!"

In Brazil, the fastest growing church during the last few years has been the Universal Church of the Kingdom of God, led by Edir Macedo. It now numbers more than 3 million. In Europe, the three largest churches are as follows:

1. Manna Church in Lisbon, Portugal, led by Jorge Tadeu. The central church of 25,000 members has planted 22 new churches in Portugal since it started in

1985, and it now has a cumulative membership of 75,000.

2. Kensington Temple in London, pastored by Colin Dye. People from 110 ethnic groups make up its membership of 6,000.

3. Faith Church in Budapest, Hungary, pastored by Sandor Nemeth. It counts 4,500 members, but has a total constituency of 15,000.

Pastor E. A. Adeboye, a former professor of hydrodynamics, leads the Redeemed Church of God network in Nigeria. At km.46 of the Lagos-Ibadan expressway, Adeboye has built a pillars-and-roof, open-sided facility that measures 1 km. by .5 km. On the first Friday of every month, a crowd of 500,000 gathers for a dusk-to-dawn "Holy Ghost Night!"

The Waves of Love and Peace Church of Buenos Aires, which estimates some 150,000 members, purchased a 2,500-seat theater as its church facility, and five days a week they hold services 18 hours a day. On weekends, they hold services 23 hours a day, closing only from 12 midnight to 1:00 A.M. for cleaning. Just before almost every service, the crowds waiting outside fill the sidewalk and partially block traffic in the street.

Cesar Castellanos's International Charismatic Mission in Bogotá, Colombia, finished 1996 having 10,000 home cell groups. His goal for the end of 1997 was 30,000 groups. However, in early 1997, Cesar and his wife, Claudia, were machine-gunned by terrorists bent on killing the pastor of the nation's largest church. Cesar took four bullets and Claudia took three, and they had to spend several months in Houston for treatment. What about the home cell groups? The infrastructure had been so carefully laid that they reached the 30,000 cells they had projected!

I could go on, but I just wanted to enter a few of these numbers into the record because in the past we were not able to cite figures of this magnitude in our reporting of traditional church growth. David Martin, a sociologist, wrote an interesting article in *The National Review*, titled "Wesley's World Revolution." He says the following:

> Over the past thirty or so years the religious map of the world has changed dramatically. In the developed West the liberal religious establishment have seen their constituencies shrink relative to the conservative evangelicals. In the Third World, the World Council of Churches' share of the Protestant constituency has dropped, and a protean indigenous Christianity has emerged indifferent to the Western theological intelligentsia. More often than not, this shift is toward a Pentecostal faith in the gifts of the Holy Spirit—healing, tongues, exorcism, prophecy, holiness. Overall, perhaps a quarter of a billion people are involved.[11]

THE BIG PICTURE

Research about the New Apostolic Reformation is just beginning. Many Christian leaders still have no idea that this movement even exists. Some have stereotypes that relegate it to the lunatic fringe of Christianity. It is even threatening to some because of the radical differences in style as contrasted to the traditional churches most of us have known.

One traditional scholar, Wilbert Shenk, a Mennonite missiologist, is among the first to declare a wake-up call to those who may still be sleeping through this revolution. He says we must now open our minds to what is actually happening. "We must move beyond the conventional framework, which is governed by the assumption that what happened in the course of Western Christendom is universally normative for Christian history."[12]

Part of our inbred Western arrogance tends to evaluate whatever happens by using our own set of experiences and our own scale of values as the criteria. This must and will change. I want to be among those who applaud whatever the Holy Spirit does, even if it may be radically different from the way I think it should be done.

The rest of this book is essentially a description and analysis of the distinctives of the New Apostolic Reformation. Each chapter will detail certain ones. Before we delve into those descriptions, however, I want to project the big picture and display some overall conclusions of well-known people who have been researching the movement. One thing that will be obvious is how much overlapping there is on the various lists of distinctives. This is reassuring because by that we know we are observing many of the same things and that even in this early stage there is an emerging consensus.

Donald Miller of the University of Southern California in Los Angeles conducted a study of Vineyard, Calvary Chapel and Hope Chapel, reporting his findings in *Reinventing American Protestantism*. In it, he lists 12 distinctives of what he calls "new paradigm churches":

1. They were started after the mid-1960s.
2. The majority of congregation members were born after 1945.
3. Seminary training of clergy is optional.
4. Worship is contemporary.
5. Lay leadership is highly valued.
6. They have extensive small group ministries.
7. Clergy and congregants usually dress informally.
8. Tolerance of different personal styles is prized.
9. Pastors tend to be understated, humble and self-revealing.
10. Bodily, rather than mere cognitive, participation in worship is the norm.
11. The "gifts of the Holy Spirit" are affirmed.
12. Bible-centered teaching predominates over topical sermonizing.

Miller goes on to say, "Overarching all of these characteristics is a spirit of joy and celebration that contrasts strongly with the sterner Protestant (especially Puritan) tradition."[13]

George G. Hunter III of Asbury Theological Seminary in Wilmore, Kentucky, sets forth what he calls "ten features of apostolic congregations":

1. Strong biblical content.
2. Earnest in prayer.
3. Compassion for the lost.
4. Obedience to the Great Commission.
5. Vision for what people can become.
6. Cultural adaptation to the target population.
7. Small groups.
8. Strong lay ministries.
9. Every member and every seeker receives regular pastoral care—from a layperson.
10. Many ministries to the unchurched.[14]

Elmer L. Towns of Liberty University in Lynchburg, Virginia, considers the following eight characteristics as significant in the new apostolic churches:

1. Large size.
2. Family feeling, but not exclusive.
3. Cross socioeconomic classes.
4. Led by "charismatic" pastor-leaders.
5. Congregation both independent and interdependent.
6. Reflect New Testament theological bias.
7. Passion for outpouring of God's Spirit.
8. Bonded by methodology, not theology.[15]

C. Peter Wagner of Fuller Theological Seminary in Pasadena, California. Here is my list of nine salient characteristics of the New Apostolic Reformation:

1. New name.
2. New authority structure.
3. New leadership training.

4. New ministry focus.
5. New worship style.
6. New prayer forms.
7. New financing.
8. New outreach.
9. New power priorities.[16]

FROM THE OLD TO THE NEW

For most readers, me included, our point of reference for the focus of this book is traditional Christianity. I have made a list of 20 of our traditional emphases, and I have contrasted each with the counterpart we are now observing in the New Apostolic Reformation. True, these are only words and phrases, but a few moments of meditation about the implications of each could be time well spent in preparing for the remainder of this book:

- From *Christ as Savior* to *Jesus as Lord.*
- From *Jesus the Lamb* to *Jesus the Lion.*
- From the *cross* to the *crown.*
- From *justification* to *sanctification.*
- From saved *from death* to saved *for life.*
- From *water* baptism to *Spirit* baptism.
- From *living in the desert* to *crossing the Jordan.*
- From *saying prayers* to *praying in the Spirit.*
- From *denying or fearing evil* to *doing spiritual warfare.*
- From *counseling* to *deliverance.*
- From *training* to *anointing.*
- From *guilt for sins* to *victory over sins.*
- From *liturgy* to *spontaneity.*
- From singing *in the choir* to singing *in the Spirit.*
- From *pipe organ* to *keyboard.*
- From *hymns* to *praise and worship songs.*
- From *staff ministry* to *body ministry.*
- From *predicting* to *prophesying.*

+ From *telling* to *showing.*
+ From *seeing and hearing* to *discerning.*[17]

Notes

1. Lyle E. Schaller, *The New Reformation: Tomorrow Arrived Yesterday* (Nashville: Abingdon Press, 1995), p. 13.

2. Donald E. Miller, *Reinventing American Protestantism: Christianity in the New Millennium* (Berkeley, Calif.: University of California Press, 1997), p. 11.

3. Personal correspondence from Joseph C. Wongsak, December 15, 1994.

4. Dan Simpson, "Why Not Call It Neo-Denominationalism?" *Ministry Advantage* (July-August 1996), p. 5.

5. Miller, *Reinventing American Protestantism*, p. 1.

6. Charles Trueheart, "The Next Church," *Atlantic Monthly* (August 1996), p. 37.

7. Frederick O. Burklin, "The New Apostolic Church," *Dynamic Religious Movements*, David J. Hesselgrave, ed. (Grand Rapids: Baker Book House, 1978), p. 68.

8. Harvey Cox, *Fire from Heaven* (Reading, Mass.: Addison-Wesley Publishing Co., 1995), p. 246.

9. Charles Nienkirchen, "Conflicting Views of the Past," *Charismatic Christianity as a Global Culture*, Karla Poewe, ed. (Columbia, S.C.: University of South Carolina Press, 1994), p. 119.

10. George G. Hunter III, personal correspondence with the author, April 12, 1996.

11. David Martin, "Wesley's World Revolution," *The National Review* (December 31, 1995), p. 26.

12. Wilbert Shenk, "Toward a Global Church History," *International Bulletin of Missionary Research* (April 1996), p. 50.

13. Miller, *Reinventing American Protestantism*, p. 20.

14. George G. Hunter III, in *Leadership Network Forum*, no date, but mailed in 1996.

15. Elmer L. Towns, "Understanding the Cycles of Church Renewal," *Ministry Advantage* (July-August 1996), p. 3.

16. See C. Peter Wagner, ed., *The New Apostolic Churches* (Ventura, Calif.: Regal Books, 1997), pp. 18-25.

17. Adapted by C. Peter Wagner from a scale originally designed by Hans Schnabel and published in the June 1993 *ENDSEARCH* newsletter. Used with permission.

CHAPTER THREE

Churches Driven by
Vision and Values

New apostolic leaders live in the future.

I clearly recall back in 1996 conversing with a new apostolic pastor. At one point I asked him, "How many home cell groups do you have?"

His answer? "In the year 2000 we will have 600!"

It did not seem to make any difference at all to him that he did not answer my question. The number of cell groups he had in 1996 was of little consequence to him. He considered those 600 cell groups, four years in the future, as real. They existed! This was the most significant reality to him at the moment.

Awhile later, when I thought back on the conversation, I was flabbergasted and even a bit embarrassed when I realized I never did find out how many cell groups that church had at the time! It was a good lesson to me on the compelling force of the future in new apostolic thinking. Let's take a closer look.

THE COMPELLING FORCE OF THE FUTURE

My friend John Maxwell told me awhile ago that I should read the book *Go for the Magic* written by Pat Williams, the general manager of the Orlando Magic professional basketball team. I am glad I read the book. Williams's philosophy helped me understand why the number of cell groups in the future would be more compelling to my pastor friend than the number of cell groups today.

Pat Williams says, "We all have three blocks of time in our lives: *Yesterday, today,* and *tomorrow.* Those three blocks of time are there for all of us to take and use as we see fit....Everyone gets sixty seconds per minute, sixty minutes per hour, twenty-four hours per day, no more, no less. I am convinced that the secret that allows certain people to rise above the pack is *the way they choose to deal with those three blocks of time.*"[1]

Williams's thought levels the playing field. I don't know how many losers I have heard say, "I wish I had the time to do what so-and-so does." I always want to reply that the fact of the matter is: you *do* have the time. You simply choose to use it in a different way.

Listen to what Williams says about the past: "We should take a realistic look at yesterday. Yesterday is a canceled check. We can never get it back. As the great humorist Will Rogers said, 'Don't let yesterday take up too much of today.' We don't want to forget the past, because that is where we find lessons for today. But neither do we want to get stuck in the past."[2] I couldn't agree more.

HOW NEW APOSTOLIC LEADERS FOCUS THEIR MINDS

Traditional church leaders begin with the present and then look to the past. New apostolic leaders begin with the future and then look to the present. Most denominations are *heritage driven.* Most apostolic networks are *vision driven.* The difference is enormous.

Traditional leaders long for the past, live in the present and fear the future. New apostolic leaders appreciate the past, live in the present and long for the future. Pat Williams says, "Yesterday shapes who we are today, just as what we do today shapes who we will be tomorrow. Look at it this way: Life is like driving a car. It's wise to check the rearview mirror now and then, but the rearview mirror is there only for us to glance at, not to stare at. Staring at where you've been will only land you in a ditch."[3]

The way pastors and other church leaders decide to focus their minds will deeply affect their personal attitudes, which in turn affect everyday decisions and priorities of ministry. For example, those who choose to focus on the past for the most part are *reactive*, they readily see obstacles and they have a low tolerance of risk. Those who choose to focus on the future are more likely to be *proactive*, they readily see opportunities and they have a high tolerance of risk.

MAINTAINING THE COMFORT ZONE

For more than a quarter of a century, I have been a teacher of pastors. My home base is a fairly prestigious theological seminary, although I do as much or more teaching in pastors' conferences and seminars across the nation and in various parts of the world. The vast majority of pastors in every state and in many other countries have settled into a comfort zone. The present and the past mold their daily lives. The future is vague, misty and unsure.

When I was in England recently, I met an Anglican pastor, Kerry Thorpe, who is senior minister of Holy Trinity, Margate. He gave me a copy of his book *Doing Things Differently*, in which he summarizes, better than anything else I have seen, the distinctive values of comfort zone devotees. As I looked at them, I realized these values are exactly what many pastors have learned in seminary, my seminary included.

The following are some of the things we have been teaching pastors as guiding principles for ministry:

1. THE MODERATE MIDDLE. Thorpe says, "The middle way has an attractiveness about it that suggests the avoidance of extremes."[4] When you think about this, you have to wonder where first-century Christianity would have gone if Jesus and the apostles had determined to avoid extremes and remain in the comfortable middle. This is not only where most pastors and denominational executives I know actually are, but it is also where they *want to be*.

2. AVOIDING OFFENSE. Many church leaders will go almost any distance to avoid criticism. Kerry Thorpe says, "Many of us, for psychological reasons, have a deep investment in being liked by others. It matters to us that we are approved. We create an atmosphere in which it is considered bad manners to speak of matters that might be controversial."[5]

3. PRESERVING UNITY. Unity becomes an end in itself, and we begin to strive for unity for the sake of unity. When the desire to keep everyone happy molds our planning and our priorities, we tend to ease into a plain vanilla, least-common-denominatorism, which effectively preserves the status quo and chokes growth potential.

4. VALUING THE NORMAL. It is better to be normal than abnormal. What is normal? The way we have done things in the past. Change is a threat to the stability of the comfort zone, therefore, it is something at least to be suspicious of and to avoid if at all possible.

5. GRADUALISM. If, by chance, change does become inevitable, then the *rate* of change should be kept under strict control. Thorpe says, "There is another deeply honored myth, that the best changes take place slowly."[6] Let's not *jump* into the future; let's *ease* into the future. This reminds me of what one of my senior citizen friends said: "My goal is to become a very old man as slowly as possible."

John Maxwell says, "Losers yearn for the past and get stuck in it. Winners learn from the past and let go of it."

I once heard John Maxwell sum it up in one of his unforgettable contemporary proverbs: "Losers yearn for the past and get stuck in it; winners learn from the past and let go of it." New apostolic leaders will take that one to the bank.

FAITH AND THE FUTURE

We need faith if we are going to be everything God wants us to be. The Bible says, "Without faith it is impossible to please [God]" (Heb. 11:6).

What is the faith the author of Hebrews is talking about here? "Faith is the substance of things hoped for" (Heb. 11:1). Keep in mind that nothing past or present is hoped for—only the future is hoped for. This faith we read about in Hebrews 11 is not for yesterday or today; it is for tomorrow. It is the faith Noah had when he built the ark on dry ground. It operates when we put *substance* on the future.

One who could put substance on the future as well as any was Walt Disney. Pat Williams tells this revealing story: "Walt Disney didn't live to walk down the Main Street of his new Magic Kingdom or to stroll from pavilion to pavilion in Epcot Center. He died in 1965, almost five years before Walt Disney World opened. On the day the Florida park opened, someone commented to Mike Vance, creative director of Walt Disney Studios, 'Isn't it too bad Walt Disney didn't live to see this?'

"'He did see it,' Vance replied simply. 'That's why it's here.'"[7]

I like what Ed Delph says about new apostolic pastors and church leaders: "Most of them feel that they are called to *take ground* and not to *hold ground*." John Richardson said, "When it comes to the future, there are three kinds of people: those who let it happen, those who make it happen, and those who wonder what happened."[8]

SACRIFICING A SACRED COW

Michael Regele, president of Percept, a foremost geodemographic research firm serving churches of all kinds, is a household name among denominational executives. His desire is that denominations will continue to play a vital role in the future of American Christianity. Regele is a researcher who does not sugarcoat the pill. He realizes that several things, which he calls "sacred cows," will have to change if denominations hope to remain viable.

One of the sacred cows to which he refers is: "What Matters Most Is Our Tradition." Regele's comment: "To say that one's tradition matters is part of one's identity. However, when our historic tradition becomes a barrier to making sense to our contemporary society, then we have the formula for extinction."9 More often than not, instead of becoming a *faith booster*, tradition becomes a *faith blocker*.

THE OTHER SIDE OF YEARNING FOR REVIVAL

This presents the other side of the calls we frequently hear for "revival." I realize that cautionary words about yearning for "revival" are akin to knocking mom and apple pie. As readers of my book *The Rising Revival* (Regal Books) will know, I desire the great outpouring of the Spirit of God on our nation and on the world as much as anyone I am aware of. However, much revival thinking these days is overly locked into yesterday, at least in my opinion.

Much of the talk about revival I am hearing tends to be nostalgic, focusing backward on Azusa Street or the Welsh Revival or what happened under Jonathan Edwards or Charles Finney. The fact is that many revival fires have been ignited by testimonies of what the Holy Spirit is doing *today*, but few, if any, have been ignited by contemplating and recounting what happened *yesterday*.

Speaking of Jonathan Edwards, it would be more advisable to attempt to apply his *principles* today rather than to imitate his *procedures*. Jonathan Edwards did not look back to the past for his vision. Rather, he defended what was called the "new light," much to the dismay of his detractors who preferred the status quo. Edwards's vision consistently was toward the future.

For example, in chapter 1, I mentioned how the Assemblies of God growth rate had slowed down in the 1990s, which was projected to be their "Decade of Harvest." Here is the way the denomination chose to report progress to their constituency in mid-decade, 1995: "The Harvest Task Force, in its first meeting under the new leadership structure, issued a clarion call to 'retool and refocus for the harvest.' Specific directives include (1) A spiritual call to revival....While number goals can serve as a measure of progress, the emphasis needs to return to the basics."[10]

Notice how the language of this report focuses on yesterday: "Re-tool," "Re-focus," "Re-vival," "Re-turn." The prefix "re" means to reinstate something from the past. "Revival" literally means to bring back to life. What life? The life of the past. Help is obviously needed. Where will this help come from? The past! This sort of appeal is extremely common whenever evangelism bogs down. On the other hand, when evangelism is powerful, when soul saving is on a roll, you simply don't hear this kind of language from leaders of growing churches and apostolic networks.

THE DEAD-END STREET CALLED "RENEWAL"

Efforts toward renewal have more often than not ended up in a dead-end street. Despite decades of talk about "renewal," documented accounts of denominations that actually have been renewed are few and far between. I have seen only one—the Australian Assemblies of God, which is detailed in chapter 5. Renewal more often than not is a lofty thought, apparently having very little substance. It goes back to the questions of old versus new wineskins.

Consider, for example, the experience of Ralph Neighbour: "Finally, in 1985," he writes, "when that twenty-first pastor called me from California to tell me his three-year-long struggle to develop relational church structures had ended in his forced resignation, I began to ask myself a serious question: *Can new wine be put into old skins?* The answer is, 'No!'

"Attempts at renewal don't work for one reason," Ralph Neighbour adds. "Our Lord told us over 2,000 years ago *it could not be done.* Every time we try to ignore His clear teaching, we fail. In retrospect, I could have saved myself 24 years of dreaming an impossible dream if I had taken His admonition literally. While I was trying to *renew*, He was shaping something *brand new.*"[11] Neighbour's words may be stronger than many others who have arrived at similar conclusions would use, but the principle remains that looking back rarely delivers a substantial payoff.

THE ESCAPE HATCH OF DENIAL

Some pastors and denominational executives choose to ignore these kinds of facts. For many, it is a case of vocational survival. Facing the facts could cost them their jobs! Lyle Schaller comments on this: "Many denominational agencies today exist in a state of denial...and denial is never, never a source of creativity and innovation." If denominations are going to survive in any sort of viable way, Schaller thinks they must be realistic and face the facts. He says, "What I would see as the first step in terms of the adaptation of denominations to a new day would be to move out of the denial stage."[12]

As a concrete example, consider the findings of Ronald Vallet and Charles Zech as reported in their book *The Mainline Church's Funding Crisis*: "The evidence is overpowering that mainline denominations in North America—both the United States and Canada—are undergoing a mission funding crisis."[13]

The study found that the United Church of Christ (UCC) in the period 1970-1992 lost 24 percent in giving. However, "In March 1994, stewardship officials of the UCC were asked whether or not a mission funding crisis existed. One wrote that 'my perception of this United Church of Christ does not reach to 'crisis categories and language.'"[14] If leaders refuse to admit there is a problem, the likelihood is they will soon be experiencing another 24 percent decline in finances.

THE VISION OF THE FUTURE CHURCH

I have taken a good bit of space to explain the mind-set of traditional Christian leaders. I thought it was necessary if we are going to understand just how radical is the change from where we have been in the past to New Apostolic Reformation thinking.

The first time I came into contact with this new kind of thinking was in the early 1980s when my wife, Doris, and I spent some time in Argentina with Omar and Marfa Cabrera. They are the founders of what is one of the dozen largest churches in the world with 145,000 members.

In those days, I had few mental grids through which I could analyze what I was really observing. However, I should have gotten my first cue from the name Omar Cabrera had given to his church: Vision of the Future. He was not locked into yesterday; he was launching into tomorrow. In fact, he did so many new things that he was publicly ostracized by the established Protestant leaders in Argentina for more than a decade. Fortunately, the wounds have now been healed through repentance and reconciliation, and Cabrera is widely honored and admired as one of the chief apostles of the Argentine church.

What are some of the core values of new apostolic leaders that have arisen as they have attempted to fulfill their "vision for the future"? Let's take a look.

FIVE COMPASS-POINT NEW APOSTOLIC VALUES

There is great diversity among new apostolic churches. Each network has a distinctive DNA as a component of the whole Body of Christ. Given all their diversity, these churches, generally speaking, are heading in the same directions. They have a common set of values. Because they are heading in similar directions, I call these values "compass-point values." I would not presume to say that every one of these new apostolic churches agrees with every other one in the way they see and interpret these values. They definitely do form a pattern, however. I am bold enough to say that the churches that deviate from them could be considered exceptions to the rule.

These five compass-point values are nonnegotiable. They are not the only nonnegotiable values among new apostolic churches. Who knows? Someone could probably make a list of 50. However, these are five principal values that, according to my observation, most set the New Apostolic Reformation apart from much of traditional Christianity. I realize we are not concerned entirely with black-and-white kind of distinctions. The differences fall along a spectrum. There are many shades of gray; but the general outlines of these differences are clear.

Three of these values relate to faith: theology, ecclesiology and eschatology. The other two relate to practice: organization and leadership. Let's explore them.

1. THEOLOGY HAS ABSOLUTE NORMS

Arguably, one of the most influential books about religion in the last half of the twentieth century was Dean Kelley's *Why Conservative Churches Are Growing*. Kelley's main thesis did not primarily relate to conservative-liberal theological differences, but to "strictness." His research uncovered the fact that strict churches grow more rapidly than lenient churches. Why? Because, according to Kelley, they provide their members with better explanations of the meaning of life.

Kelley says, "Whatever undertakings make life meaningful in ultimate terms for their members, those enterprises are serving the religious function, irrespective of their ideology or structure, whether they claim to be doing so or not....This suggests a different measure of success among religious groups.

Those are successful which are explaining life to their members so that it makes sense to them."[15]

If strictness is so important, then what, exactly, constitutes strictness? Kelley's first "trait of strictness" is *absolutism*. He says, "If the members of a religious group show high commitment to its goals or beliefs, and willingness to suffer and sacrifice for them, etc., they also tend to show a kind of absolutism about those aims, beliefs, explanations of life."[16]

Later on, Kelley delineates what he calls "minimal maxims of strictness," saying that those who are serious about their faith "do not confuse it with other beliefs/loyalties/practices, or mingle them together indiscriminately, or pretend they are alike, of equal merit, or mutually compatible if they are not."[17]

TRADITIONAL CHURCHES DEABSOLUTIZE THEOLOGY AND ETHICS

In chapter 1, I explained the differences between contextual factors and institutional factors and how the leaders of declining denominations attempted to blame their woes on contextual factors because they wanted to avoid taking the blame. Dean Kelley's book, which highlights *institutional* factors as primary determinants of growth or nongrowth, blindsided many of them back in the early 1970s, and they did their best to discredit Kelley. As we have seen, they were ultimately unsuccessful in that effort.

One of the most consequential decisions church leaders made, thereby causing their churches to enter into severe decline beginning in 1965, was to deabsolutize their theology and ethics. They were setting their sails in a direction completely opposite to Kelley's principle of strictness. Many of them took pride in their "liberated" version of Christianity.

Thomas Oden, a credentialed mainline insider and professor of theology at Drew University in Madison, New Jersey, describes in vivid terms how this has ended up for many:

> Much of what has been studied in liberated religion
> under the heading of "theology" has nothing whatso-

ever to do with God or God's revelation or God's church or the worship of God....God has become a joke in the university. The "theo" in theological can mean jazz or recycling or Tarot cards or mung bean experiments. Anything can be put in the slot called "theology" with complete immunity and without anyone's ever questioning whether the subject matter is God or whether it is possible any longer to speak plausibly of God....I am worried about the future trajectory of something called theology in which professors who are paid to teach about God have decided that the idea of God is absurd.[18]

To suggest that theological absolutes are nonnegotiable is offensive to many mainline church leaders. Tolerance is equated with godliness, and Bible-centered theology is regarded as intrinsically intolerant. Heresy? Here is what Oden says about that: "No heresy of any kind any longer exists....Not only is there no concept of heresy, but also there is no way even to raise the question of where the boundaries of legitimate Christian belief lie, when absolute relativism holds sway."[19]

Three researchers, Benton Johnson, Dean Hoge and Donald Luidens, recently undertook a study of mainline churches to try to determine what they called in the title of their report "The Real Reason for Decline." One of their conclusions was: "The single best predictor of church participation turned out to be belief—orthodox Christian *belief,* and especially the teaching that a person can be saved only through Jesus Christ."[20]

THERE ARE THEOLOGICAL ABSOLUTES

Most new apostolic leaders would have predicted what Johnson, Hoge and Luidens discovered. It is interesting that new apostolic churches are not *creedal,* but they do agree on the *core* of theology.

In his excellent book *Primary Purpose,* Ted Haggard, pastor of New Life Church in Colorado Springs, Colorado, distinguishes between absolutes, interpretations and deductions affecting our belief. It is characteristic of new apostolic leaders to keep the core list of absolutes as short as possible.

For example, Ed Delph once developed a list of guidelines for alignment of apostolic leaders, one of which was "Basic and essential doctrinal beliefs are the same or similar enough." I love that "similar enough"! This is far different from the days when I was a recognized fundamentalist and advocated an extremely long list of absolutes. Donald Miller concludes that "New paradigm Christians are *doctrinal minimalists*."[21]

The point is not how long the list of absolutes might be, but: Are there absolutes? The answer is, yes there are, and they are *strict* absolutes in Dean Kelley's sense of strictness. They are things church members are willing to suffer and sacrifice for if need be. My observation is that there are three generally agreed-upon theological absolutes in new apostolic churches:

1. The Bible is true and normative. It is the absolute authority for faith and practice.
2. Jesus Christ is God and Lord.
3. An individual's personal relationship with Jesus Christ makes the difference between heaven and hell. Note that each one of these relates to what Dean Kelley would call "the meaning of life in ultimate terms."

If I were to select three of the *moral* nonnegotiables I have observed in new apostolic churches, they would be the following:

1. Human life begins at conception.
2. Homosexuality is sin against God.
3. Extramarital heterosexual relationships are also sin.

HOW STRICT ARE NEW APOSTOLIC CHURCHES?
This raises an issue that needs to be addressed, if only briefly. Now that the significant role of new apostolic churches in contemporary Christianity is becoming more widely recognized,

they have increasingly become the objects of study by sociologists of religion. Some of them, applying Dean Kelley's criteria of strictness, have concluded that new apostolic churches are lenient and, therefore, they may have an inherent weakness.

One of these is Mark Shibley, a sociologist at Loyola University in Chicago, Illinois. Shibley's study of a midwestern Vineyard church surfaces "traits of leniency," including relativism, tolerance of cultural diversity and a desire for dialogue rather than monologue. He concludes, "While Vineyard is clearly a strong church, it is not clearly strict."[22]

I think Shibley accurately describes these aspects of Vineyard, but I would argue that, despite these characteristics, Vineyard is strict. As Shibley observes, one of the strengths of Vineyard is that it has allowed itself to be molded to a considerable extent by contemporary culture. In missiological terms, it is a contextualized church.

Shibley says, "In a pluralistic society, strong churches will not continue to grow if their strictness moves them too far from the cultural norms that surround their institutions."[23] This is true. He could have mentioned the lack of conversion growth among the Amish to help reinforce his point.

CULTURAL CONFORMITY PLUS NONNEGOTIABLES

Further examination will, undoubtedly, indicate that Vineyard and other new apostolic churches are culturally conformist. However, they still retain certain core nonnegotiable values relating to the ultimate meaning of life that locate them on the strict side of the line. The theological and ethical convictions I mentioned could be a part of that core, and they could all be regarded as countercultural, especially outside the Bible Belt.

Donald Miller's studies of Vineyard, Calvary Chapel and Hope Chapel, which he calls new paradigm churches, support my contention. Instead of using Kelley's lenient-strict typology, he uses Ernst Troeltsch's church-sect typology, and he concludes that, indeed, new apostolic churches are sects, meaning that they are strict.

Miller says, "What makes new paradigm Christians sectlike is their insistence that there is one truth, not many, and that authority is a meaningful category, not simply a social construction rooted in material self-interest. Yet, although they impose high moral standards on their members, new paradigm Christians are anything but sober and life-denying in their demeanor."[24] It is probably because of this casual demeanor that some might conclude these churches are on the lenient side.

Here is another helpful elaboration from Donald Miller: "New paradigm churches are 'high-demand' institutions, however relaxed and contemporary their music and organizational structure may appear. They provide a structure of mentoring and accountability for individuals who are serious about the tough challenge of changing their lives."[25]

A notable trait of strictness is the new apostolic insistence that church members be born-again.

Miller says, "In contrast to many mainline churches, new paradigm churches are highly conversion-oriented; they believe that they have an answer to people's felt needs, and this conviction is perhaps intensified by the fact that so many of the pastors have drug addiction and other vices in their backgrounds."[26]

New apostolic Christians passionately believe that Jesus is the answer to life's problems and that if individuals need personal help or help for their families, the first essential step is to become a believer. In other words, they fervently address the ultimate meaning of life.

2. Ecclesiology Looks Outward

Another trait of new apostolic strictness is a burning desire to win the lost to Christ. This is a corollary to the issue of heaven and hell, which was listed among the theological nonnegotiables above. A characteristic of many traditional churches is that the church exists primarily to serve its members, and when that is done it may or may not choose to reach out. If there is no such thing as hell, though, why bother? This issue surfaced in a study of diminished giving in mainline and evangelical churches. The researchers found that "the de-emphasis of hell, with no equally compelling alternative, has not only under-mined the traditional evangelistic focus of the church but has also removed part of the clergy's job description—to call people to action to avoid consequences—and the implied authority that went with it."27

The subtitle of Ted Haggard's book *Primary Purpose* (Creation House) sums up the heart desire of new apostolic Christians as well as anything I have observed: *Making It Hard to Go to Hell from Your City*. Churches looking outward are so much a part of the fabric of the New Apostolic Reformation that I will include a whole chapter about outreach later on.

3. ESCHATOLOGY IS OPTIMISTIC

The third new apostolic compass-point value is that Satan is being defeated, that things are going well for the kingdom of God and that spiritual victories will continue to exceed spiritu-al defeats. New apostolic leaders recognize that society is crum-bling, that demons infest our environment and that people are hurting more and more. However, they hold what Frank Damazio calls a "visionary eschatology." In other words, they strongly believe that more souls than ever are being saved, that churches will continue to multiply, that demonic strongholds will be torn down, that the powers of darkness will crack open and that the advance of God's kingdom is inexorable.

As I move among new apostolic leaders, I hear surprisingly little conversation relating to pre-millennialism or post-millen-nialism or a-millennialism, and even less about pre-tribulation or mid-tribulation or post-tribulation rapture. These eschato-logical issues, once high on the agendas of many conservative church leaders, do not seem to be that important today.

Robert Schuller's advice to young church leaders would

seem to apply to new apostolic Christians: "Don't let eschatology stifle your long-term thinking."[28]

4. ORGANIZATION EMERGES FROM PERSONAL RELATIONSHIPS

The first three compass-point values relate to issues of faith. These last two relate to practice.

How are new apostolic organizations organized? Let's begin by looking at this fascinating observation made by Lyle Schaller:

> Why do units of local government in northern Italy excel when compared to units of local government in southern Italy? In a remarkable analysis of the local governments of Italy, Robert D. Putnam and his colleagues concluded that the key variable was in their social and political culture. For nearly a millennium southern Italy had been organized in a rigidly hierarchical system with a heavy emphasis on "vertical bonds." By contrast, the social and political culture of northern Italy had been organized around "horizontal bonds." The small organizations in the North resembles voluntary associations built on the trust of people for one another.[29]

Schaller's account could apply equally to the organizational patterns of traditional denominations (like southern Italy) and apostolic networks (like northern Italy). The basic issue is whether an organization is based on control (southern Italy) or trust (northern Italy). Let's apply this by first looking at the theory and then at the practice.

THE THEORY

My theoretical framework for understanding the organizational structure of the New Apostolic Reformation follows *The New*

Organization by Colin Hastings, the most helpful book I have found on the subject. Here is how Hastings describes the old way of organizing. All of us who have spent years in denominational structures will immediately recognize what he is talking about.

> The way that we organize our enterprises and public bodies has remained essentially unchanged for several thousand years. Perhaps more importantly, the way we picture organizations in our minds and the way we think about how they work is deeply ingrained in every one of us. Which is why, when this traditional way of organizing begins to let us down, begins to show its inability to deal with quite momentous levels of change, we all find it difficult to see alternatives, let alone comprehend or implement them.[30]

Denominational structures that worked only a couple of decades ago are now becoming obsolete. God is pouring out new wine, and many of the old wineskins are proving dysfunctional. A call for "renewal" of the old wineskins will be inadequate in most cases. Only a determination for "reinventing" or "re-engineering," which means, to all intents and purposes, starting from scratch, may prove to be a viable solution.

The alternatives are so new that many well-entrenched church leaders are either unaware of them or they do not comprehend them. Hastings says, "It is only in the last 50 years or so that the traditional command and control model, derived from ancient military practice, has been seriously questioned."[31]

RELATIONSHIPS ARE CENTRAL

What, then, is called for? Hastings says, "When we start seeing an organization as a constantly changing kaleidoscope of relationships between people, we begin to get a better flavor of what might be involved."[32] The operative word here is *relationships*. Some refer to the change as the transition from modern to post-modern culture, which has many parallel trends in our society as a whole. Here are some of the concrete ways changes might work out in everyday church life:

> From *traditional Protestantism* to the *New Apostolic Reformation*;
> From *position based* to *vision and values*;
> From *inhibition of talent* to *exhibition of talent*;
> From *rigid* to *flexible*;
> From *passion for order* to *tolerance of ambiguity*;
> From *control* to *coordination*;
> From *Why?* to *Why not?*
> From *boundary making* to *boundary breaking*;
> From *permission withholding* to *empowerment*.

It is not uncommon at three-day annual conventions of churches belonging to an apostolic network to spend a large amount of time in worship, in coffee breaks, in meals together, in a few upbeat, motivational messages, in playing golf and in a semi-casual 30- to 45-minute business meeting. The best way to spend time, most new apostolic leaders will agree, is in building relationships.

Hastings says, "It is investment in the ability of people who know each other within the corporation to make quick contact, know how each other is likely to think, assemble resources rapidly and make quick decisions based on having worked together before, that will be the key to retaining the benefits of smallness."[33]

THE PRACTICE

Lyle Schaller takes a long look at mainline church polity, especially examining his own United Methodist Church, in a highly significant recent book, *Tattered Trust*. By way of analogy, he discusses the pioneer wagon trains that brought the first settlers to the west. Every wagon train had a wagon master, who, at the beginning of each day, would point west and say, "There is where we are going today!" He would invariably be pointing to new, unexplored, risky territory.

Picking up from here, Schaller says, "The polity of The United Methodist Church, which is organized around distrust of individuals, makes it impossible for anyone to serve as the wagon master."[34] Schaller then gives a long list of examples of "systemic distrust" of leaders. Here is my paraphrase of a few of them:

- The district cabinet is more qualified to choose a church's pastor than are congregational leaders.
- The denomination is better equipped to determine the training a pastor needs than the candidate is.
- Ministers cannot be trusted to choose where they can serve most effectively.
- Donors cannot be trusted to designate their benevolence dollars.
- Congregational leaders cannot be trusted to choose where their church should be located.

The outcome of distrust of individuals, rampant among traditional denominations, looks something like this, according to Schaller:

> The number one responsibility of a denominational system is to regulate the role, behavior, and beliefs of individuals, congregations, and regional judicatories. This normally calls for a legalistic polity designed to facilitate permission withholding. The system also will include provisions for appealing decisions to higher courts of the church. The denomination will determine the standards for ordination, the criteria for determining the final destination of financial contributions, the organizational structure for congregations, the role, responsibilities of regional judicatories, and a thousand other issues. Law moves ahead of grace.[35]

By way of example, the manual setting forth the rules and regulations of The Christian and Missionary Alliance contains 83,500 words, and the manual for the Church of the Nazarene contains 96,000 words. The minutes alone of the 1993 General Council of the Assemblies of God contain 55,500 words.

New apostolic leaders have reacted decisively against the kind of top-down control Lyle Schaller describes and is emulated by denominations in general. They do trust individuals. They do have wagon masters. This leads to the final one of the five new apostolic compass-point values:

5. LEADERS CAN BE TRUSTED

Of all the radical elements of change in the New Apostolic Reformation, I regard one of them to be the most radical of all. It is so important that I have chosen these words very carefully:

> *The amount of spiritual authority*
> *delegated by the Holy Spirit*
> *to individuals.*

The two operative words in that statement are *authority* and *individuals*. The authority derives from trust, which in this case is not tattered, but intact. The authority is invested in individuals as contrasted to bureaucracies, judicatories, sessions, vestries, boards, committees and similar groups formed to make decisions. This plays out specifically on two levels: the local church level (pastors) and the translocal level (apostles). I will discuss each level in detail in the next two chapters.

Meanwhile, delegating authority to individuals has two outstanding advantages, namely, focusing vision and releasing creativity.

A. FOCUSING VISION. It is axiomatic that the more diffused the vision, the weaker the organization.

To apply this to a concrete case of a denomination, let's study the Presbyterian Church (U.S.A.), which has been in a steady decline since 1965. Back in 1992, someone raised the question of what might be the real vision of the denomination. Because of established church polity, no one person in the organization could have been entrusted to give the answer. So a convocation of leaders was called in Chicago from October 30 to November 1, 1992. Its mandate: to identify the mission priorities of the church.

The result of that convocation was a 256-page document, detailing 143 denominational priorities! When there is no leader to cast the vision, the vision can become so diffused that it is next to meaningless. Most new apostolic leaders I know would have a difficult time believing such a convocation could actually occur.

Some committed denominationalists, such as Tony Campolo (an American Baptist), have begun to observe this from the inside. In his book *Can Mainline Denominations Make a Comeback?* he says: "I do not know how mainline denominations are going to do it, but there is little doubt among those experts in sociology of religion that the realignment of their churches is essential. Too much diversity within any denomination paralyzes its growth and development. And right now there is too much diversity in all of them!"[36]

I suspect one of the reasons Campolo says he doesn't know how they could implement this is that he realizes that within present denominational structures there is virtually no possibility of trusting *individuals* enough to delegate to them vision-casting authority for the whole organization. Methodists could use a new John Wesley, Presbyterians could use a new John Knox and Lutherans could use a new Martin Luther. All of them, in their day, had extraordinary authority as individual leaders, and their vision was clear and unquestioned by their followers.

Here is the way George Barna sees it: "Vision is entrusted to an individual. Did you notice in the Bible that God never gave vision to a committee? In every case, God selected a person for whom He tailored a vision for a better future."[37]

B. RELEASING CREATIVITY. When individual leaders have freedom from permission withholders, they can be as creative as God wants them to be. They can take risks. They can make mistakes. They can explore new territory. They can color outside the lines. They can push back boundaries. They can butcher sacred cows. They can shake up the status quo. They can break rules. They can soar to new heights.

When leaders have freedom from permission withholders, they can be as creative as God wants them to be.

I love the way Roberts Liardon, a new apostolic leader, explains it in an article he calls "Extremists, Radicals, and Non-Conformists: Please Be One!"

> An "extremist" is someone like Jesus, filled with His principles. They go a "little farther," leaving the average and acceptable norm of the day...If making a bold statement *glorifies the principles of God* but labels you as an extremist, radical or non-conformist, then wear those words as a medal!...God never calls you to be average. Average is a mixture of good and bad. Nowhere in the Bible did God call anyone and keep them average. Instead, they built an ark in the midst of chaos; they parted the sea; they marched around walls, causing them to fall; they walked on the water; and people were totally healed as their shadow passed by. Many times, He even changed their names to assure the victory.[38]

It would be difficult for most traditional evangelical leaders to say words such as these. In fact, some would want to scold Liardon for doing it. However, the price for choosing the least common denominator is diminished creativity. As an illustration of how this manifests itself, *Christianity Today* published a special issue in 1996, featuring pictures and bios of what they called "Up and Comers: Fifty evangelical leaders 40 and under."[39]

It was notable that out of the 50 young leaders who were the cream of the crop of traditional evangelicals, only 6 of them identified their primary ministry as a local church. Why? I suspect the reason was that these individuals, who would not have been included if they were not somewhere above average in creativity, quickly learned that their creativity would be unacceptably stifled in their traditional denominations and local churches. Therefore, 88 percent of them chose to minister outside a local church structure to be able to release their creativity.

I may be wrong, but I would guess that a similar roster of new apostolic leaders would show something like 88 percent in local churches, rather than in parachurch ministries. New apostolic leaders can be supervised by a local church or an apostolic network covering and still be "extremists or radicals," as Roberts Liardon would say.

By way of summary, I love this quote from Wolfgang Simson:

> Yesterday's despised revolutionaries have often become today's trusted pillars of the church. Are you ready for this? The unbalanced ones, the ones who are called by God to do the ridiculous, the unbelievable, the never-heard-of, the ones that break the rules, the spiritual pioneers inventing new ways and breaking through the walls *do* change the world. The play-safe, normal, balanced, spiritual middle-class maintain it.[40]

As any new apostolic leader will tell you, suspicion and distrust feed the status quo; trust and empowerment shape the future!

Notes
1. Pat Williams, *Go for the Magic* (Nashville: Thomas Nelson, 1995), p. 17.
2. Ibid.

3. Ibid., p. 22.

4. Kerry Thorpe, *Doing Things Differently: Changing the Heart of the Church* (Cambridge, England: Grove Books Limited, 1997), p. 9.

5. Ibid., p. 10.

6. Ibid., p. 11.

7. Williams, *Go For the Magic*, p. 88.

8. Quoted by George Barna, *Turning Vision into Action* (Ventura, Calif.: Regal Books, 1996), p. 17.

9. Michael Regele, "Sacrificing Some Sacred Cows," *Viewpoint* (Fall 1994), p. 1.

10. General Council of the Assemblies of God, *Biennial Report 1993-1995*, p. 12.

11. Ralph Neighbour, *Where Do We Go From Here?* (Houston, Tex.: Touch Publications, 1990), p. 92.

12. Lyle E. Schaller, "Is There a Future for Denominations?" *Forum Files* (Leadership Network) (November 1994), p. 1.

13. Ronald Vallet and Charles Zech, *The Mainline Church's Funding Crisis* (Grand Rapids: Eerdmans Publishing House, 1995), p. 66.

14. Ibid., p. 8.

15. Dean M. Kelley, *Why Conservative Churches Are Growing* (Macon, Ga.: Mercer University Press, 1986), p. 45.

16. Ibid., p. 78.

17. Ibid., p. 121.

18. Thomas C. Oden, *Requiem: A Lament in Three Movements* (Nashville: Abingdon Press, 1995), pp. 44, 45.

19. Ibid., p. 47.

20. Benton Johnson, Dean R. Hoge and Donald A. Luidens, "Mainline Churches: The Real Reason for Decline," *First Things: A Monthly Journal of Religion and Public Life* (March 1993), p. 15.

21. Donald E. Miller, *Reinventing American Protestantism* (Berkeley, Calif.: University of California Press, 1997), p. 121.

22. Mark A. Shibley, *Resurgent Evangelicalism in the United States* (Columbia, S.C.: University of South Carolina Press, 1996), p. 135.

23. Ibid., p. 136.

24. Miller, *Reinventing American Protestantism*, p. 154.

25. Ibid., p. 79.

26. Ibid.

27. John and Sylvia Ronsvalle, *Behind Stained Glass Windows: Money Dynamics in the Church* (Grand Rapids: Baker Books, 1996), p. 61.

28. "How Schuller Shaped Your Ministry," interview by *Leadership* magazine (Spring 1997), p. 14.

29. Lyle E. Schaller, *Tattered Trust* (Nashville: Abingdon Press, 1996), p. 43.

30. Colin Hastings, *The New Organization* (London, England: McGraw-Hill, 1993), p. 3.

31. Ibid., p. xvi.
32. Ibid.
33. Ibid., p. 87.
34. Schaller, *Tattered Trust*, p. 42.
35. Ibid., p. 59.
36. Tony Campolo, *Can Mainline Denominations Make a Comeback?* (Valley Forge, Pa.: Judson Press, 1995), p. 163.
37. Barna, *Turning Vision into Action*, p. 75.
38. Roberts Liardon, "Extremists, Radicals and Non-Conformists: Please Be One!" *Spirit Life International* (Summer 1996), p. 2.
39. "Up and Comers: Fifty evangelical leaders 40 and under," *Christianity Today* (November 11, 1996), pp. 20-30.
40. Wolfgang Simson, *British Church Growth Digest* (Spring 1996), p. 3.

CHAPTER FOUR

The Pastor Leads
the Church

Remember, the most radical change in the New Apostolic Reformation, in my opinion, is the recognition of the amount of spiritual authority delegated by the Holy Spirit to individuals.

THE LOCUS OF CORPORATE TRUST

In most churches in the United States—I would guess more than 90 percent—the pastor is regarded as an employee of the church. What this means is that the locus of corporate trust is not the pastor, but rather the deacon board, the trustees, the session, the vestry, the congregation, the elected church board, the presbytery, the district cabinet or whatever other body that might have developed within the local church or the denominational system. There is a general mind-set that individuals are not worthy of a great deal of trust on any level. Groups, somehow or other, appear to be much safer.

Trust, then, is the key factor, the root of the role of pastors in new apostolic churches. If trust is the root, authority is the fruit. The members of new apostolic congregations are at least as intelligent and committed across the board as members of traditional congregations, and they exhibit a surprisingly high level of trust in their pastors. They willingly submit to the pastor's authority and judgment concerning church matters.

For example, in New Life Church of Colorado Springs

where my wife and I give our tithe, we trust our pastor, Ted Haggard, with sole discretion of 65 percent of the annual budget of more than $5 million. The remaining 35 percent is available to the trustees for buildings, land and such items as needed, and the pastor also chairs the board of trustees.

TRADITIONAL VIEWS OF THE PASTOR'S ROLE

I suspect that most readers of this book are, or have been at one time, adult members of traditional churches, as I have for most of my Christian life. We have uncritically accepted traditional concepts of the role of our pastors as if they had been derived from biblical mandates. Understandably, we find ourselves uncomfortable with things such as trusting pastors to manage million-dollar budgets by themselves. We have developed a rhetoric to express this discomfort, referring to new apostolic pastors as "autocratic," "dictators," "empire builders," "manipulative," "tyrants" or "power hungry."

We have been much more accustomed to such traditional assumptions as the following:

1. AS EMPLOYEES OF THE CHURCH, PASTORS ARE PAID A SALARY TO MINISTER. In many denominations, the pastors are commonly referred to as their "ministers." This has also carried over to the U.S. government, because we clergy list our vocation on our 1040 forms as "minister." The implication? The pastor's job is to do the ministry of the church.

2. PASTORS COME AND PASTORS GO. Limited pastoral tenure is the rule. Some denominations such as the Salvation Army or Seventh-day Adventists find themselves on the shorter end of the pastoral tenure scale at around two to four years. Southern Baptists average two years and three months.[1] In 1995, United Methodist clergy averaged 4.3 years in their current

appointments. Presbyterians expect a slightly longer tenure. Lutheran pastors change less frequently than most. In every case, however, the assumption is that our current pastor is not here for life. This is why so many pastors have, at one time or another, heard a deacon speak the disheartening words: "Son, I was here a long time before you came, and I'll be here a long time after you're gone!"

3. PASTORS ARE ENABLERS. When they come into a church, new pastors in traditional churches are expected to spend as much time as necessary in getting to know the church members and finding out what they want to do and where they want to go. The pastors' responsibility from then on is to enable the members to accomplish what they desire.

4. PASTORS ARE, TO BORROW AN ANTHROPOLOGICAL TERM, THE CHURCH "MEDICINE MEN." This is a term Lyle Schaller uses from time to time to contrast the "medicine man" with the "tribal chief." The medicine man does the religious things: praying, baptizing, explaining the Bible, representing the church to the public, blessing church suppers and Sunday School picnics, visiting hospitals, conducting marriages and funerals, dedicating children and the like. However, the pastor should not expect to function as the tribal chief. The true tribal chief of the congregation has long since achieved that status, although rarely is the role allowed to be explicit. Sometimes that person (or occasionally that family) is found in the formal elected church structures, but sometimes they are in the virtually invisible informal structure. Wherever they are located, they diligently propagate the idea that the pastor functions as our paid chaplain.

By way of example, until recently the Presbyterian Church (U.S.A.) had formalized the medicine man pastoral role. The local church board, called the session, is composed of a number of elders who are elected by the congregation, the pastor serving as the moderator. For years, the pastor was called the *"teaching elder,"* and the others were the *"ruling* elders." These designations have been officially dropped, but functionally the relationship continues in most Presbyterian churches.

I could not help but chuckle when I recently read in a prominent mainline-oriented Christian magazine a classified advertisement for a pastor. It read: "Our strong committee structure will enable you to focus on spiritual leadership." The church clearly wanted a medicine man, not a tribal chief!

5. PASTORS ARE SUBJECT TO PERFORMANCE REVIEWS. Because pastors are employees, the church considers itself responsible to hire, fire and supervise. Therefore, responsible churches think they should periodically take stock to assess whether their current pastors are doing well enough to stay or whether the time might have come for them to move on. Some do this on an ad hoc basis, but others institutionalize the process. For years the Church of the Nazarene, for example, required each congregation to conduct an annual pastoral review. This has now been extended to four years, but the underlying threat that the congregation can fire the pastor on the spot easily instills the idea that a "good" pastor's chief goal should be to maintain the status quo, promote harmony and keep everybody happy.

I will not soon forget a Nazarene pastor who enrolled in one of my two-week doctor of ministry courses. In the class prayer time on the Monday of the second week, he shared his heart with the other pastors in the class. During the Sunday service the day before, an irate church member had taken the pulpit away from the guest speaker whom the pastor had invited and had proceeded to deliver a fierce diatribe against my student and his ministry, suggesting he be fired and asked to leave town when he returned from the class. Although some, undoubtedly, considered this to be out of order, the established system had opened the door for such behavior. Not surprisingly, the pastor soon resigned and went on to plant a new apostolic church.

NEW APOSTOLIC CHURCHES ARE DIFFERENT

My friend David (Kwang Shin) Kim was a successful Korean-American landscape architect when he was converted to Christ and called to plant a church in Southern California. His vision was to plant a church that would have foreign mission outreach as its primary goal. He found three other families who would join him and his wife in starting the church, and he called a meeting of the four men. In the meeting Kim said, "Next Sunday we will have our first service, and a new church will be born. We must decide now how we can best serve the Lord. I have a friend who feels called to Guam as a missionary if he can raise $800 a month as support. I propose that we add $400, and pledge $1,200 a month as support."

When I heard David Kim tell this story, he added, smiling, "I wish I had a camera there to catch the expressions on the faces of the committee members!"

After sometime of shocked silence, one man said, "Pastor, you can't run a church like that."

So Kim replied, "Well, then, how should I run the church?"

The man said, "This is May and we are starting a new church. We have to wait until the end of the year. We have to take stock of our first year's growth and our cash flow and make a budget for next year. After we subtract our expenses from our projected income we can then decide what kind of mission work we can afford."

Kim responded, "If you don't want to do the Lord's work, why do you want to join with me in starting a new church? We already have 400 Korean churches in the Los Angeles area, and they are more than enough to minister to the Korean population. We don't need another church for Koreans, but we do need a church that will do mission work. I am a businessman and I know how much each one of you makes. I can easily calculate our church's cash flow if each one of you tithes. I'm relying on the heavenly Father to use your pocketbooks."

He then turned to a committee member named Mr. Oh, who at the time knew nothing about church administration, and said, "Mr. Oh, who do you think is right?"

Mr. Oh blinked and hesitatingly said, "Well, Pastor, I think you're right."

David Kim later commented, "With that, I won the debate!"

What was the upshot of that striking decision-making process? Grace Korean Church now has 2,500 members, the annual budget is $6.5 million and $5 million of it goes to missions! They fully support 154 missionaries to 43 different countries. They have planted 720 churches in the former Soviet Union, 2,000 house churches in mainland China all registered with the government, 700 churches in East Africa and 280 churches in Vietnam, just as examples. David Kim's current goal is to move into a larger facility so the church can grow and eventually fully support 2,000 missionaries!

SIX FUNDAMENTAL ASSUMPTIONS

Not all new apostolic pastors will lead their churches the same way as David Kim does, but virtually all of them will agree on six fundamental assumptions regarding the role of the pastor in a church. None of the six characterizes pastors of most traditional churches.

1. THE PASTORS CAST THE VISION.
Unlike traditional pastors who consider themselves "enablers," most new apostolic pastors would never think of approaching

the members of the congregation to ask them the direction they think the church should go. Instead, they begin by asking God where He thinks the church should go. They fully expect God to answer their prayer and to impart to their minds the vision for the church He has called them to lead. To make sure they have accurately heard from God, the pastors will, of course, test their ideas along with certain selected individuals, usually the elders, before announcing the vision to the whole congregation. Once they have the degree of consensus they believe they need, they boldly cast the vision, and that is it.

New apostolic pastors take the biblical analogy of the sheep and the shepherd seriously. On a given day, the sheep do not decide where they will go to find food. The pastor makes the decision and the sheep follow the pastor.

People consider and maintain their membership in new apostolic churches basically because they have bought into the vision of the pastor.

Apostle John Eckhardt of Chicago says, "The people in the church as well as the elders tend to believe that the vision that the leader has is from God, and they don't have any problem following that vision. They trust the strong leader. There is a level of trust that this person is called by God and given a vision by God. Therefore, they will follow the pastor and lend whatever assistance is necessary to accomplish the pastor's priorities."[2]

A basic reason people consider and maintain their membership in new apostolic churches is that they have bought into the vision of the pastor.

One implication of this is that the enabler model, diligently taught in seminaries in the 1960s, 1970s and 1980s, and persisting in some in the 1990s, is out. Research has shown that it inhibits church growth, and that it will rather consistently prevent churches from breaking the 200 barrier.

On an even deeper level, the enabler model frequently works

to prevent pastors from being the persons God wants them to be. Ted Haggard says that these kind of structures can "restrain godliness and inadvertently provide a voice for ungodliness. Too many structures unnecessarily give a platform to the whiners, manipulators and controllers within the Body in the wholesome name of accountability."[3]

Lyle Schaller says, "The enabler style of pastoral leadership is appropriate in perhaps 75,000 Protestant churches in the United States. These congregations average forty or fewer at worship. Most of them want a loving shepherd, not an initiating leader. That may explain, in part, why they are small. Another 75,000 Protestant congregations average 125 or more at worship. In these, the guiding generalization is that the larger the size of the congregation, the more important it is for the pastor to accept and fill the role of initiating leader."[4]

This is contrary to what many of today's pastors were taught in seminaries. A fundamental reason for this is that seminary professors are rarely initiating leaders themselves. Seminaries tend to prize bureaucratic structures. I clearly remember hearing David Hubbard, the late president of Fuller Seminary, say to his faculty, "The *process* is much more important than the *outcome*." Strong, visionary leadership is often referred to pejoratively by seminary professors as "entrepreneurship."

Here, for example, is the way Frank Damazio describes the typical new apostolic senior pastor: "He can fire the imagination and create a sense of dedication for a vision which motivates followers into effective, meaningful service. He guards the identity and direction of the congregation, clarifying and emphasizing purpose. The visionary is a spiritual pacesetter. The visionary develops strategies for implementing the mission of the church and constantly generates momentum to achieve goals."[5]

2. PASTORS MAJOR IN LEADERSHIP AND MINOR IN MANAGEMENT.
Few visionary, initiating leaders have the patience to manage. In small churches, they have no choice; pastors have to manage as well as lead. As soon as the church is large enough to begin

adding staff, though, new apostolic pastors add managers to the team.

This is an implicit application of the biblical principle of spiritual gifts. I say *implicit* because I have observed that, strangely enough, the level of *explicit* teaching and application of the biblical doctrine of spiritual gifts among new apostolic churches is relatively low. Be that as it may, the gift of *leadership* is mentioned in Romans 12:8, and the gift of management (or administration) is mentioned in 1 Corinthians 12:28. The analogy in the original Greek is that the *leader* is the owner of the ship, and the *manager* is the helmsman. One decides where the ship is to go and the other figures out how to get it there. New apostolic pastors are generally seen as the ship's owner.

3. PASTORS MAKE TOP-DRAWER POLICY DECISIONS AND DELEGATE THE REST.

The larger the church, the truer it is that the pastor is the principal decision maker on the highest levels. In fact, most new apostolic pastors have a veto power on any decision at all through the whole church system, although they tend to use it only occasionally. Even in smaller new apostolic churches this is the rule. Donald Miller observes, "The senior pastor sets the vision and defines the spiritual culture of the institution, but he typically gives substantial autonomy to individual staff members in overseeing specific programs."[6]

I realize that some will say, "What happened to democracy?" This is precisely the point. In their understanding of biblical ecclesiology, new apostolic pastors do not consider churches as democratic institutions. Many will argue that a *culturally*, rather than a *biblically*, directed imposition of democracy is a principal factor that has weakened denominational churches through the years.

Rick Warren says it as well as any: "What do the words *committees, elections, majority rule, boards, board members, parliamentary procedures, voting,* and *vote* have in common? None of these words is found in the New Testament! We have imposed an

American form of government on the church and, as a result, most churches are as bogged down in bureaucracy as our government is. It takes forever to get anything done."[7]

James Emery White picks up on this, saying, "The Bible teaches that the church is a family. In most family structures, the immature members (children) outnumber or at least equal the mature members (parents). In my family, there are two parents and four children. If we voted on everything, we would have ice cream for dinner every night, never go to bed, and live at Disney World."[8]

One of the results of delegating management responsibilities to staff members is that, especially in the large new apostolic churches, the senior pastors themselves do not know all that is happening in their own churches. Rick Warren says, "I haven't known everything that happens at Saddleback for years. I don't need to know about it all! You might ask, 'Then how do you control it?' My answer is: 'I don't. It's not my job to control the church. It's my job to *lead* it.'"[9]

This readily will be seen as a major point of departure from the traditional assumption that the pastor is an employee of the church. Apostle John Kelly once told me how surprised he was in the early years when he was called to be the pastor of a small traditional church run by a board of elders. He was not there long, implementing some innovative ideas, until the board wanted to fire him. John, a former officer in the Marine Corps special services division, called the board together and summarily informed them: "You don't fire me, I fire you!" It rather quickly transitioned to a new apostolic church.

4. PASTORS BUILD A SOLID, COMPETENT MANAGEMENT TEAM.

The functional equivalents of traditional church boards in new apostolic churches are management teams organized to manage ministry, not to set the direction of the church. They are teams called to serve the pastor. In most cases, they take the forms of elder boards and pastoral staff.

Elders. What is the typical role of elders? Apostle Emmanuele

Cannistraci says, "Normally the pastor is a highly visionary leader who spends time in prayer seeking God's plan for the church. When the resulting vision is presented to the elders, they amplify it to the people, rather than changing it or blocking it. They may provide cautions or additional insight that is helpful. The vision is then presented to the church by the leadership, and when there is unity, the plan can be accomplished."[10]

Dick Iverson describes "eldership management" as follows: "Several ministers (spiritual elders) work in shepherding the congregation of the local church. Together as a team, they minister to the people whom God has set into the local body. This form of government could be termed team ministry. I believe this is a biblical form of local church government—and of church ministry."[11] Notice that Iverson refers to "eldership *management*," not "elder *leadership*." This is a key point in understanding the role of new apostolic elders.

Dick Iverson's disciple and successor as pastor of City Bible Church, Frank Damazio, clearly defines this. He says, "The senior pastor is the key leader in God's leadership structure. His office and ministry may be described as general overseer, presiding elder, first among equals, senior pastor, senior minister, or as the Set Man. He is the person in charge, the one with the God-given responsibility to lead and direct the local church."[12]

How, then, does Frank Damazio view the role of elders? "The vision or direction of the church is set by the Set Man or senior pastor of the church. His eldership team does not originate the vision, but often shares a partnership with him in setting it....The senior pastor should be the presiding elder or chairperson at all eldership meetings. The eldership should not convene for business or decision-making meetings without the presence or permission of the senior pastor."[13]

Staff. In new apostolic churches, staff members are considered employees of the senior pastor. This is a departure from the traditional model in which certain boards or committees have been empowered to hire new staff. They ordinarily do this with the consent of the senior pastor, but it is not unusual for a traditional board to hire a staff member over the objection of the senior pastor. As a matter of fact, some argue that it is healthy to have staff members who do not necessarily agree with each other. New apostolic pastors view it differently. They are the ones who hire and fire staff.

Here is the way George Barna, a researcher, describes visionary leadership: "These leaders invariably surround themselves with a small cadre of intensely loyal, zealous, capable, driven peers who form a tightly knit leadership team. Much of the revolutionary activity is delegated to and conceived by members of that team. Through verbal skill, emotional resonance, and strategic effort, revolutionary leaders blatantly defy that which contradicts their own doctrine, exhorting others to follow suit. Their goals are audacious, and their gifts and skills feed people's hopes for a sudden, major change."[14] Although Barna here is describing "revolutionary leaders of recent history," this is also the profile of the more successful new apostolic pastors and their staffs.

5. PASTORS ARE CALLED FOR LIFE.

Many new apostolic pastors have planted the church they pastor. Neither they, nor their congregation, have any thought that they will eventually move on to another church. This is also the case when transitions are made from one senior pastor to another in existing churches. For example, when the by-laws of Evangel Christian Fellowship in San Jose, California, were drafted, they designated Emmanuele Cannistraci, their founding pastor, "pastor for life." His nephew, David Cannistraci, now pastors the church from day-to-day as "copastor," and he is also "pastor for life." Emmanuele and his wife will continue to be supported by the church financially as long as either one of them lives.

This rather radical departure from traditional concepts of pastoral tenure carries two *important* implications and two other *interesting* implications:

The first *important* implication is that by doing this, new apostolic churches are incorporating a tested principle of church growth. Growing churches are characterized by pastors who have longer tenures than they have in typical plateaued or declining churches. This is one of many reasons new apostolic churches are growing faster than others across the board.

Territorial Commitment. The second *important* implication relates to spiritual authority. In his outstanding book, Commitment to Conquer (Chosen Books), Bob Beckett makes a persuasive case that pastoral authority increases in proportion to the pastor's commitment to the community as well as to his church. Virtually every conscientious pastor is committed to the church he serves. Few and far between are those pastors who are equally committed to the community in which their church is located.

Bob Beckett and his wife, Susan, long considered Hemet, California, just a stepping stone to bigger and better things down the road. However, their church, The Dwelling Place, kept splitting, it wouldn't grow, finances were always a problem and they were so frustrated that they found themselves just going through the routine of week-to-week pastoral work.

Serving as pastor for life carries with it a strong territorial commitment, accompanied by awesome levels of spiritual authority.

Then God spoke to them and told them they were to stay in Hemet for the rest of their lives. They obeyed and they publicly announced that they were buying cemetery plots to seal their decision. That was the turning point, and from that day on the church has grown, prospered and provided Bob a platform for a fruitful national and international ministry. The principle is that serving as pastor for life carries with it a strong territorial commitment, which is accompanied by awesome new levels of spiritual authority.

The first *interesting* application of a lifetime call is that new apostolic churches are frequently known by insiders and out-siders alike by the pastor's name. It is commonplace to speak of Robert Schuller's church or of Bill Hybels's church or of Jack Hayford's church or of T. D. Jakes's church or of John Osteen's church. This is not a theological statement, because there is no question that these churches ultimately belong to Jesus. It is a statement of identity, however, reflecting the long-term, lifetime commitment these pastors have to such churches. In contrast, few have ever referred to the First United Methodist Church of Pumphandle, Nebraska, by the name of any of the pastors who happened to be occupying the parsonage at the time.

Mom-and-Pop Churches. The second *interesting* application is that new apostolic churches are often classic mom-and-pop outfits. The pastor's spouse is frequently ordained and serves as copastor or has a similar title. I believe I am correct in saying that we find more active clergy couples in new apostolic churches than in any other kind of churches except the Salvation Army. Their children and other relatives frequently go on staff as a matter of course, so it is not unusual to find several family members on the staff of large new apostolic churches. This leads to the last characteristic of new apostolic pastors:

6. PASTORS CHOOSE THEIR SUCCESSORS.

I just mentioned that Emmanuele Cannistraci turned Evangel Christian Fellowship over to his nephew, David Cannistraci. The decision to do that was Emmanuele's, no one else's. Likewise, Dick Iverson turned over the senior pastorate of City Bible Church (formerly Bible Temple) of Portland, Oregon, to his disciple, Frank Damazio.

I was privileged to be present at Damazio's "passing the baton" ceremony in 1995, and I heard Iverson say, "There are several here with us today who are well qualified to take the responsibility of Bible Temple. I considered many of you as I was in prayer for my successor. The reason I chose Frank Damazio was in obedience to the voice of God in my spirit."

Here is the announcement Frank Damazio read to his congregation in the church he was then pastoring in Eugene, Oregon: "Pastors Frank and Sharon Damazio have accepted the invitation of Pastor Dick Iverson to be his successors and take the church in Portland, Oregon. The move will take place by September 1. My successor here will be Gary Clark whom I have appointed and the eldership has confirmed to be my replacement."[15]

The assumption behind that announcement is that senior pastors choose their successors. Frank Damazio says, "The senior pastor must accept the responsibility to raise a successor, and the eldership must understand and support the process."[16] He recommends that the pastor receive the nomination from the Lord, that the elders approve and that it be taken to the congregation for their approval. "Then," he says, "they will have a threefold witness: the pastor's heart, the eldership's heart, and the heart of the congregation."[17]

Frequently, the outgoing senior pastor will turn the church over to a son. This is, and, undoubtedly, will remain, the exception and not a rule. Many pastors, however, have fervently prayed that their anointing will be carried through the generations, and when God answers that prayer they are more than ready to name a son as their successor, provided, of course, that the son fulfills the requirements for ministry. Billy Graham did it with Franklin, Oral Roberts did it with Richard, Paul Walker did it with Mark, Bill Hamon did it with Tom, Lester Sumrall did it with Stephen, just to list some of the high-profile names.

Because the son is, by definition, an insider to the church, the succession is frequently more gradual and natural than bringing in an outsider might be. For example, in the Cathedral of Faith in San Jose, California, senior pastor Kenny Foreman commissioned his son Ken as copastor seven years ago. At first, Ken preached once a month. Later it expanded to 16 times a year, and at this writing he preaches three times a month on the average.

Kenny has installed Ken's younger brother, Kurt, as church administrator and business manager and one of his daughters heads the media department. All the Foreman children have earned college degrees in their respective areas of ministry, and they are well qualified for their positions. When the time comes for Kenny and his wife, Shirley, to move on, they will be sure the church is in good hands.

MODALITIES AND SODALITIES

When I wrote my book *Leading Your Church to Growth* (Regal Books) several years ago, I included a chapter titled "Why Bill Bright Is Not Your Pastor." I used Bill Bright's name because he is a high-visibility prototype of a classic sodality leader. That was about 15 years ago. I am delighted to report that as I write this, we do have many more Bill Bright kind of sodality leaders heading local churches than we have ever had before.

For those unfamiliar with modality-sodality theory, "modality" is the term used for congregational structures. It can be an individual congregation in a local church or a group of churches that form a traditional denominational judicatory. "Sodality" refers to mission structures or parachurch organizations. Modalities, by nature, are people-oriented entities. New members are usually born into or socialized into the group. On the other hand, sodalities are more task oriented. No one is born into a sodality. New members are recruited, ordinarily on the basis of whether they can contribute to the task. All people are valued, but those who can contribute to the task are the ones who are recruited into a sodality.

Through the years, observers have noticed that sodality (parachurch) leaders have characteristics that are different from average pastors. If they are effective sodality leaders they have the following characteristics:

1. They think their particular task is the most important task in God's kingdom.
2. They believe they are accomplishing this task better

than anyone else. (This often irritates modality leaders and even other sodality leaders.)
3. They have a relatively low need for people.

To say that some Christian leaders may have a low need for people may sound strange and even harsh at first. For modality leaders, though, mostly local church pastors, people are primary and the task is secondary. On the other hand, for sodality leaders the task is primary and people are secondary.

New apostolic pastors, particularly if they are gifted to be large-church pastors, tend to be more like sodality leaders. The reason this important difference is not more frequently noticed is that their *task*, unlike the task of many parachurch leaders, is to serve *people*. It is ironic that their relatively low need for people helps them serve people better. This is much like many surgeons. Their task is also to help people, but it is not unusual for a surgeon to lack "people skills."

In a traditional church, when a prominent church member comes to the pastor saying words to the effect, "Pastor, I don't like the direction that the church is heading right now," the pastor will typically reply, "Let's refer your opinion to the church board and see if we need to change our direction." New apostolic pastors take a totally different approach. They tend to say, "My friend, I respect your opinion. Let's pray about it, and I will do my best to help you find a church in our community where you do agree with the direction it is headed!"

Bob Beckett tells the story of a new family who moved to Hemet, California, and joined The Dwelling Place church. They had come from a church that had a $250,000 pipe organ. They made an appointment with Bob and said, "Pastor, we would like to contribute to a fund for a pipe organ in our church."

Bob replied, "No one here would even know how to plug one in!"

"But," they said, "the music is so beautiful. We need organ music!"

"All right," Bob said. "Tomorrow I'll send you a list of all the churches in town with pipe organs!"

Bob Beckett does not have such a high need for people that he would consider changing his church's philosophy of worship to keep a family, good Christians and generous tithers that they might be, in his church.

George Barna agrees. He says, "Invite dissidents to leave. This may sound harsh, but follow the logic. Invite stubborn people to find a church home that suits them better. Don't portray them as enemies or ignorant or problematic....Your job is to help them make a decision, which is to get on board and sail in harmony with the rest of the crew or find a ship sailing to a destination they find amenable....If you allow these problem people to cling to your ship, I guarantee that they will be anchors that drag down your expedition. They won't be happy, you won't be happy, the church won't be happy, visitors won't be happy. Nobody wins."[18]

In Lima, Peru, awhile ago, I met new apostolic pastor Manuel Gutierrez of the *Iglesia Cristiana Viva*. He told me that when he began transitioning his church into a cell-based church, an elder opposed his vision and created a conflict. He began accusing the pastor to other elders, saying, "Our pastor is becoming a pope!"

Manuel called him in and said, "Brother, you are a leader in this church for three reasons: (1) You're my friend, (2) You agree with my vision, and (3) You are loyal to me. If any of the three are missing, you are no longer a leader!" The next week the man was looking for a new church.

THE THORNY SUBJECT OF ACCOUNTABILITY

As I probed a bit more deeply into why Manuel Gutierrez would dismiss an elder, he said, "Sheep do not discipline pastors; pastors discipline pastors." His elder was attempting to control him. I have thought about this a good deal because it raises the thorny question of new apostolic accountability.

If new apostolic leaders have so much authority, to whom are they ultimately accountable? I am not referring to their accountability to God, but to their place in the God-given human accountability structure here on earth. The question about the accountability of *apostles* will be discussed in the next chapter. However, to whom are new apostolic *pastors* accountable?

Are they accountable to the congregation? No. Dissident church members are expected to leave.

Are they accountable to the elders? Almost all pastors will say they are. This is good biblical theory, but it rarely works out in practice. It works in Presbyterian churches, for example, when the elders are elected by the congregation. In new apostolic churches, however, when the elders are either appointed or dismissed by the senior pastor, it functions only in healthy churches. When the church gets sick, this accountability structure is rarely strong enough to carry the day.

Are they accountable to apostles? If the church is integrated into an apostolic network, the answer is yes. This is both biblically sound and operationally functional.

One denominational critic of the New Apostolic Reformation, who shall go unnamed, wrote to me and said, "These individualistic ministries *are accountable to no one.* Each leader is doing what is right in his own eyes. Since there are no reins to control and direct these leaders, we may be in for an unprecedented outbreak of heretical teachings, manipulative leadership, and can-you-top-this manifestations of the miraculous. This is what I already see happening."

It is comforting to know that new apostolic leaders are very much aware of this problem, and although it is not totally resolved at this writing, most intend to keep working on it until it is.

For example, Apostle John Kelly of Antioch Churches and Ministries writes to pastors in a column titled "Words from a Father":

> We all need a spiritual cover over us—a person or group
> to give counsel or advice when necessary; a person or

group that we have enough trust in that we would allow them to speak into our lives, knowing that they would always have our best interest at heart; someone to speak the truth in love and hold us accountable to the Scriptures for Christ's sake. We should covet the counsel and correction of this group of godly men. None of us are lone-rangers and we don't want to be perceived as such.[19]

ACCOUNTABILITY STRUCTURES

Not all new apostolic leaders do it the same way, but some patterns are beginning to emerge. Manuel Gutierrez, who said, "Sheep do not discipline pastors; pastors discipline pastors," holds himself publicly accountable to Mac Hammond, an apostle based in Minneapolis, Minnesota, and to Jim Kaseman, an apostle in the Association of Faith Churches and Ministries in Tulsa, Oklahoma. Locally, Gutierrez is accountable to the *Fraternidad Internacional de Pastores Cristianos* (FIPC–International Brotherhood of Christian Pastors), which he, along with other apostolic leaders

---

Manuel Gutierrez said, "Sheep do not discipline pastors; pastors discipline pastors."

---

in Lima, Peru, such as Humberto Lay and Juan Capuro, founded in 1991 precisely as a local accountability structure. Manuel told me he also said to his rebellious elder, "If I need discipline, report me to the FIPC."

Does the FIPC function as it should? Will pastors really discipline other pastors when the crunch comes? In this case, yes. The FIPC has already disciplined two of its members—one on morals charges, and one on financial charges. These members both submitted to the discipline and removed themselves from active ministry for the specified periods of time.

As another example, Pastor Mel Green of Word of Life Church in Red Deer, Alberta, Canada, also supervises 20 other churches. He says, "No man should be independent or isolated." He has announced to his congregation that he has a group of three individuals who are "his pastors" and to whom he submits. They are Mel Davis, Emmanuele Cannistraci and Charles Green, all recognized leaders who are not members of his church.

My pastor, Ted Haggard, calls the operation of New Life Church a "pain-free church government." The only decision in the hands of the congregation is to give final approval to the call of a senior pastor when a new one is eventually needed. The call is presumably for life. Meanwhile, the pastor names a board of trustees to look after the financial matters of the church and a board of elders to look after the spiritual ministry of the church. Both are named to support the vision of the senior pastor.

Ted has an external board of overseers "nominated by the pastor and confirmed by the elders" (per New Life Church by-laws), to whom he personally submits and holds himself accountable. It is headed up by Larry Stockstill of Bethany World Prayer Center in Baker, Louisiana, which was the parent church of New Life, and includes four other local pastors. Any discipline problem is to be reported to them, and any three of them can discipline or fire Ted Haggard.

As in most other facets of new apostolic ecclesiology, pastoral accountability stands or falls on personal relationships, not legal decrees.

Notes

1. See Elmer Towns, C. Peter Wagner and Thom S. Rainer, *The Everychurch Guide to Growth* (Nashville: Broadman & Holman Publishers, 1998), p. 91.
2. John Eckhardt, personal correspondence with the author, December 1995.
3. Ted Haggard, *The Life Giving Church* (Ventura, Calif.: Regal Books, 1998), p. 1 of introduction.
4. Lyle E. Schaller, "You Can't Believe Everything You Hear About Church Growth," *Leadership* (Winter 1997): 48.

5. Frank Damazio, *Effective Keys to Successful Leadership* (Portland, Oreg.: Bible Temple Publishing, 1993), p. 114.

6. Donald E. Miller, *Reinventing American Protestantism* (Berkeley, Calif.: University of California Press, 1997), p. 138.

7. Rick Warren, *The Purpose Driven Church* (Grand Rapids: Zondervan Publishing House, 1995), p. 377.

8. James Emery White, *Rethinking the Church* (Grand Rapids: Baker Books, 1997), p. 100.

9. Warren, *The Purpose Driven Church*, p. 378.

10. Message delivered at Evangel Temple in San Jose, California, on December 13, 1995.

11. Dick Iverson, *Team Ministry* (Portland, Oreg.: Bible Temple Publishing, 1984), p. 19.

12. Damazio, *Effective Keys to Successful Leadership*, p. xiii.

13. Ibid., pp. 15, 16.

14. George Barna, *The Second Coming of the Church* (Nashville: Word Publishing, 1998), p. 201.

15. Frank Damazio, *The Vanguard Leader* (Portland, Oreg.: Bible Temple Publishing, 1994), p. 282.

16. Ibid., p. 309.

17. Ibid., p. 290.

18. George Barna, *Turning Vision into Action* (Ventura, Calif.: Regal Books, 1996), pp. 148, 149.

19. John Kelly, "Words from a Father," *The Networker* (April 1997), p. 3.

Five Crucial Questions About Apostolic Ministry

I imagine many readers will begin this book by turning to this chapter. They will have chosen well. Clearly, a book about the New *Apostolic* Reformation requires, as its centerpiece, a careful explanation of what is meant by the word "apostle" and how the concept of apostle is being revealed in contemporary Christianity.

As I have said more than once, the most radical difference between what I am calling *new apostolic* Christianity and *traditional* Christianity revolves around the amount of authority the Holy Spirit is perceived to delegate to *individuals* as opposed to groups such as boards or committees or presbyteries. The last chapter focused mainly on the *local* authority delegated to pastors; this chapter focuses on *translocal* authority delegated to apostles.

To help us grasp the whole picture, I will list five of what I consider to be among the most crucial questions about apostolic ministry before I explain them one by one:

1. What is an apostle?
2. Are there apostles today?

3. How important are apostles?
4. How does an apostle gain authority?
5. What are the qualities of a genuine apostle?

QUESTION 1: WHAT IS AN APOSTLE?

Our English word "apostle" is derived from the Greek *apóstolos*. *Apóstolos* is a noun and the corresponding verb is *apostello*, to send. Another, more common, biblical word meaning "to send" is *pempo*, but there is an important difference between the two. *Apostello* means to be sent with a particular purpose or with a specified commission from the one who does the sending. When this is done, "the envoy has full powers and is the personal representative of the one sending him."[1] The ancient Greeks also used *apostello* from time to time to indicate being sent out with divine authorization. This is what we are referring to in this chapter.

The New Testament uses *apóstolos* for the twelve apostles chosen personally by Jesus. They are the ones with whom we are most familiar, but they are not the only ones. At least twelve others are also called "apostle" in the New Testament, including Andronicus, Apollos, Barnabas, Epaphroditus, James (the brother of Jesus), Junia, Matthias, Paul, Silas, Timothy and two others referred to but not specifically named.

A SPIRITUAL GIFT

Apostle is a spiritual gift. It appears along with several other gifts in 1 Corinthians 12, which Paul introduces by saying, "Now concerning spiritual gifts, brethren, I do not want you to be ignorant" (1 Cor. 12:1). Apostles are mentioned in 1 Corinthians 12:28 and 29 along with other spiritual gifts such as miracles, healings, helps, administration and tongues. They are also listed in Ephesians 4:11 along with prophets, evangelists, pastors and teachers.

Some may observe that this list in Ephesians 4:11 is a list of the kinds of individuals God gives as gifts to the Church as a whole—they constitute offices. This is technically correct. It is also assumed, for example, that the teachers would have the gift of teaching and the prophets would have the gift of prophecy as a chief qualification for that particular office. Both prophecy and teaching are specifically designated as spiritual gifts; in fact they both appear in the two major New Testament lists, Romans 12 (see verses 6 and 7) and 1 Corinthians 12 (see verses 10 and 28). So a reasonable inference would be that apostles have also received their office because they have been given the spiritual gift of apostle.

Here is the definition I have been using for the spiritual gift of apostle: *The gift of apostle is the special ability that God gives to certain members of the Body of Christ to assume and exercise general leadership over a number of churches with an extraordinary authority in spiritual matters that is spontaneously recognized and appreciated by those churches.*[2]

As I have continued to study the New Apostolic Reformation, however, it has become clear that this definition applies to many, perhaps the majority of apostles, but not to all. I was hoping that by the time I finished this book I would have satisfactory terminology to name and define however many other kinds of apostles there might be. This has not happened as I wished, so we will simply leave the matter pending for further research.

A key word in my basic definition is "authority." I do not want to overstress this, but viewing an apostle through the grid of authority is essential. It helps us avoid the common mistake some have made by confusing the gift of apostle with the gift of missionary. Let me explain.

APOSTLE VERSUS MISSIONARY

Our English word "missionary" comes from the Latin *missionarius*, which means a person sent into an area to do religious work. This gives it a close affinity with the concept of "apostle" as a sent one. Kenneth Taylor in *The Living Bible* frequently translated *apóstolos* as "missionary," such as in Romans 1:1 where *The Living Bible* says, "Paul...chosen to be a missionary." However, when the same Kenneth Taylor later called together a team of professional Bible scholars to do the *New Living Translation*, they thought Romans 1:1 should read: "Paul...chosen...to be an apostle."

I agree. I believe Paul was describing the spiritual gift of missionary when he wrote Ephesians 3:6-9:

> That the Gentiles should be fellow heirs, of the same body, and partakers of His promise in Christ through the gospel, of which I became a minister according to *the gift of the grace of God* given to me by the effective working of His power. To me, who am less than the least of all the saints, this grace was given, that I should preach among the Gentiles the unsearchable riches of Christ (emphasis mine).

In other words, Paul attributes the ability he had as a Jew, a Hebrew of the Hebrews no less, to minister cross-culturally to Gentiles to a "gift of the grace of God" (i.e., a spiritual gift). This was the missionary gift.

Here is how I define it: *The gift of missionary is the special ability that God gives to certain members of the Body of Christ to minister whatever other spiritual gifts they have in a second culture.*[3]

Notice the contrast between Peter and Paul. They were both apostles; but Peter was not cross-cultural. He was the apostle to the *circumcision*, namely, to his fellow Jews. Paul was an apostle primarily to the *uncircumcision*, the Gentiles, who had an entirely different culture from the one in which he had been raised. Peter had the gift of apostle, but not the gift of missionary. Paul had both the gift of apostle and the gift of missionary.

AMBASSADORIAL AUTHORITY

David Cannistraci, the author of the outstanding book *Apostles and the Emerging Apostolic Movement*, defines "apostle" as "one who is called and sent by Christ to have the spiritual authority, character, gifts and abilities to successfully reach and establish people in Kingdom truth and order, especially through founding and overseeing local churches."[4]

Planting and overseeing new churches is an important dimension of most apostolic ministries. Virtually any individual who does this over a period of time would be correctly seen as an apostle, although there might also be some bona fide apostles who are not directly involved in church planting per se.

Apostles should be thought of as ambassadors. Bill Hamon, author of *Apostles, Prophets and the Coming Moves of God*, sees this clearly. He says, "The basic root meaning [of 'apostle'] is 'one sent as representative of another,' with the power and authority of the representative coming from the one who sent him. They are like ambassadors who represent a country."[5]

It is important to remember that apostles are human beings. They have their good days and their bad days. Because they do not have divine natures, they make their share of mistakes. I recall hearing John Kelly say, "Some people think that apostles glow in the dark. They don't!"

Apostle John Eckhardt puts it this way: "There are those who think a person has to be perfect and infallible to walk in the call of an Apostle. But we must realize that all of the ministry gifts are grace gifts. They are given by grace and not earned. You either have it or you don't. Paul recognized that he was not worthy to be called an apostle, and was such only by the grace of God."[6]

QUESTION 2: ARE THERE APOSTLES TODAY?

Although their number has been diminishing significantly over the last couple of decades, some Christian leaders still consider themselves "cessationists." They hold the position that many of the spiritual gifts that were in operation in the first-century Church were designed by God so that their use would "cease" with the close of the Apostolic Age and with the completion of the New Testament canon of Scripture. The lists of the gifts that would have ceased vary among various schools of cessationism, but prophets and apostles, whether considered as spiritual gifts or offices or both, appear on many of the lists.

Those who process data through such a paradigm naturally would affirm that there are no such things as apostles, in the biblical sense of the word, in churches today. They might concede that missionaries could be referred to as apostles because they are sent out, but, as I have indicated, that is quite different from the way I am using the term in this chapter.

Differences of opinion also exist among those who are not cessationists. For example, Professor George Batson of Continental Theological Seminary in Belgium, himself a Pentecostal, says, "It seems better to take 'apostle' as a technical term, not transferable to an office in the post-apostolic age. This precludes the 'apostolic succession' of authority in the Church of Rome."[7]

THE GIFT VERSUS THE TITLE

Others admit that apostolic ministry is in place today, but the *title* should no longer be used. For example, Reinhold Ulonska, a German Pentecostal theologian, says, "If we understand that [apostle] means the ministry and not so much the title we may say: 'Yes, there are apostles today.'...Today the title *apostle* seems to have a ring of glory and authority, which true apostles would never claim for themselves."[8]

Felipe Ferrez of the Church of the Foursquare Gospel in the Philippines agrees: "That is to say that the *apostolic office* foundational to the NT church may have ceased, but the *gift of apostle* remains as a continuing endowment on the Body of Christ."[9]

Some have marginalized the office of apostle through what could be interpreted as a form of benign neglect. An example is the Assemblies of God in the U.S.A. Article VII of their bylaws reads as follows: "Section 1. Ministry Described. Christ's gifts to the Church include apostles, prophets, evangelists, pastors and teachers (Ephesians 4:11), exhorters, administrators, leaders, and helpers (Romans 12:7,8). We understand God's call to these ministry gifts is totally within His sovereign discretion without regard to gender, race, disability, or national origin."[10]

In practice, the Assemblies of God recognizes leaders having the title "Pastor So-and-so," "Evangelist So-and-so" and "Doctor or Professor So-and-so," but not "Prophet So-and-so" or "Apostle So-and-so." The choice that has been made, not only by Assemblies of God, but by the great majority of other traditional denominations as well, to recognize evangelists, pastors and teachers, but not to recognize apostles and prophets does not derive from biblical exegesis, but rather from entrenched ecclesiastical traditions.

Along these lines, it may be enlightening to recognize that the term "evangelist," so common today, was not generally accepted in our country until the times of Charles Finney, who ministered from 1825-1875. Finney ignited a good deal of controversy when he first accepted the office of evangelist. Theologians of the time strenuously argued against what they were calling these "New Measures."

I agree with Bishop Carlis Moody of the Church of God in Christ, who says, "Yes, there are Apostles in the church today! They manifest extraordinary spiritual leadership, and are anointed with the power of the Holy Spirit to confront the powers of Satan, by confirming the gospel by signs and miracles and establishing churches according to the New Testament pattern and doctrine of the Apostles."[11]

THE OFFICE OF APOSTLE

It is important to understand the difference between the *gift* of apostle and the *office* of apostle. Any office is the public recognition by the Body of Christ that an individual has a certain gift and is authorized to minister that gift in what might be termed an "official" capacity. Most of us are accustomed to the ordination of pastors, which officially sets pastors into public ministry. The same concept should be applied to apostles.

Bill Hamon says, "[Christ] gave some to be apostles, not have an occasionally functioning gift of apostle. Apostles are to minister as ambassadors of Christ—being the apostolic ministry that Jesus would be if He were here personally."[12]

We are witnessing a fairly rapid change in the attitude of church leaders toward accepting the contemporary office of apostle. Some theologians are still arguing against it, much as they argued against calling Finney an "evangelist" in a past generation. The trend is clear, though, and my guess is that in a few years the controversy will begin to die down. For example, a recent letter written to Apostle John Eckhardt was copied to me. It began, "Dear Apostle John," and the opening paragraph said, "First, I want to say that I get a real bang out of starting out a letter with this salutation. You have to know that I never expected to be able to say those words this side of the resurrection."

QUESTION 3: HOW IMPORTANT ARE APOSTLES?

I expect that some for whom this idea of apostle is new will be saying, "The church has gotten along fine for many generations without recognizing the office of apostle. Why make such a big deal of it now at this late date?" That question deserves as careful an answer as possible.

My hypothesis is that the bride of Christ, the Church, has been maturing through a discernible process during the past few centuries in preparation for completing the task of the Great Commission. My starting point is the Protestant Reformation in which the theological underpinnings were firmly established: the authority of Scripture, justification by faith and the priesthood of all believers. The Wesleyan movement then introduced the demand for personal and corporate holiness.

The Pentecostal movement later profiled the supernatural work of the Holy Spirit in a variety of power ministries. The office of intercessor was restored in the 1970s and the office of prophet was restored in the 1980s. The final piece came into place in the 1990s with the recognition of the gift and office of apostle.

The Church is prepared to advance
the Kingdom with a speed and intensity that
has not been possible in previous generations.

This is not to say that the Church is perfect. It is to say that the infrastructure of the Church, so to speak, may now be complete. The Church is much more prepared to advance the Kingdom with a speed and intensity that has not been possible in previous generations.

Apostles Are Unique

It could be argued, quite convincingly, that the Church has always had apostles, but that they have not been recognized as such. Nevertheless, true as this assertion might be, once the apostles receive the recognition they deserve, the Church is prepared to move to a higher level. This is what is happening in our day.

John Eckhardt puts it this way: "There is no substitute for the apostle. The prophet, evangelist, pastor or teacher cannot do what the apostle can do. Neither can the apostle do what the other gifts can do. Each gift is needed and has a unique purpose. They are not optional. God gave them to us because we need them all."[13]

Predictably, recognizing apostles and thereby bringing the church to a new level will stir up opposition in the invisible world. I like what David Cannistraci says: "How the enemy dreads the apostle! How he fears the full restoration of this ministry! A New Testament apostolic function fully deployed within the Church today would significantly impact the dominion of darkness. Satan knows this, and I'm sure all of hell shudders at the prospect of a revitalization of apostles and apostolic people."[14]

APOSTOLIC ROCKET BOOSTERS!

This is all to say that apostles are extremely important for the answer to our prayer, "'Your kingdom come. Your will be done on earth as it is in heaven'" (Matt. 6:10).

Bill Hamon says, "When the apostles are restored in their fullness, it will activate many things. It will cause many prophecies concerning the end times to start coming to pass at an accelerated rate. The apostle is the last of the fivefold ministries to be restored. It is like a great machine that needs five things to happen in sequence before it will fully work. It could be compared to a space rocket booster that must have five switches turned on before it can launch the space shuttle—the Church. Each switch or button represents one of the fivefold ministries."[15]

Keep in mind that the premise on which the importance of apostolic ministry is predicated is the completion of the Great Commission. John Kelly agrees: "We live in a critical hour. There needs to be a demonstration in this generation of the ministry of the apostle with miraculous, prophetic power and world-changing productivity. When the apostles begin to arise by the thousands, we will be able to take the nations for Jesus Christ. The harvest cannot be brought in apart from this foundational office."[16] If Kelly is right, the apostolic office is so important that it can mean the difference between heaven and hell for multitudes!

QUESTION 4: HOW DOES AN APOSTLE GAIN AUTHORITY?

Apostles, compared to most traditional church leaders, possess and exercise unusual authority. Where do they get this authority? If we can understand and accept the answer to this question, a large number of the doubts that some continue to harbor regarding the validity of true apostolic ministry will evaporate.

"SELF-APPOINTED" APOSTLES

Some, who have not yet understood the question of authority, attempt to dismiss the issue by using the term "self-appointed apostles." The implication is that the so-called apostolic office has no basis other than an internal personal desire for an imposing title or for undue power. If such were the case, however, apostles would have very few followers, and there would be no movement we could label the New Apostolic Reformation.

On the contrary, the initiative for the whole process begins with God, as it does with any of the other spiritual gifts. In explaining the matter of spiritual gifts to the Corinthians, Paul says, "But now God has set the members, each one of them, in the body just as He pleased" (1 Cor. 12:18).

Paul then goes on to say, "And God has appointed these in the church: first apostles, second prophets, third teachers" (1 Cor. 12:28). If we are going to label apostles as "self-appointed," we might as well do the same with teachers, but for some reason we are not inclined to do that. I have been a teacher for more than 40 years, for example, and no one has yet suggested I am a "self-appointed teacher."

God is the one who does the appointing, and recognizing that He has done so rests with the Body of Christ. We are used to having the Church operate in this manner with our pastors, and we call that "ordination." Every ordination committee I know of understands that its role is to confirm publicly what God has already done. We rarely use the term "self-appointed pastors."

Some of the derogatory attitudes toward apostles undoubtedly emerge from negative experiences of the past. Bill Hamon says, "During the last few years, I have seen some young pastors of small churches receive prophecies that they are called to be apostles. Some immediately changed their name cards from 'Reverend' or 'Pastor' to 'Apostle' and began trying to plant churches and solicit other ministers whom they can father....They have more presumption than faith; more zeal than wisdom....This type of person usually makes the wrong response and causes an improper representation of the divine ministry of an apostle."[17]

Admitting, then, that there are some spurious apostles out there, let's take a look at how the genuine ones receive their authority.

APOSTLES ARE CHARISMATIC LEADERS

I am using the term "charismatic" here, not in the theological sense, but in the sociological sense. Max Weber, the German sociologist regarded by many as the father of modern sociology, defines the term "charisma" as follows:

> The term "charisma" will be applied to a certain quality of an individual personality by virtue of which he is set apart from ordinary men and treated as endowed with supernatural, superhuman, or at least specifically exceptional powers or qualities. These are such as are not accessible to the ordinary person, but are regarded as of divine origin or as exemplary, and on the basis of them the individual concerned is treated as a leader.[18]

I will return to Max Weber from time to time because his seminal insights about leadership are very *apropos* to the New Apostolic Reformation.

Such leadership charisma, as Weber defines it, cannot derive from an organizational or bureaucratic promotion to some "position of leadership." It cannot be generated within a corporate system, such as a denomination, but it must come from outside, namely, from God.

DENOMINATIONS AND THE PETER PRINCIPLE

In denominations, as we have known them, the Peter Principle operates freely. This happens when authority is presumed to derive from promotion to a higher rank. The Peter Principle was formulated by Dr. Laurence J. Peter, who describes it as follows: "*In a hierarchy, every employee tends to rise to his or her level of incompetence.*"[19] I realize that this sounds strange when one first hears it. Without even reading the well-formulated arguments of Peter's book, the validity of the principle becomes convincing after a bit of serious thought. Peter says, "For each individual, for you, for me, the final promotion is from a level of competence to a level of incompetence."[20]

Why would this be true? It is very simple. Only competent people get chosen for promotion. Incompetents do not get chosen. When you no longer get chosen for promotion, you have presumably reached your level of incompetence.

Not all new apostolic leaders would have known the term "Peter Principle," but they are very much aware that it has characterized certain denominational bureaucracies. Bill Hamon speaks for many when he says, "Apostles have the delegated authority to represent the kingdom of God in a governmental, official capacity. It is not a religious, hierarchical authority given by man but a spiritual authority given by Christ."[21]

APOSTOLIC AUTHORITY IS VALIDATED BY FRUIT

Jesus once said that we shall know them by their fruit (see Matt. 7:16,20). This, obviously, applies to apostles as well as to others. It goes without saying that a fruitless apostle has not been activated and energized by God. Bill Hamon puts it this way: "The only way a fivefold minister's calling can be determined is by receiving a revelation from God, training for that ministry and then evidencing the fruit of that ministry."[22]

John Eckhardt agrees: "You don't have to force yourself on anyone or try to prove to anyone that you have a gift. If you are an Apostle, then as you preach and teach, your gift will be evident. Others in the Body will perceive the grace given unto you."[23]

As an illustration of how the office of apostle can be publicly recognized, let me refer to the Sacred Consecration Service of my friend Luciano Padilla, Jr., to the office of apostle. This occurred on July 22, 1995, at Padilla's church, Bay Ridge Christian Center of Brooklyn, New York. Four bishops from other churches presided at the service and consecrated Luciano as an apostle. Their first question to the elder representing Padilla's congregation was, "Do you have a word from the Lord?" This is in line with Bill Hamon's statement that the apostolic calling should first come through receiving a revelation from God.

The elder affirmed that they had such a revelation, and he proceeded to quote verbatim three prophecies, one in 1986 through Pastor Padilla himself, one in 1992 through Mari Luz Dones and one in 1994 through Patricia Rodgers. The next question was to the congregation asking if they affirmed God's call on their pastor to the office of apostle, and they unanimously responded that they did. A solemn ceremony of laying on of hands and anointing with oil followed.

The congregation of Bay Ridge Christian Center affirmed the apostolic office in this case, only after carefully observing the fruit of Luciano Padilla's ministry for more than 25 years.

BACK TO THE ISSUE OF TRUST

Just as trust in individuals plays a large role in the ministry of new apostolic pastors as contrasted to traditional pastors, so the same is true for apostolic ministry in church leadership. Recognizing the relatively low level of trust the constituency of most denominations places in their leaders, Lyle Schaller wrote a whole book on the subject: *Tattered Trust*. In it he says, "Every society chooses between two paths. One is to trust people. The other is to trust those institutions the people have created."[24]

One of the purposes of this book is to explore why new apostolic churches are growing so much faster today than denominational churches. Here is one of the reasons in the words of Lyle Schaller:

> Who can be trusted? In the 1950s, the cultural environment in the Unites States made it easy for adults born before 1935 to say that they trust "Scripture, the denominational system, and the people whom God

has called to staff that system." Forty years later, younger adults are more likely to say that they trust "The leading of the Holy Spirit, Jesus Christ, Scriptures, me, and those individuals who have earned my trust."[25]

In light of this, it is no wonder new apostolic churches are populated with baby boomers while, year after year, the age profile of traditional denominations continues to rise. The late John Wimber, founder of the Vineyard movement, sums up the source of his apostolic (even though he chose not to use the term) authority well: "If leadership is influence, I intend to continue to lead our movement by influencing it in the directions I feel it should go. This does not require structural authority in my opinion. I have the voluntary acceptance of all the leaders that are at this time leading our movement worldwide."[26]

QUESTION 5: WHAT ARE THE QUALITIES OF A GENUINE APOSTLE?

I use the term "genuine apostle" because I recognize that there are and will continue to be false apostles. Paul once said, "For such are false apostles, deceitful workers, transforming themselves into apostles of Christ. And no wonder! For Satan himself transforms himself into an angel of light" (2 Cor. 11:13,14).

Having recognized that there are false apostles, it is helpful also to recognize that Satan does not limit himself to counterfeiting the apostolic ministry. He also counterfeits prophets, evangelists, pastors and teachers. For example, Matthew 7:15 says, "Beware of false *prophets*." Galatians 1:9 describes false *evangelists* as "if anyone preaches any other gospel to you than what you have received, let him be accursed." In John 10:12, Jesus speaks of the one who is "a hireling, he who is not the shepherd [or *pastor*]." Peter says, "There will be false *teachers* among you" (2 Pet. 2:1).

Undoubtedly, the devil will go to any extreme possible to derail the New Apostolic Reformation, including an attempt to raise up false apostles. David Cannistraci sees this clearly:

> Satan's chief aim through these false apostles will be threefold: to *dilute, defile* and *discredit* the apostle and the apostolic movement. Many will be bewitched into rejecting true apostles because of the inevitable failure of false apostles. Critics of apostolic ministry will likely point out the problems of the false apostles in an attempt to dismiss the validity of apostolic activity. This effort may well become the single greatest threat to the apostolic movement's success.[27]

APOSTLES HAVE GODLY CHARACTER

Although the New Testament does not have a specific list of personal qualifications for an apostle, the qualifications for bishop clearly apply. No one should be recognized as an apostle who does not display character traits such as "blameless, the husband of one wife, temperate, sober-minded, of good behavior, hospitable, able to teach; not given to wine, not violent, not greedy for money, but gentle, not quarrelsome, not covetous; one who rules his own house well, having his children in submission with all reverence (for if a man does not know how to rule his own house, how will he take care of the church of God?); not a novice" (1 Tim. 3:2-6).

Genuine humility is one of the chief characteristics of an apostle. Many will question whether it is possible to exercise the extraordinary authority apostles have and still be humble. It cannot be otherwise. According to Max Weber, there is a clear distinction between *legal-rational* leadership in which the *position* confers the power and *charismatic* leadership in which the *person* has been entrusted with the power. Jesus explicitly delineated the difference.

Jesus said that the rulers of the Gentiles (legal-rational leadership) "lord it over them, and those who are great exercise authority over them." This was not the way He wanted His followers to lead. He went on to say, "whoever desires to be great among you, let him be your servant" (Matt. 20:25,26). On another occasion Jesus said, "Whoever exalts himself will be humbled, and he who humbles himself will be exalted" (Luke 14:11). The phrase "humbles himself" places the initiative for humility squarely on the shoulders of the leader. The more authority, the more *intentional* humility is called for.

If biblical principles hold true, genuine apostles
cannot be apostles unless they are
perceived by their followers as servants.

If biblical principles hold true, genuine apostles could not be apostles unless they were perceived by their followers as servants. When this happens, authority is released because the followers believe that every decision the apostle makes will be for their ultimate benefit.

I like the way Bill Hamon puts it:

> This forever settles the issue of who is greatest and least in the Church. The greatest is not one who has the highest title, position, authority or thousands serving him. The greatest in the Church is the one who is the most humble, serves the most people and doesn't even concern him or herself with thoughts of whether he or she is the greatest or highest in position.[28]

APOSTLES ARE PARENTS

Apostolic networks frequently like to consider themselves a family, the apostle being the father, or parent, of the family. For example, Leo Lawson describes Morning Star International as having "a spiritual DNA that is shared among those in our particular 'family' of churches....The 'father' of the apostolic family...is seen as imparting his spiritual DNA to those joined to him, and those joined to him see themselves as sharing both a common history as well as a common destiny."[29]

How does this work out? Lawson goes on:

> Acknowledging the "fatherly" function of Morning Star President, Rice Broocks, our pastors respond to his leadership much as they expect those in their churches to follow their own pastoral leadership. While the pastors dialog and consult with Rice and the apostolic team members, like a parent functioning in a natural family, once Rice announces the decision arrived at after consultation with the apostolic team, pastors are trusted to accept and support the decision.[30]

I am using the word "parent" as well as "father" so as not to overstress the gender issue. Empirically, the great majority of apostles have been male so they naturally feel like fathers, but there is a mother dimension to the apostolic function as well. When Paul writes to the Thessalonians, at one point he says, "We were gentle among you, just as a nursing *mother* cherishes her own children" (1 Thess. 2:7). Later he also says, "As you know how we exhorted, and comforted, and charged every one of you, as a *father* does his own children" (v. 11). Paul sets the tone for gender-inclusive apostolic roles.

RELEASING THE SPIRITUAL CHILDREN

Spiritual parents provide four services that all members of the spiritual family highly value. They provide (1) protection, (2) role modeling, (3) correction (accountability) and (4) empowerment. This parental role of empowerment, when taken seriously and exercised wisely, will raise up children in the faith, many of whom will subsequently be released for their own parental ministry.

Unfortunately, cases have recently been observed in which certain new apostolic leaders have not been able to do this with grace, and that has become a major factor leading to the stagnation and routinization of some apostolic networks. This is a major consideration for mapping the future of the New Apostolic Reformation, and I will discuss it in much more detail in the next chapter.

Meanwhile, Paul Daniel, the apostolic leader of His People in South Africa, sees it as well as anyone. He says, "God has called the 'fathers' of the ministry to identify the gifts and callings on young people's lives and to serve that calling so they may become everything God wants them to be. If these young people do greater things for God in their lives than we ourselves accomplish, we will rejoice. Fathers, I believe, should never by threatened by sons, but should rejoice when they excel."[31]

Bill Hamon adds: "Mature apostles are fathers. Mature human fathers are more concerned about their children's well-being and success than their own. True prophetic and apostolic fathers are more interested in seeing those that they are fathering come into their ministry than in magnifying their own ministry."[32]

TRUE APOSTLES ARE HOLY

Most apostles do not find themselves among those believers who, day in and day out, are struggling and wondering whether they are pleasing God or not. Their character, a prerequisite for being recognized as an apostle, has caused them to rise above the pack. They recognize that they have become more accountable to God than the average believer. They take James 3:1 literally: "My brethren, let not many of you become teachers, knowing that we shall receive a stricter judgment."

The best apostles are not proud or boastful, but they do recognize that, by the grace of God, they must be an example in their godliness and holiness of everyday life. If they lose that, they lose their authority. They want to be able to say, with the apostle Paul: "For I know nothing against myself, yet I am not justified by this; but He who judges me is the Lord" (1 Cor. 4:4). Once they look inside themselves and find nothing impure or offensive to God, they can then say, as Paul did, "Therefore I urge you, imitate me" (v. 16). There is no other way to serve as legitimate apostolic role models.

WHAT ABOUT APOSTOLIC ACCOUNTABILITY?

The question of how apostles are accountable is even more sensitive than the issue of the accountability of new apostolic pastors. We dwelt on pastoral accountability at the end of the last chapter, and apostolic accountability must be discussed before this chapter comes to a close.

I wish I had a more definitive word. For local church pastors who are in apostolic networks, the accountability structure is relatively simple. They are accountable to their apostles. To whom are the apostles accountable? In my association with some of the top leaders of the New Apostolic Reformation, I frequently raise the question of accountability, and I must say I have not received consistently clear answers. One thing, however, is clearly consistent: apostolic leaders, virtually without exception, recognize that they need genuine accountability. Most of them also recognize that whatever accountability structure they are using, if any, does not meet the standards of strictness they ultimately desire.

Some have formed apostolic teams or apostolic councils within their networks, with whom they work closely. This provides a certain level of accountability, but to a point. It is still essentially the relationship of a leader to subordinates, just as is the pastor's role with the local church elders.

Barney Coombs, in his fine book *Apostles Today*, does talk briefly about the problem. He says that apostles are accountable in three directions: (1) They are accountable to God; (2) They are accountable to peers; and (3) They are accountable to the local church that originally sent them out.[33] In my opinion, the peer-level accountability is the one level on which the future integrity of the New Apostolic Reformation will undoubtedly stand or fall.

David Cannistraci analyzes this in some detail:

> What we observe in the New Testament is this principle of mutual accountability wherein the "generals" become accountable *to one another*. This principle mandates that people become accountable to their top-level peers as well as to their ultimate head. It creates an effective relational network whereby authorities (especially in positions of headship) maintain openness, communication and teachability with one another. Within this arrangement, submission to one another is practiced and abuses are avoided.[34]

As we will see in the next chapter, some apostolic networks are being formed by bringing together a number of already recognized apostles under the leadership of an overseeing apostle. This is a step in the right direction, because the apostles who decide to join such a network have thereby placed themselves under the authority of the overseeing apostle and have accepted the accompanying accountability. The question remains: To whom is the overseeing apostle accountable?

Fortunately, several dynamics are now under way that are providing opportunities for apostles to relate creatively and in depth to their peers who lead other apostolic networks. To the degree that friendship and trust can develop from this process, there is realistic hope that many apostles will voluntarily and publicly submit themselves to an accountability structure of legitimate apostolic peers. On this one, the jury is still out.

Notes

1. E. von Eicken, H. Linder, "Apostle," *The New International Dictionary of New Testament Theology, Vol. 1*, Colin Brown, ed. (Grand Rapids: Zondervan Publishing House, 1975), p. 127.
2. C. Peter Wagner, *Your Spiritual Gifts Can Help Your Church Grow* (Ventura, Calif.: Regal Books, 1979; rev. ed., 1994), p. 231.
3. Ibid., p. 233.

4. David Cannistraci, *Apostles and the Emerging Apostolic Movement* (formerly *The Gift of Apostle*) (Ventura, Calif.: Regal Books, 1996), p. 29.

5. Bill Hamon, *Apostles, Prophets and the Coming Moves of God* (Shippensburg, Pa.: Destiny Image, 1997), p. 124.

6. John Eckhardt, *The Ministry Anointing of the Apostle* (Chicago: Crusaders Publications, 1993), p. 40.

7. George Batson, *World Pentecost* (Autumn 1996), p. 16.

8. Reinhold Ulonska, Ibid., p. 17.

9. Felipe S. Ferrez, Ibid., p. 18.

10. Bylaws of the General Council of the Assemblies of God, revised August 10, 1993.

11. Carlis L. Moody, *World Pentecost* (Autumn 1996), p. 18.

12. Hamon, *Apostles, Prophets and the Coming Moves of God*, p. 31.

13. John Eckhardt, *50 Truths Concerning Apostolic Ministry* (Chicago: Crusaders Ministries, 1994), p. 8.

14. Cannistraci, *Apostles and the Emerging Apostolic Movement*, p. 79.

15. Hamon, *Apostles, Prophets and the Coming Moves of God*, p. 221.

16. John Kelly in an informational packet for Antioch Churches and Ministries, n.p., n.d.

17. Hamon, *Apostles, Prophets and the Coming Moves of God*, pp. 73, 74.

18. Max Weber, *The Theory of Social and Economic Organization* (New York: The Free Press, 1947), pp. 358, 359.

19. Laurence J. Peter, *The Peter Principle* (New York: Bantam Books, 1969), p. 7.

20. Ibid., p. 8.

21. Hamon, *Apostles, Prophets and the Coming Moves of God*, p. 32.

22. Ibid., p. 164.

23. Eckhardt, *The Ministry Anointing of the Apostle*, pp. 40, 41.

24. Lyle E. Schaller, *Tattered Trust* (Nashville: Abingdon Press, 1996), p. 44.

25. Ibid., p. 45.

26. John Wimber, "Leaving but Not Quitting," *Equipping the Saints* (3rd Quarter 1996), p. 23.

27. Cannistraci, *Apostles and the Emerging Apostolic Movement*, p. 130.

28. Hamon, *Apostles, Prophets and the Coming Moves of God*, pp. 216, 217.

29. Leo Lawson, "The New Apostolic Paradigm and Morning Star International Churches" (master's paper, Fuller Theological Seminary School of World Mission, December 1997), p. 38.

30. Ibid., p. 41.

31. Paul Daniel, "His People Christian Ministries," *The New Apostolic Churches*, C. Peter Wagner, ed. (Ventura, Calif.: Regal Books, 1998), p. 237.

32. Hamon, *Apostles, Prophets and the Coming Moves of God*, p. 40.

33. Barney Coombs, *Apostles Today* (Tunbridge, Kent, England: Sovereign World, 1996), pp. 212, 213.

34. Cannistraci, *Apostles and the Emerging Apostolic Movement*, pp. 151, 152.

CHAPTER SIX

The Nuts and Bolts of
Apostolic Networks

Not long ago, I spent a couple of days in an apostolic delivery room. A new apostolic network was being born. The parent of the new network is Greg Dickow, founder and senior pastor of Life Changers International Church of Barrington Hills, Illinois, just west of Chicago. In four years, the church has become one of the fastest growing churches in the Chicago area, and they had just moved into a new $3.5 million facility.

For some time, Greg had felt the apostolic calling on his life, and in 1998 he decided to go public with the Life Changers Association. Around 300 interested pastors and church leaders from several states attended the event. Some were already committed to join Dickow's network, and others were exploring the possibilities.

Why were these leaders interested? Obviously, Greg Dickow was meeting a felt need. Most of those attending were either pastors of small new apostolic churches or denominational pastors looking for other options. Greg's experience in new apostolic circles had made him well aware of the felt needs of the pastors. To help us understand this, I will cite several quotes from the Life Changers Association informational brochure:

+ Life Changers Association is not just looking forward to the 21st century, we are destined to help shape it.

- Draw on the expertise and anointing of some of today's more progressive thinkers and ministry leaders as they help you with worship, youth and children's ministry, financial administration, staff recruiting and development, church growth, strategic planning, successful marketing, media planning, fund raising and more.
- The mandate of the association is to help you discover, develop and distribute your gifts, talents, abilities, and ultimate life purpose.
- People consumed with a passion to see lives changed and eager to seize their God-given destiny are the kind of people involved in the association.
- The association offers a world-class training center that hosts leadership seminars, conferences, worship seminars, conventions, evangelism workshops, and financial seminars.[1]

No one knows how many apostolic networks are in existence today. Nor can anyone count the number of births, such as Life Changers Association, that are constantly occurring in many parts of the world. Some researchers estimate that two to three new networks are being formed in Africa alone every day. Whatever the number, it is certain that apostolic networks constitute one of the most significant new wineskins in worldwide Protestantism today.

COMMON CHARACTERISTICS OF APOSTOLIC NETWORKS

APOSTOLIC NETWORKS ARE TRANSLOCAL

Apostolic networks are composed of local churches that, for one reason or another, voluntarily decide to affiliate with the network. Their heartfelt desire is to relate to one another in a satisfying way.

I like David Cannistraci's definition: "An apostolic network can take many forms. Essentially, it is a band of autonomous churches and individual ministries that are voluntarily united in an organized structure. The framework of human relationships is sufficient to facilitate interdependency between network members and their apostolic oversight."[2] The operative words here are "autonomous," "voluntarily," "relationships," "interdependency" and "apostolic oversight." Virtually every apostolic network, regardless of the form it might take, would display those characteristics.

Although apostolic networks are translocal, their spheres are limited. God usually assigns certain territorial spheres to the apostolic leaders He chooses.

Roberts Liardon says, "We know that apostles are divinely appointed to a given territory or region. Some of these territories make up cities or counties while others are regional, national or international. No man can determine his appointed territory; only God makes such appointments."[3]

This statement seems to fit what the apostle Paul wrote to the Corinthians: "If I am not an apostle to others, yet doubtless I am to you" (1 Cor. 9:2). Later he says, "We, however, will not boast beyond measure, but within the limits of the sphere which God appointed us—a sphere which especially includes you" (2 Cor. 10:13).

APOSTOLIC NETWORKS ARE BASED ON RELATIONSHIPS

Local church pastors relate personally to the apostle. Frequently, the churches in the network were planted by or are under the supervision of the apostle, so the affiliation is a natural one. In other cases, the desire to join a network can be traced back to a personal friendship with other pastors in the network, or relationships that have developed, one way or another, with the apostle. A strong motivation for joining comes from a God-given desire on the part of pastors not to be an independent church, but to relate dynamically to other churches in interdependence.

Greg Dickow appeals to this desire. In his brochure designed to recruit pastors, he writes: "Many of us have tried various networks, coalitions, denominations, and fellowships with the hope of filling our need for real relationship with others. For whatever reason it may not have worked out as you had planned. I believe there is hope! The Life Changers Association is a fresh new breed of visionaries and leaders who are aggressively committed to covenant relationships."[4] Just to keep the contrast in mind, there is no doubt that such language would be considered inappropriate or even offensive by many traditional denominational executives.

David Cannistraci helps us see the differences:

> Apostolic networks are different from most denominations because in networks, *relationships* (not policies and rules) are the main source of organizational strength. Only minimal legal and financial control are imposed. In the apostolic network to which I belong, the function of government is accomplished largely through the partnership of prayer, discussion, planning and visionary leadership. The most effective networks are more than mere ministerial fellowships, because the purpose is to accomplish apostolic ministry and not merely to facilitate camaraderie.[5]

APOSTOLIC NETWORKS HAVE ONE LEADER

I have mentioned the matter of trust several times. In new apostolic thinking, trust is in individuals, not in boards, committees, teams or councils. Networks stand or fall on personal relationships, and the most crucial relationship for a network is the relationship of the individual pastors to the apostolic leader. In some cases, the apostle has gathered an inner circle called an "apostolic team."

The members of the team, in their own right, are considered apostles or, if that label is not a label of choice, a functional equivalent with whatever name may be preferred. Even in such cases, though, the apostolic team is not a committee that follows Roberts Rules of Order, but ordinarily a team that has voluntarily submitted to the final authority of one leader.

This is an important way apostolic networks differ from ministerial fellowships that view themselves as a grouping of peers, any one of whom can serve as its leader for a given period of time. I will return to this point later in the chapter when we examine factors that can determine whether apostolic networks will sputter and stall or whether they will energetically grow and multiply.

AUTHORITY FLOWS FROM THE BOTTOM UP
I introduced Michael Regele of Percept in chapter 3. He is the one who wrote the article directed to governing bodies of historic denominations, entitled "Sacrificing Some Sacred Cows." One of what he calls "sacred cows" is: Lower Serves the Higher.

Here is how Regele explains it:

> Early in my training as a candidate for ordination in the Presbyterian Church USA, I was introduced to the concept of being a connectional church (a concept I found positive and meaningful, given my origins in the unaffiliated movement). A corollary to our "connectionalism" was the concept that within our governing body structures was the principle that the lower body is responsible to the higher, culminating ultimately in the General Assembly, the final arbiter for the church. (Each historic denomination has a similar concept.) In *practice* and too often in *attitude*, this principle translates into the lower exists to *serve* the higher.[6]

Regele's observation is that this manner of applying the principle of denominational connectionalism may have seen its day. He goes on to say, "Regardless of what one thinks about this, at the local level there is an increasing disenchantment with the principle. Many local congregations are simply choosing not to play anymore. We expect this trend to persist."[7]

Chuck Smith, one of the prototypes of new apostolic leaders in the United States, and founder of the Calvary Chapel movement, must have held the same viewpoint back in the 1960s when he chose to terminate his affiliation with the International Church of the Foursquare Gospel.

Donald Miller of the University of Southern California reports what he found in his research of Calvary Chapel:

> After investigating several other denominations, Smith concluded that his criticisms of the Foursquare were, in fact, endemic to all denominations: "I saw them as ultimately coming under control of those who are not necessarily the most spiritual men..." In Smith's analysis, it is power-oriented people who end up leading denominations, and "once they have achieved a position of power, then they become protective and they want to protect themselves in this position of power."[8]

THE NETWORK SERVES; IT DOES NOT CONTROL

New apostolic thinking views the local church as the essential building block of the apostolic network. The network exists to serve the churches, and the churches empower the apostle. Because affiliation is voluntary and so loosely structured, the minute the network begins to serve itself and not the churches, it will begin to crumble.

Dick Iverson, founder of Ministers Fellowship International (M.F.I.), puts it this way:

> We have built several features into M.F.I. from the beginning that we believed would enable us to avoid denominationalism. We are committed to doing whatever we have to do to maintain our fellowship as a network and to avoid any kind of controlling hier-

archy. We don't oppose denominations or those who are in them. We thank God for what He has done and for what He continues to do for the kingdom through denominations. However, we share among ourselves a personal conviction that a central headquarters will not dictate policy for local churches. Every church is to be autonomous, and yet the pastors also can enjoy the security of meaningful accountability and checks and balances in their leadership.[9]

APOSTOLIC NETWORKS ADD VALUE TO LOCAL CHURCH LEADERSHIP
Apostolic networks perceive themselves in the role of adding value to those who pastor local churches. Apostle John Kelly, for example, makes his case in an informational brochure about Antioch Churches and Ministries, answering the question: "Why should a minister be a part of Antioch Churches and Ministries?" Kelly says,

> The answer is that ACM is unique in its approach to the pastor. The goal of the Network is to build the pastor and his church, not to create a centralized "Mecca." Ministers in the Network will benefit tangibly from being a part. A few of the blessings people are deriving from being involved in ACM include:
> - The blessing of committed relationships
> - The blessing of vision and mission
> - The blessing of covering (accountability)
> - The blessing of opportunity
> - The blessing of challenge
> - The blessing of synergy
> - The blessing of life[10]

Local churches flow in and out of apostolic networks. They remain in them as long as they perceive they are receiving added value. For example, during the 12-month period from June 1991 to June 1992, 76 congregations joined the Calvary Chapel network led by Chuck Smith, while 35 congregations were removed from "the list," as they call it. That is why a certain kind of marketing approach is frequently used by the networks. They believe they need to get the word out that they do, in fact, add value to local churches. To illustrate this, consider John Kelly's motivational appeal:

> If you have been seeking a network of fellow ministers and local churches that are committed to relationships, believe in the authority of local church government, do cooperative missions work with other local churches, practice teamwork, and value fivefold ministry with apostles who are fathers and not bureaucrats or autocrats, you can relate to us at Antioch Churches and Ministries.[11]

DO APOSTOLIC NETWORKS BECOME DENOMINATIONS?

If anyone were to ask me which is the most important section of this book, I would unhesitatingly say that this is it. Most of the rest of the book reports and analyzes what the New Apostolic Reformation *is*. This section sets forth the options of what it may or may not *be* in the future. To illustrate, let me quote from one prominent Christian leader in the United States writing to another one and discussing my book *The New Apostolic Churches*.

Without naming either of the parties, this is what was said: "As I told you, there was some talk at the beginning of calling this movement 'postdenominationalism.' In a way, this new apostolic movement may actually turn out to be *predenominational* as it grows and expands."

This statement accurately depicts a real danger. As we have just seen, the last thing new apostolic leaders want is denominationalism, but can they avoid it? Donald Miller, for one, thinks they cannot. He foresees "the inevitable evolution of new paradigm [his term for 'new apostolic'] groups toward denominationalism. In time, they will start centralizing authority, insisting on uniform practices, and creating bureaucratic layers of approval for acts that previously were spontaneous and spirit-led."[12]

Sociologists of religion of past generations such as Ernst Troeltsch and H. Richard Neibuhr, with whom Donald Miller is very familiar, have found it useful to distinguish between the "church" and the "sect." The church connotes the religious establishment that, in our day, could be applied to the traditional denominations. The sect is the upstart new movement that could be applied to new apostolic churches and apostolic networks. The church typically opposes the emerging sect, sometimes quite strenuously, as the Catholic church did in the counter-Reformation. I fully expect that history will repeat itself and that many denominational executives will find themselves quite upset when they begin to learn about certain characteristics of the New Apostolic Reformation. Some, indeed, may not even like this book!

THE ROUTINIZATION OF CHARISMA

The historical trend is for sects eventually to evolve into churches, and when they do, new sects can be expected to appear on the scene. That is why many would agree with Donald Miller that there is no way for apostolic networks to avoid eventually becoming denominations. In his book *Reinventing American Protestantism*, Miller works more out of the paradigm established by sociologist Max Weber than that of Troeltsch/ Neibuhr. Max Weber, in his classic *The Theory of Social and Economic Organization* (The Free Press), develops the principle of what he calls "routinization of charisma."

In the last chapter, we looked at Weber's definition of "charisma," and how clearly it applies to today's apostolic leaders. The charismatic leader possesses qualities the followers perceive as emanating from superhuman sources. This is one of the reasons the apostle who founds an apostolic network carries so much authority. This is the person who casts the vision others will voluntarily and unreservedly give themselves to implement. When the charismatic leader dies, the followers then feel obligated to devise ways and means to perpetuate the charisma. Weber observes that in the Western world, the tendency is for the followers to develop rational, bureaucratic, democratic structures in their attempt to preserve the charisma and to remain true to the vision of their founder.

---

*The charismatic leader possesses qualities
the followers perceive as emanating
from superhuman sources.*

However, the trade-off is that when democratic structures are developed, the leaders then gain their positions of power by the will (meaning the votes) of the followers. When this happens, the source of power subtly shifts from God to a group. The group that elected the leader can also presumably fire the leader at will. So the trust is now in a group, no longer in an individual charismatic leader.

Donald Miller says, "According to Weber, the routinization of charisma is not merely inevitable but absolutely necessary if a movement is to survive after the departure of the founding leader."[13]

THE ASSEMBLIES OF GOD AT THE CROSSROADS

Another sociologist of religion, Margaret M. Poloma, also working from Weber's paradigm, studied the largest of the white Pentecostal denominations in the United States, the Assemblies of God. In her book *The Assemblies of God at the Crossroads*, Poloma says the following:

Despite the evidence of ongoing religious experiences, few observers would question that the charismatic fervor of the early Pentecostals had been domesticated over the decades. Although charisma is still very much part of the Assemblies of God, in theory as well as in practice, there has been a noteworthy shift from an emphasis on "magical charisma" supported by prophetic leaders to priestly or more routinized forms. The very success of the Assemblies and the inevitable development of a bureaucratic organization has produced certain tensions.[14]

To illustrate what is occurring, I recall being in a church meeting when one member was reporting about her recent trip to Canada and to San Diego. She was thrilled that what she saw reflected what she perceived as a wholesome unity within the Body of Christ. She had visited an Assemblies of God church in Canada (known there as Pentecostal Assemblies of Canada) and a Presbyterian church in San Diego. Her enthusiastic report was that "the services were practically identical—it was hard to tell the difference." Little did she realize that she was describing a classic case of a sect becoming a church.

It needs to be clear that the Assemblies of God is not being singled out because it is any better or worse than other denominations. It just happens to be one of those that has been more thoroughly studied and documented than others. The Assemblies of God is not *making* history as much as it is *repeating* history. Poloma goes on to say, "Just as other once-charismatic religious institutions have been led down the path of over-institutionalization and over-regulation, which in turn has destroyed much of the original charisma, the Assemblies of God too faces threats from routinization."[15]

Understanding that the Assemblies of God (AOG) has begun to travel down the road of the sect becoming a church may help explain why it would reject the sectlike Latter Rain Movement of the post-World War II era, and the sectlike Charismatic Movement that began in the early 1960s. It also may throw some light on why the denomination could not absorb the visions of some of the younger AOG charismatic leaders such as Loren Cunningham, founder of Youth With A Mission.

ADMINISTRATORS CLAMP ON THE LID

Specifically, what happens in the typical church system when charisma is routinized? Harold Eberle says, "The downfall of a ministry first occurs when the apostles and/or prophets are replaced."[16] This is invariably the case, even in church traditions in which the titles or offices of apostle and prophet are not formally recognized. Then, what follows?

Eberle says, "The control invariably ends up in the hands of those with gifts of administrations, with pastors serving under them. The apostolic anointing is replaced by superintendents, district representatives, overseers, bishops, and others with various titles, but all of whom have administrative hearts. The prophetic voice is replaced by doctrinal statements and accepted forms of practice."[17]

This, then, becomes self-perpetuating because the administrators in control build staffs of other administrators indefinitely. Eberle goes on: "The Holy Spirit is restricted through well-meant rules and programs. Administrators become a 'lid' on the people involved under them."[18]

VINEYARD DECLARES ITSELF A DENOMINATION

Although the time line is not fixed, routinization of charisma, or the transition from sect to church, ordinarily requires a generation or two after the demise of the founder. In light of this, it is remarkable that the Association of Vineyard Churches, one of the early prototypes of the New Apostolic Reformation in the United States, declared itself a denomination in the first generation. In fact, several years before he passed away, John

Wimber, the founder, thought it was advisable to move into the denominational stream.

In 1993, Wimber wrote:

> The Association of Vineyard Churches—for better or worse—is a denomination. We see this primarily in the area of relational structure that provides accountability, cohesion, and encouragement....By 1984 the number of Vineyards was growing rapidly. We made the decision to formalize the structure that had evolved. Until then, we really worked under Vineyard Ministries International. But VMI was a renewal organization, so we formed AVC for church planting and to provide oversight. Historically, we probably became a denomination when we incorporated AVC, appointed Regional Overseers, called a board of directors, and began ordaining ministers.[19]

In taking this step, Wimber was very much aware of the need to stop short of some of the trappings of denominationalism that new apostolic leaders collectively dread. This is reflected in the subtitle of the paper just quoted, "Steering a Course Between Chaos & Traditional Denominationalism." Before Wimber died, he appointed Todd Hunter as national director of the Association of Vineyard Churches. About six months after Wimber's death, Hunter convened a council of Vineyard leaders, which produced "The AVC-USA Columbus Accords." One of the more significant statements in this accord is: "We are determined to resist the routinization of charisma."[20] I will return to this later.

THE CASE OF THE CHRISTIAN AND MISSIONARY ALLIANCE

Back in the 1880s, The Christian and Missionary Alliance (C&MA) was founded by A. B. Simpson in New York City. It was a classic sect emerging from a church. After 18 years as a Presbyterian minister, Simpson thought that to reach the masses in New York City more effectively, he had to break the denominational ties, which he did. The new "society," as he called it, was designed to stand independently of any denomination.

For decades, later on, the chief public voice for the C&MA was that of prolific author A. W. Tozer. In 1943 he wrote, "[A. B. Simpson] never intended his society to become a denomination. Whether this proves superior insight or the total lack of it, history will decide. He sought to provide fellowship only, and looked with suspicion upon anything like rigid organization."[21] Simpson had the characteristics of an apostle, and his society had the characteristics of an apostolic network. He certainly would be regarded, in anybody's book, as a charismatic leader in the Weberian sense.

Tozer later comments, "The society had not been long in existence before normal developments within it began to upset the idyllic simplicity of the original plan." Decades later, in his own day, Tozer reports: "[The Christian and Missionary Alliance] gently but persistently declares that it is not a denomination, and yet it exercises every spiritual and ecclesiastical function of any Protestant body in the world—without one exception."[22]

So it was inevitable that, in 1974, the General Council would reorganize the structure of the Alliance and formalize the denomination. *Eternity* magazine reported: "After 87 years as a para-denominational organization dedicated to missionary activity, the Christian and Missionary Alliance has officially recognized what many people have known for years: the Alliance is a denomination. By a vote of 834 to 98, delegates to the Alliance's General Council meeting in Atlanta (Georgia) adopted a new constitution and by-laws, making the Alliance a denomination."[23]

WHAT DO APOSTLES WANT TO AVOID?

These kinds of case studies are what lead scholars such as Donald Miller to predict that current apostolic networks will eventually become denominations. Is this necessarily so? Is it really inevitable that the groupings of churches I have been describing in this book will turn out to be a few more regulatory, permission-withholding bureaucracies? I am sure the apostles with whom I am personally acquainted sincerely want to avoid becoming denominations every bit as much as A. B. Simpson did.

Lyle Schaller vividly details what the apostolic networks are attempting to avoid:

> [A denomination] adopts rules and regulations that must be followed by individuals, congregations, and regional judicatories as well as by national agencies. Examples include the credentials required for ordination; procedures for removing a member's name from a congregational membership roster; permission to relocate a congregation's meeting place; a requirement that race, gender, age, color, nationality, or marital status cannot be considered as factors in filling a vacant pulpit; quotas for selecting delegates to regional and national conventions and to denominational boards; the adoption of a minimum salary for pastors; minimum standards for congregational contributions to the denominational treasury; mandatory retirement at a specified age; requirements for continuing education for pastors; restrictions on designated second-mile giving by contributors; regulations on marriage, divorce, remarriage, sexual orientation, abortion and cohabitation; restrictions on who will be admitted to the table for the Lord's Supper; restrictions on involvement in interchurch activities; and criteria for selection of volunteers to serve on committees and boards.[24]

ROUTINIZATION OF CHARISMA
CAN BE PREVENTED

At this point, I feel a personal responsibility not just to diagnose, but also to prescribe. Most sociologists of religion agree that routinization of charisma is inevitable, and the history of religion seems to support this. However, I doubt that it is as inexorable as some may imagine.

Brenda Brasher, a young, postmodern sociologist of religion, who studied under Donald Miller, agrees with me. After researching Chuck Smith's Calvary Chapel movement in depth, Brasher concludes: "Routinization of charismatic authority in the postmodern religious world appears in this instance as an ongoing, developmental option which the movement can elect not to pursue rather than an inevitable, postcharismatic crisis survival response which, if it wishes to be successful, it must inevitably make."[25]

THE PRESCRIPTION FOR PRESERVING VITALITY

I realize that in doing this I am moving into uncharted waters. If I am going to prescribe, however, let me write out, as clearly as I can, my prescription for the preservation of the vitality of new apostolic networks as they have been emerging in our times. The prescription has three mandates. If these are applied with boldness and passed on faithfully to the next generation of apostles, the New Apostolic Reformation can continue serving the kingdom of God indefinitely. At least that is my opinion at the moment.

- ◆ Mandate One: Keep a ceiling on the number of churches in each network.
- ◆ Mandate Two: Constantly cultivate new charisma.
- ◆ Mandate Three: Multiply apostolic networks.

Let's look at these one at a time.

MANDATE ONE: KEEP A CEILING ON THE NUMBER OF CHURCHES IN EACH NETWORK

My hypothesis is that there is a numerical limit to the number of churches one apostolic individual can meaningfully oversee.

If apostolic networks stand or fall on personal relationships, as we have stated many times, how many such personal relationships can a given apostle maintain long range? Obviously, there has to be a limit. It cannot be an infinite number. Could anyone relate to 1,000 churches? Or 500?

This brings to mind the doctoral research of Bill Sullivan, founder and director of the Church Growth Department of the Church of the Nazarene in Kansas City, whom I had the privilege of mentoring. Knowing the principle of church growth that the best way to evangelize an area is to plant new churches, Bill wondered if that principle could be applied to a higher level, namely, that of multiplying Nazarene districts across the United States. His research revealed that when Nazarene *districts* reached 70 churches, their growth rate tended to decrease. One of the reasons was that the effectiveness of the district superintendent to supervise churches could be sustained satisfactorily up to about 70, but for most that was the limit.

FROM RELATIONSHIPS TO REGIMENTATION

Awhile ago, I quoted John Wimber's statement declaring that The Association of Vineyard Churches had become a denomination. You may have noted that, in his paper, Wimber noted that "By 1984 the number of Vineyards was growing rapidly." As I recall, the number at that time had reached around 200 churches, and new ones were being added. My point is that a certain *number* of churches was one of the factors that had persuaded John Wimber he needed to formalize the Vineyard structure. The earlier Vineyard movement had functioned well because every one of the pastors had enjoyed a personal relationship with Wimber. He would return their calls. The apostle was able to keep in touch with the churches.

Then the time came when this was no longer the case. Wimber could not keep up with the churches because there were too many. I imagine that frustration had begun to set in some time before the number of churches reached 200. By then, it had become obvious that the organization needed to move from *relationships* to *regimentation*.

THE RANGE: 50 TO 150 CHURCHES

What is the optimum number of churches in a given apostolic network? Let me say first of all that a bit more research on this matter could give us better answers. Let me say, second, that we should undoubtedly be looking at a range rather than one specific *number*. My best guess at the moment is that most apostles can handle up to 50 churches fairly well. Few could handle as many as 150 without creating some kind of bureaucracy to help make it happen. So it could well be that further research will confirm that our range is from 50 to 150 churches per network, or something in that vicinity.

If this turns out to be the case, we must then ask what the variables are that would determine whether a given network will likely peak out at the *lower* end of the range or at the *higher* end of the range. This is another point on which more research is needed, but, meanwhile, here are my observations:

1. The personality of the apostle is undoubtedly the most important variable. Some individuals by nature can establish and sustain more personal relationships than others. Experience counts as well. The more mature and seasoned the apostle, the more churches can be handled.
2. If the apostle can build and manage a peer-level apostolic team, the number of churches can be higher. For example, a team of five apostles overseeing 50 churches each would already raise the number of churches in the network to 250.

3. If the churches of the network are in close geographical proximity, the total number can be larger. One of the prerequisites for keeping in touch with the churches of a network is to visit them personally, because the network is based on personal relationships. Geographical proximity allows what would otherwise be used as travel time instead of "hanging out" time, to use an apostolic vernacular.

4. Apostles who have a lower need for quality control can probably oversee more churches. In this respect, a sanguine apostle might have an advantage over a melancholic apostle.

5. An apostolic network that has a highly efficient administrative staff, which has developed a well-oiled communications system throughout the network, can be larger than one that leans more toward the chaotic side.

6. Apostolic networks that insist on stricter standards of genuine accountability will tend to be smaller than the looser networks.

MANDATE TWO: CONSTANTLY CULTIVATE NEW CHARISMA

I will not soon forget that when I read Brenda Brasher's report about Calvary Chapel and came to her section "Cultivation of New Charisma," I felt like a prospector who had stumbled on a 20-pound gold nugget. This was something I had not found in Max Weber's writings, who had postulated the *routinization* of charisma without suggesting the other option of *cultivating* charisma. Cultivating charisma, if done well and persistently, can prove to be the salvation of the New Apostolic Reformation. Fortunately, one of the early and most visible new apostolic leaders in the United States, Chuck Smith, has provided a model we can follow.

Brasher discovered that the principal way Chuck Smith cultivates charisma in the Calvary Chapel movement is through the megachurches. She says, "With its large number of megas, Calvary supports not a single source of charismatic authority, but multiple ones."[26]

Cultivating charisma, if done well and persistently, can prove to be the salvation of the New Apostolic Reformation.

How does Chuck Smith do this? First, he publicly acknowledges and encourages the charismatic pastors of the megachurches. It also includes "allowing or accepting the megachurches to use original names such as Horizon and Harvest, and allowing or accepting megas to develop their own programs, start their own ministry schools and differentiate their styles to such an extent that connections between Calvary and its most successful megas are now fuzzy at best."[27]

A consistent theme among new apostolic leaders is that they are not there to control. Some live up to this ideal better than others. Chuck Smith is a role model for how it can be done well. The other apostles in the Calvary Chapel movement, namely, the megachurch pastors, have liberty that some other networks would not allow. These liberties include implementing their own foreign missions programs, educating their own pastors and planting daughter churches that do not necessarily affiliate with the Calvary Chapel movement.

Brenda Brasher says, "At major Calvary meetings, I have observed warm, personal interactions between most mega pastors and Smith. In interviews, mega pastors describe an active and affectionate relationship with Smith which deeply influences his life; but the unfolding ministry of the megachurches makes the gentle accountability between megas and the movement increasingly difficult to perceive."[28]

In contrast to Chuck Smith's modus operandi, John

Wimber, who ironically began as one of Calvary's megachurch pastors, but who later decided to leave and join Ken Gullickson's Vineyard movement, developed a history of severe conflict with many of his apostolic-level Vineyard megachurch pastors. Wimber's relationship with peer-level apostles was much like Paul's relationship to Barnabas.

In Paul's network, there was apparently room for only one apostle, so he split from Barnabas about a relatively trivial matter regarding whether John Mark should travel with them. In like manner, several megachurch pastors such as Tom Stipe, Mike Bickle, Ken Blue, John Arnott, Ché Ahn and Ken Gullickson himself, found themselves forced to leave the Association of Vineyard Churches after they discovered that their charisma, at least from their point of view, was not being affirmed, encouraged and cultivated by their apostle.

This may have been a factor contributing to one of the contrasts between the two movements Donald Miller has noticed: "The Vineyard now identifies itself as a denomination, whereas Calvary Chapel prefers to view itself as a close-knit fellowship of churches."[29] Apostolic leaders who are determined not to allow their networks to routinize into denominations will be cultivators of charisma. This leads to the third mandate.

MANDATE THREE:
MULTIPLY APOSTOLIC NETWORKS

If apostles constantly cultivate charisma within their networks, one of the inevitable products will be more apostles. It is clear, although not as yet well defined, that a variety of apostolic roles are possible in the kingdom of God. The kind of apostle I have been describing in this book is an overseeing apostle who has authority over a number of churches. Undoubtedly, several other kinds of apostles function authoritatively in certain areas of Kingdom ministry or within certain social alignments or in certain geographical regions such as cities, but do not have direct oversight of several local churches. I hope we soon will have a typology that will help us recognize and better understand these differing roles.

Be that as it may, many apostles are of the kind God has called to lead apostolic networks of their own. It is, therefore, imperative that existing apostles proactively take whatever steps might be necessary to empower the rising charismatic leaders within their sphere of influence to *start their own apostolic networks*.

If this is done, it will help immunize the New Apostolic Reformation from the routinization of charisma for two reasons:

1. It will keep the number of churches per network lower and more manageable.
2. It will provide first-generation, unroutinized, charismatic leadership for each new network.

In such a case, the only network susceptible to routinization of charisma would be what remains of the founding network. The new ones will have at least a generation more to function under the founding charismatic leader. If the apostle of the original founding network takes pains to choose a peer-level (not a subordinate) successor in whom charisma has been genuinely cultivated, rather than let a group choose the successor, the odds for routinization even of that network will measurably decrease.

Here is how Brenda Brasher views Calvary Chapel:

> Many pastors perceived the potential for the megas to branch off from the movement after Smith retires. Some considered it likely. One pastor, in his response, identified the groups he thought most likely to do so: "What I am saying is that it is possible that groups such as Horizon Christian Fellowship of San Diego, Harvest Crusade of Riverside, Applegate Christian Fellowship, or Calvary San Jose may actually become individual Calvary Chapel movements of their own."[30]

PARENTS GIVE THEIR CHILDREN AWAY

My question would be related to why such a thing could not be encouraged to happen while the founding apostle is still alive. It seems to me that the more the apostle is a true parent, the more likely it could happen. Why don't apostles, as a part of their vision, routinely spawn off and give away new apostolic networks? Paul Daniel was quoted in the last chapter as saying: "Fathers, I believe, should never be threatened by sons, but should rejoice when they excel."[31]

My wife and I have parented three girls. We invested much time, huge amounts of energy and a considerable portion of our lifetime earnings in raising them. We became emotionally attached to all of them; *and we gave them all away*. This was always my understanding of what parents were supposed to do.

Larry Kreider of Dove Christian Fellowship International says:

> Only a dysfunctional parent will try to hang on to his children and use them to fulfill his own vision. Healthy parents expect their children to leave their home to start their own families. Healthy spiritual parents must think the same way. This generation of Christian leaders are called to "give away" many of the believers in their churches to start their own spiritual families—new cell groups and new churches.[32]

Many of today's apostles will fully agree with Kreider's principle. They will usually apply it, however, as does Kreider, only to the level of multiplying churches within a given network. I believe that to prevent the generational routinization of charisma in the New Apostolic Reformation, this same principle needs to be applied to multiplying *networks*. Presumably, when churches are multiplied they relate to each other in the apostolic network that spawned them, forming a family of churches having similar DNA. The apostolic network is a *family of local churches*.

How about networks of networks? How about several over-seeing apostles who have similar spiritual DNA relating to each other as peer-level leaders of their own networks in a *family of networks?* Such a thing would not only avoid the routinization of charisma, but it would also go a long way toward solving the recurring problem of the accountability of overseeing apostles.

Can Denominations Change?

A major question, and a legitimate one, that will be raised by many readers of this book is whether routinized denomina-tions can reverse the trend and become apostolic networks. Another way of phrasing the question could relate to whether old wineskins can be reconditioned in order to hold the new wine. My understanding of the culture in New Testament times is that many old wineskins could be and were treated in a spe-cial way by soaking them in brine, rubbing in oil and restoring their flexibility so that they could contain new wine. Of course, certain old wineskins were so cracked or decomposed that they had seen their day. Some old ones could be made useful with effort, but the wineskins of preference were the new ones being used for the first time.

Some of today's apostolic networks are aware of this, and they strive to keep their wineskin flexible so that it will not become cracked and useless. Don Atkin describes Antioch Churches and Ministries in this light:

> John Kelly, our Overseeing Apostle, is a wise strate-gist. God is seeing that Apostle Kelly is surrounded by quality people with the necessary expertise to con-tinually "work the oil of the Holy Spirit" into our wineskin. This assures us that the wine, or the ministry, will continually dictate the shape of the ministry. It ain't the way it used to be. And, it ain't the way it's gonna be! But we have chosen to "go with the

flow" of wine, and make daily, weekly and monthly adjustments in the wineskin. In this way we will remain contemporary, on the cutting edge of the move of God.[33]

THE ASSEMBLIES OF GOD IN AUSTRALIA: IT CAN BE DONE!

Especially since the 1960s, denominational "renewal movements" have proliferated in almost every traditional denomination. They have all sensed a call of God to remain in their denomination in order to pray for and work for renewal. None that I am aware of has been successful. The denominational leaders, true to their ideal of pluralism, have tolerated them, but the problems of control, power, and particularly management of financial resources have caused them to domesticate the renewal movements, a skill at which they are rather competent. What renewal might have taken place is largely cosmetic.

Other denominations have restructured organizationally to be relieved of the cumbersome bureaucracies and agencies that have multiplied through the years. However, when all the study commissions have reported, when the consultants have been paid, when the often emotionally charged conventions and assemblies have ended and when the new structure is announced, little has usually changed. The old wineskin may look a bit different, but it is still the old wineskin. The denomination has not become an apostolic network, and usually the growth rate of the denomination has not changed.

Given this background, you can imagine my delight when my friend David Cartledge began informing me that the Assemblies of God in Australia, clearly an old wineskin, had actually done it. They had made the transition from a traditional denomination to an apostolic network. The fruit of the change is dramatically depicted in the denominational graph of growth.

Let's begin with the graph:

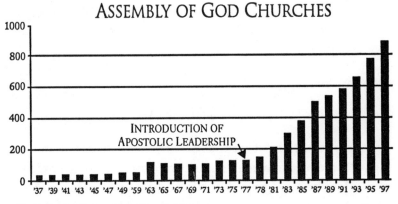

ASSEMBLY OF GOD CHURCHES

INTRODUCTION OF
APOSTOLIC LEADERSHIP

THE APOSTOLIC REVOLUTION

The process that took place is documented in a paper by David Cartledge, president of Southern Cross College, titled, "The Apostolic Revolution in the Assemblies of God in Australia." The Assemblies of God in Australia began in 1937 and functioned for forty years as a typical denomination. "Most conferences from 1937 to 1977 were characterized by adding rules, changing the constitution, and eroding the autonomy of the churches."[34] The growth pattern reflected this with a lackluster increase from 50 churches in 1937 to 150 in 1997, an average of two to three churches being added a year.

A crisis arose in the early 1970s when some Assembly of God leaders intuitively observed their movement's charisma being routinized, and they launched an aggressive effort to return to their roots. This overt, and somewhat primitive, Pentecostalism, perhaps tinged with "Latter Rain" influence, took root, among many other places, in David Cartledge's Townsville Assembly of God. Within a short time, the church had become the largest church in the city. This caused a great deal of concern among Assemblies of God denominational officials, particularly when new worship styles, a product of some New Zealand churches, began spreading to other assemblies outside of Townsville.

Cartledge reports: "A special and unprecedented Presbytery conference was called in 1972 to try to stem the tide. The controversy continued unabated with more churches being renewed and finding themselves at odds with the Executive leaders who opposed both the manifestations and the ministries that the renewed churches invited to preach."[35] In the next national conference, motions were (unsuccessfully) introduced to attempt to expel all pastors of the renewed churches from the denomination.

Cartledge says, "In reality, the debate on the manifestations of the Spirit was quite superficial. The real issue that emerged at that conference was the autonomy of the churches and their rights to engage in forms of worship that were not approved by the Executive. The other major issues were the recognition of ministry gifts beyond the pastor, teacher, and evangelist."[36] Keep in mind that the implication of this last statement was that the Assemblies of God had persisted in refusing to recognize and encourage the ministry of prophets and apostles within their churches.

The change came at the national conference of 1977, when voices crying "We want apostolic ministries to lead us" began to be heard by the delegates. Cartledge says, "Although there was no rule made about the type of ministers that should comprise the Executive, each conference since that time had always appointed proven apostolic and prophetic ministries as the national leadership of the movement."[37]

LEADERSHIP FROM MEGACHURCH PASTORS

Who were these new leaders? Just as we have observed in the case study of Calvary Chapel, they were the megachurch pastors. Previously, the Assemblies of God had no megachurches, and pastors normally moved to a new pastorate every few years. Reginald Klimionok, for example, changed the pattern by staying at Garden City Christian Church in Brisbane for 20 years, and built it from 100 to 3,000 members.

Andrew Evans went to Paradise Assembly in Adelaide in 1970 having a congregation of 150, and has 4,000 today. David Cartledge built his church in Townsville from 60 to more than

1,000 members. Frank Houston planted the Christian Life Centre in Sydney and now has 2,500 members. His son, Brian, started a daughter church from Christian Life Centre, and now has 5,000 members, the largest church in Australia. These kinds of charismatic leaders form the leadership of the renewed Assemblies of God in Australia. Brian Houston is currently the national superintendent.

Remarkable changes have occurred. For example, the Australian Assemblies now allow their pastors to plant churches and develop apostolic networks that can choose not to affiliate with the Assemblies of God, if they so desire. Cartledge says, "This created movements within the Movement, but to this point it has not been a negative value, and has contributed to the Assemblies of God's rapid growth."[38]

The denomination also allows its ministers to establish and operate their own itinerant parachurch-type organizations, and many of them are advertised as having prophetic and apostolic ministries, something that would have been impossible prior to 1977. For example, Brian Houston, the national superintendent, holds his own national conference each year and draws more participants than the Assemblies of God national conference itself.

It is possible, therefore, for old wineskins to be massaged enough by the oil of the Holy Spirit so they can receive the new wine God desires to pour out. If other denominations could take some of the bold and decisive steps that the Australian Assemblies of God have taken, the future would look bright. How many will actually choose to do so remains to be seen.

Notes
1. Greg Dickow, "Fulfilling Our God-Given Destiny" (promotional brochure for Life Changers Association, 1998).
2. David Cannistraci, *Apostles and the Emerging Apostolic Movement* (Ventura, Calif.: Regal Books, 1996), p. 190.
3. Roberts Liardon, "From Pastor Roberts," *The High Life: Embassy Christian Center's News Source* (January 1997), p. 3.
4. Greg Dickow, "A New Breed of Leaders" (promotional brochure for Life Changers Association, 1998).

5. Cannistraci, *Apostles and the Emerging Apostolic Movement*, p. 190.

6. Michael Regele, "Sacrificing Some Sacred Cows," *Viewpoint* (Fall 1994), p. 1.

7. Ibid.

8. Donald E. Miller, *Reinventing American Protestantism* (Berkeley, Calif.: University of California Press, 1997), p. 32.

9. Dick Iverson, "Ministers Fellowship International," *The New Apostolic Churches*, C. Peter Wagner, ed. (Ventura, Calif.: Regal Books, 1998), p. 176.

10. John Kelly, "Benefits of Involvement" (informational brochure for Antioch Churches and Ministries, n.d).

11. Ibid.

12. Miller, *Reinventing American Protestantism*, p. 181.

13. Ibid., p. 26.

14. Margaret M. Poloma, *The Assemblies of God at the Crossroads* (Knoxville, Tenn.: University of Tennessee Press, 1989), p. 94.

15. Ibid.

16. Harold R. Eberle, *The Complete Wineskin* (Yakima, Wash.: Winepress Publishing, 1993), p. 74.

17. Ibid.

18. Ibid., p. 76.

19. John Wimber, "The Vineyard Movement: Steering a Course Between Chaos & Traditional Denominationalism," *Vineyard Reflections* (October/November/December 1993), p. 1.

20. Association of Vineyard Churches—USA, "The AVC-USA Columbus Accords," third draft (April 27, 1998), p. 2.

21. A. W. Tozer, *Wingspread* (Harrisburg, Pa.: Christian Publications, 1943), p. 130.

22. Ibid., pp. 104, 105.

23. "C&M Alliance Converts to Denominational Status," *Eternity* (August 1974), p. 8.

24. Lyle E. Schaller, *21 Bridges to the 21st Century* (Nashville: Abingdon Press, 1994), pp. 139, 140.

25. Brenda E. Brasher, "Calvary Chapel and the Megachurch Phenomenon" (paper presented at the annual meeting of the Society for the Scientific Study of Religion, Washington, D.C., November 6-8, 1992), p. 4.

26. Ibid., p. 23.

27. Ibid., pp. 23, 24.

28. Ibid., pp. 17, 18.

29. Miller, *Reinventing American Protestantism*, pp. 50, 51.

30. Brasher, "Calvary Chapel and the Megachurch Phenomenon," p. 27.

31. Paul Daniel, "His People Christian Ministries," *The New Apostolic Churches*, C. Peter Wagner, ed. (Ventura, Calif.: Regal Books, 1998), p. 237.

32. Larry Kreider, *House to House* (Ephrata, Pa.: House to House Publications, 1995; rev. ed., 1998), p. 189.

33. Don Atkin, "Our Ever-Emerging Wineskin," *The Networker* 2, no. 1 (1998), p. 4.

34. David Cartledge, "The Apostolic Revolution in the Assemblies of God in Australia" (a privately circulated paper, 1998), p. 1.

35. Ibid., p. 2.

36. Ibid.

37. Ibid., p. 5.

38. Ibid., p. 7.

CHAPTER SEVEN

Plugged-In
Worship

I would say that, initially, the most visible difference, in the eyes of just about any observer, between traditional churches and new apostolic churches is the number of electrical cords running across the church platform in all directions. No traditional church has ever had so many microphones and such huge stacks of speakers up front. One gets the idea that if there ever were a power outage there would be no choice but to cancel worship. Someone said, "New apostolic worship is wired and inspired!"

Seeing so many electrical cords triggered the adjective "plugged-in" to describe new apostolic worship. However, it goes further. As I have been able to analyze the situation, new apostolic worship is "plugged in" to three important power sources:

- It is plugged into the sound system;
- It is plugged into the Holy Spirit;
- It is plugged into contemporary culture.

A REALITY CHECK

Not only is the contemporary worship of new apostolic churches one of the most observable differences to traditionalists, but of all the changes that are taking place, this one has also spread outside new apostolic circles more than any other change. Traditional churches of just about all denominations are beginning to realize that worship forms of past generations will not survive long into the future. However, not all have, as yet, chosen to come aboard.

George G. Hunter III, a church growth expert, says, "Eight in ten churches are stagnant or declining, in part because what they do from 11:00 to 12:00 on Sunday morning is not 'culturally relevant' to the unchurched people in the church's ministry area."[1] This will come as a reality check to many churches that up till now have not noticed or that perhaps have not liked the radical changes that have already begun.

Here is how Barry Liesch, a professor at Biola University in La Mirada, California, views it:

> Nothing short of a revolution in worship styles is sweeping across North America [He could have said "the world."]. Worship leaders, pastors and trained musicians face new and powerful forces of change—forces that bring renewal to some churches and fear to others. No denomination or group can sidestep the hot debate between the benefits of hymns versus choruses, seeker services versus worship services, choirs versus worship teams, organs versus synthesizers, and flowing praise versus singing one song at a time.[2]

WHAT DO WE MEAN BY "WORSHIP"?

Many excellent books about worship have been published during the last few years. After reading many of them, I began to notice that the authors apparently have not arrived at a consensus about what worship really is. As I was searching for a standard definition, I came to wonder if such a thing even existed. Worship leaders are, by nature, more right brained than left brained. As I read what they write, I conclude that almost all of them are *feeling* more or less the same things about worship, but that, understandably, they tend to *verbalize* these feelings differently.

I want to clarify that I am approaching this subject strictly as a nonprofessional. I am not a *producer* of worship, as most authors of these books are, but I am purely a *consumer* of worship. I have no more idea of how to lead worship than I have of how to make beef stroganoff. However, I can pretty well tell the difference between good and bad in both cases. Part of what I mean to say by this is that I will leave the matter of definitions up to the producers, and here is what some of them say:

+ LAMAR BOSCHMAN: *"Worship,* in the verb form, means the paying of homage or respect. In the Christian world, the term is used for the reverent devotion, service, or honor—whether public or individual—that is paid to God."[3]
+ SALLY MORGENTHALER: "Christian worship is not only offering all that we are to a Holy God (spirit). It is an intentional response of praise, thanksgiving, and adoration to *The* God, the One revealed in the Word, made known and accessible to us in Jesus Christ and witnessed in our hearts through the Holy Spirit (truth)."[4]
+ BRUCE LEAFBLAD: "Worship is that process in which we make God first in our lives."[5]
+ DONALD HUSTAD: "Worship is any and every worthy response to God."[6]

THE EIGHT MOST SIGNIFICANT CHANGES

In the balance of this chapter I will discuss what I consider the eight most significant changes from traditional worship to new apostolic worship:

1. From classical to contextual
2. From performance to participation

3. From hymns to songs
4. From pipe organ to percussion
5. From cerebral to celebration
6. From awe of God to intimacy with God
7. From liturgy to liberty
8. From meditation to mission

1. FROM CLASSICAL TO CONTEXTUAL

Probably the factor that has most contributed to the remarkable spread of new apostolic worship throughout the Body of Christ is the fact that it is plugged into contemporary culture. However, the decision of a particular local church to use contemporary worship does not, in itself, mean that it qualifies as a new apostolic church. Many other considerations enter the picture.

The transcultural appeal of contemporary worship interests me. For several years, as I have traveled to a variety of nations on six continents, I have been amazed that today's corporate worship sounds so much the same. This is not attributable entirely to translations of songs written in Western nations, although that happens a great deal. In most cases, the majority of worship songs have been composed by Christian musicians of that particular culture. I may not be able to read the words on the screen, but, even so, I can feel a spiritual environment and the presence of God through worship much the same way I feel them in my own home church in Colorado Springs.

I often wonder if historians of church music would not agree that right now we have the most universal sound of Christian worship since the Gregorian chant.

CULTURE IS THE DETERMINING FACTOR

New apostolic worship leaders strongly, and unapologetically, look to contemporary culture as the major determinant for the style of music they use, particularly if they are focused on reaching the unsaved in their community. In doing so, they reject the formal view of music that would hold that certain kinds of music are intrinsically superior to others. Instead, they lean much more toward the functional view of music, which is considerably more pragmatic, arguing that the best music is the music that holds the attention of those who listen to it.

George Hunter says, "All worship services are contemporary, but most are 'contemporary' to some other culture or generation."

The word "contemporary" has been used often in this discussion. I like the way George Hunter puts "contemporary" into the overall picture: "All worship services are contemporary, but most are 'contemporary' to some other culture and/or some other generation. For example, churches that feature eighteenth century German pipe organ music are 'contemporary' to German culture of the eighteenth century."[7]

THE CULTURAL ROOTS OF MOST CHURCHES

How does this apply to what we are noticing in many of our churches today? Hunter goes on:

> Two deep cultural roots shape most of our churches. First, your typical "old line" church is rooted in the European cultural soil of, say, England, Scotland, Germany or Sweden, from which the denominational tradition came. Second, the church is rooted in the 1950s, when "mainline" Christianity last prospered and significantly influenced the society. The problem is that the culture of the community around the church is different from the European culture from which the denomination came, and the community culture is increasingly different from what it was like in the 1950s.[8]

One of the churches in the United States, firmly rooted in the cultural soil of German Lutheranism, that has most made the choice to contextualize its church life to 1990s American suburban culture is a member of the Evangelical Lutheran Church of America denomination, namely, Community Church of Joy in Phoenix, Arizona. As a direct result, it has become the largest and fastest growing church in the denomination. Its pastor is Walther Kallestad, and its worship leader is Tim Wright. In his book *A Community of Joy*, Tim Wright points out that in the past most Americans chose a church on the basis of three criteria:

+ Denominational affiliation
+ Church doctrine
+ Location

This is no longer so! Tim Wright says, "People now choose churches in much the same way they make all other choices—as consumers (not necessarily as believers). They go where the action is—where they think their needs will be met—regardless of denomination, apparent doctrine, or location. For consumers, the worship service is one of the major reasons for choosing a church."9

31 FLAVORS OF WORSHIP

When I was a kid, my choices for ice cream were vanilla, chocolate or strawberry. Now, Baskin-Robbins allows me to choose from 31 flavors. Bread was white or whole wheat. Now it takes forever to stand in front of a supermarket bread section and decide what kind you will take home. Part of the culture in which we live today demands that people be given a wide variety of choices in just about every aspect of their lives.

The same thing applies to contemporary worship. Once we have decided to break from the traditional worship culture George Hunter describes, we then are faced with many further decisions. LaMar Boschman says, "There are many different styles of new apostolic worship. From the seeker-sensitive to Integrity to Vineyard to Maranatha to Promise Keepers and many others. And that proliferation of varieties of worship styles is going to grow and develop. It is a phenomenon of our digital age."[10]

"THIS IS HARMFUL IN EVERY WAY POSSIBLE"

Not everyone likes what is happening. A few years ago, I was doing a spiritual warfare seminar with Yonggi Cho in Switzerland, where the daily worship times were led by a Swiss contemporary worship team from the city of Ibeto.

Toward the end of the seminar sessions, I received a letter from one of the attendees, which said: "Worshipful praise in music is extremely important as a weapon of spiritual warfare, as you mentioned in one of your addresses. However, I feel that the extremely loud, ear-deafening noise we have heard so far by the young people from Ibeto is, in my humble opinion, very harmful spiritually, physically, and in every way possible!"

I love the quote my friend Gary McIntosh of Talbot Seminary in La Mirada, California, discovered. The words are those of an American pastor objecting to new trends in church music.

> There are several reasons for opposing it. One, it's too new. Two, it's often worldly, even blasphemous. The new Christian music is not as pleasant as the more established style. Because there are so many new songs, you can't learn them all. It puts too much emphasis on instrumental music rather than Godly lyrics. This new music creates disturbances making people act indecently and disorderly. The preceding generation got along without it. It's a money making scene and some of these new music upstarts are lewd and loose.[11]

Who said this? It was a pastor attacking Isaac Watts, now regarded as the father of American hymnody, in 1723! What else is new?

"RELIGIOUS DITTIES"? "VULGAR STREET SONGS"?

In his book *Reinventing American Protestantism*, Donald Miller picks up on a similar phenomenon 100 years later, in the early 1800s, quoting historian Nathan Hatch.

> Hatch states: "At the turn of the nineteenth century a groundswell of self-made tunesmiths, indifferent to authorized hymnody, created their own simple verses and set them to rousing popular tunes." He says that the music for these songs was borrowed indiscriminately from "a wide variety of secular tunes of love, war, homesickness, piracy, robbery, and murder." The established churches of the time (e.g., the Episcopalians, Presbyterians and Congregationalists) viewed these religious "ditties" as vulgar street songs, unfit for respectable religion.[12]

Such comments are not unusual in the 1990s. Many Christian leaders still strongly object to contemporary worship, contending, for example, that the songs do not have the theological depth of traditional hymns. If this hypothesis were tested in a serious research project, I doubt if it could be sustained. We are simply hearing good theology expressed in new ways.

THE ONGOING "WORSHIP WARS"

Frequent references are made to "worship wars" in recent literature about Christian worship.[13] I must say, however, I have yet to find a new apostolic church that considers itself to be fighting such a war, even though the warring factions tend to place the blame on their contemporary worship. It is apparent that the war occurs, not in churches that have accepted the innovation, but in those resisting the innovation, churches that social scientists would call the "later adopters."

Who are those who remain most uncomfortable with new apostolic worship? Generally speaking, they are the following groups:

- Older people, the generations known as "builders" and "seniors";
- Older congregations for which change presents itself as an insurmountable threat;
- Older pastors who are peacefully settled into their comfort zones;
- Congregations that have high European people consciousness such as Lutherans, Episcopalians, Mennonites, Salvation Army, Presbyterians, etc.;
- Classical musicians who have college degrees in music and who hold the formal, as opposed to the functional, view of music.

2. FROM PERFORMANCE TO PARTICIPATION

I worshiped in evangelical Christian churches as a spectator for 43 years. My role was to sing along with the pipe organ, to bow my head during prayer, to give an offering, to stand and sit when told, to try to pay attention to the sermon and to keep my children in order. William Easum and Thomas Bandy have it right when they say, "In the worship of Christendom [their word for what I call traditional churches], what mattered most was simply that you were there. Just being there communicated your faith in God, your commitment to membership in the church, and your comfort with the status quo of Christendom."[14] This is what I faithfully did from the time I accepted Christ in 1950 till 1993.

During the musical parts of the service, I would sit more than stand. The song leader, or "music director," would usually wave his (in my churches it was invariably a male) arms and between the hymns ad lib comments designed to keep my attention. The focus was on the choir, tastefully robed at the front and center of the sanctuary. The anthem by the choir, punctuated with fancy organ interludes, was considered the high point of worship. Polite applause was expected at the end of each performance, during which the choir director would face the audience and modestly acknowledge the acclaim.

When some began expressing a bit of discomfort with this during the 1980s, we were frequently told by the music director that the "real" choir of the church is the congregation. What did that mean? When, after hearing it a few times, I began to process it, two conclusions emerged:

1. We of the congregation were now regarded as performers the same as the choir members were. This was explained by verbalizing that we were, indeed, performers, and that the audience was God. That made good sense to me, at least intellectually.
2. We, like the choir, were programmed and controlled by a choir director who occupied the platform and who was in charge during worship. He led the congregation as if we were a choir, and he was always in control.

EXPERIENCING THE HOLY

A major change came in 1993 when our church started plugged-in worship. For the first time, I felt as though I was a *participant* rather than a *performer*. I felt as though the Holy Spirit, not the music director, was in control. I use the word "felt" because the difference is undoubtedly more in the heart than in the head. We did have a worship leader who was directing the event, but somehow he made us feel different.

William Easum and Thomas Bandy express the contrast well: "The nice, reverent, orderly, down-home, intergenerational, and carefully contained *presentation* of the Holy has been replaced by an unsettling, irreverent, unpredictable, out-of-this-world, cross-cultural and barely contained *experience* of the Holy."[15]

LaMar Boschman would agree. Here is the way he explains it:

There has been a shift from the spectator mode of the past to one of involvement. The people determine the outcome of worship because they realize that their worship experience is not dependent on professionals up front. It is the connection that individuals make with the Lord in worship that counts. And it is the active participation of each believer that jointly supplies the necessary flavor and experience of corporate worship.[16]

HIGH QUALITY REMAINS

All this is not to suggest that new apostolic worship uses lower quality music than does traditional worship. If music quality is evaluated by function rather than form, it could be argued that the new has a higher quality. The musicians who lead new apostolic worship across the board are every bit as skilled at their art as those who have led traditional worship for decades.

Barry Liesch, a music professor at Talbot, addresses the use of the word "performance" and suggests that it might be around for some time to come. He says the following:

> Pastors, nevertheless, need to understand that in their relationships to musicians, the word *performance* simply will not go away. For musicians, it's a word they have used throughout their training and they will *continue* to use it in their conversations with choirs, soloists, and worship teams—and perhaps even in the pulpit.[17]

Technically, of course, Barry Liesch is correct. At the same time, we consumers intuitively know the difference between a choir *performing* for us as the audience, and a worship team *drawing* us as participants into an experience with God.

3. FROM HYMNS TO SONGS

I had a funny feeling back in 1996. I had been invited to speak on a Sunday morning in a Baptist church in Canada. Before I preached, we sang two hymns from hymnals. As I opened the hymnal I tried, unsuccessfully, to remember when I had last sung a song from a hymnal. To all intents and purposes, I had forgotten what it was like to sing from a hymnal. In my mind, the words of the songs should have been on the overhead projector or on Power Point.

LaMar Boschman calls this phenomenon "the rebirth of music," which is the title of one of his books.

Where did this rebirth of music take origin? It did not originate with the professional musicians, but it came from the grass roots. Ordinary Christian people began hearing these new songs outside their church worship services, and they began singing them. They began buying Vineyard and Maranatha tapes because they wanted to continue worshiping in their homes and in their cars. The next thing we knew, contemporary worship became a multimillion dollar industry!

Nothing like that ever happened when we were still mainly singing hymns.

Christmas Carols Accompanied by Drums

A question that invariably surfaces in discussions relating to "worship wars" addresses the intrinsic value of older, traditional hymns. For someone like me, who is pushing 70, there is incredible personal value in the old songs. I especially love it when an old hymn is sung in a contemporary way. Month in and month out, there is a direct correlation between the moments when tears are coming out of my eyes during worship and the occasional singing of a traditional hymn.

I will never forget my first visit to New Life Church in Colorado Springs (now my home church) in December 1994. Christmas was coming and we sang "Hark the Herald Angels Sing" and "Angels We Have Heard on High," accompanied by drums! I was so overcome with emotion that I could hardly sing a word of either song.

That was okay for me, but as I glanced around I noticed that the younger people apparently weren't feeling the same things

I was. The songs, to them, were enjoyable and appropriate, but not deeply moving. I belong to a different generation.

Generation X already refers to buster music
as "old people's rock and roll"!

One of the things that greatly complicates the lives of us older people is the *rate* at which generations are changing. My generation, to be honest, was slightly different, but not *that* different from my parents' generation. Baby boomers are radically different from us. Their generation is calculated on the 18-year period between 1946 and 1964. The baby busters were down to an 11-year span, 1965 to 1976. The time span for generation X and the millennial generation will be shorter. William Easum and Thomas Bandy say, "A new generation emerges every three years—not every thirty years."[18] Generation X already refers to buster music as "old people's rock and roll"!

Facing this reality, Tim Wright says the following:

> The music used [in church] should reflect the styles of music heard on the radio *today*. Contemporary Christian music, an ever-expanding field in the music industry, offers an invaluable tool for outreach-oriented worship. The music is sophisticated, current and theologically sound. Stylistically, contemporary Christian music resembles the music played on "secular" radio stations. Lyrically, the words focus on Jesus.[19]

THIS CAN MAKE PROFESSIONAL MUSICIANS UNCOMFORTABLE
Barry Liesch, who has earned a Ph.D. in music, feels somewhat uncomfortable with the switch from hymns to songs. He considers it an "unhealthy state of affairs."

Liesch says, "I teach at a fine Christian university, and I've observed a disturbing trend. Increasingly our incoming students—which I take to be representative of the evangelical population—are ignorant of even the most well-known, historic hymns. Our young people are committed Christians and many are exemplary students, but when it comes to their knowledge of hymnody—they're ignorant! Their local churches have let them down."[20]

I imagine that few of Professor Liesch's students nowadays could either define or spell "hymnody" until they enrolled in his classes.

Barry Liesch likes and appreciates contemporary praise music. He believes, however, that each younger generation needs a worship center of gravity from which to move, and that such a center of gravity should be a repertoire of hymns.

William Easum, a United Methodist, is so irritated at professional musicians for making such a case of their formal view of music that he issues a strong statement:

> The source of the conflict comes primarily from trained musicians who often find these concepts repugnant and resist any change in the style of music. Church musicians do more to hinder congregations from sharing new life than any other staff members. Many are more interested in music appreciation than in helping people find new life. They are musicians first, and worship leaders second. Their love for music rivals their love for Christ. Making disciples is not as important as making good music. It is time we recognize this problem and deal with it accordingly.[21]

My personal opinion is that old hymns should be used regularly, from time to time, in even the most contemporary churches. I realize that "old hymns" may need explanation for some. I remember talking to a worship leader in Colombia about this. He replied, "Oh, yes. We sing the old hymns in our church. We sing 'Majesty' and 'This Is the Day That the Lord Has Made' and others like that!"

4. FROM PIPE ORGAN TO PERCUSSION

One of life's memorable occasions for me was attending the worship service on Saturday night September 24, 1993, at Lake Avenue Congregational Church in Pasadena, California. My wife and I began attending Lake Avenue in 1952, and for the first 41 years worship was business as usual. How traditional was the church? Just for fun, I once randomly selected a six-week period during which I saved the weekly church bulletins. I then looked up the dates on which the congregational hymns were written. During those six weeks, we did not sing a single hymn written in the twentieth century!

The service Doris and I attended was a new contemporary service, planned and announced by Pastor Gordon Kirk. As we entered the worship center (it seats 4,500) we immediately noticed that the choir loft and the pipe organ had been screened off from view. In the center of the platform had been placed a set of drums! I instantly knew, just visually, that we had a winner!

The switch from pipe organ to percussion was a greater sacrifice for us than it might have been for other churches. We had paid $865,000 for that pipe organ! Of course, we continued to use it on Sunday mornings.

As we have noted, generations are changing rapidly. In December 1996, I had the privilege of attending the first generation X worship service in Lake Avenue Church. It started at 11:05 A.M. (traditional services start at 11:00!), and it was held in an unfinished part of the building. The service was called "The Warehouse." The platform was void of drums! When I asked about it, I was told, "We don't like the Saturday night overload on noise hoopla. Drums are not real!"

I couldn't help also noting that correct English spelling and grammar no longer seem to be high values. One line of a song went: "I'm not gonna worry cause you're working it out today."

CHOIRS: OUT AND IN

In most new apostolic churches, synthesizers, guitars and

drums have replaced the pipe organ and worship teams have replaced the choir. The choir is coming back, however, but in a different form and function. The new apostolic choir is typically not robed, because it is not intended to be different from other worshipers or to attract attention. It does not perform. William Easum says, "When choirs are present they form a part of the worship team. They assist in leading worship the entire time they are present, not just when they sing. Their presence sets a tone and setting."[22]

5. FROM CEREBRAL TO CELEBRATION

I am indebted to Tim Wright for the phrase "from cerebral to celebration." It describes perfectly the difference between what we have known in the past and what we are experiencing in the present.

In the past, the church service was a time of quiet reverence. The church furniture was dark, and stained-glass windows were the norm. Candles were often burning. When we went to church, if we talked at all, we whispered. Some of our favorite texts were, "Be still, and know that I am God" (Ps. 46:10), and "The Lord is in His holy temple. Let all the earth keep silence before Him" (Hab. 2:20). Many churches posted a sign: Enter in silence. Worship in progress.

Tim Wright, who is a Lutheran, speaks of European traditions permeating our American churches. He says, "These traditions tend to view emotions as suspect. Christian faith is understood as an intellectual assent based on God's faithfulness, rather than an emotional feeling of security or well-being enhanced by the presence of God. As a result, worship and preaching in liturgical churches tend toward a cerebral orientation."[23]

In new apostolic churches, a worship service once characterized by *peacefulness* has become an atmosphere better described as *pulsation*. There are four major differences, including (a) music, (b) body language, (c) applause and (d) flow. Let's take a look.

(A) MUSIC

Tim Wright says, "Today's generations were raised on background music. For many, especially the unchurched, complete quiet is not the spiritual experience it may be for believers. Rather, silence intimidates. Silence makes people uncomfortable."[24]

The duration of the musical part of the new apostolic worship service is striking to those who are not accustomed to it. Thirty minutes is on the short end of the worship spectrum. Forty minutes is common. An hour is long, but not unusual, in many settings. William Easum astutely compares the past to the present with this observation:

> Music is replacing the written liturgy with which many Christians grew up. Music achieves the same results once accompanied by responsive readings, creeds, psalters, and corporate prayers. It is the vehicle or conduit through which the message is conveyed. It is a setting in which Christians praise and adore God....It is not unusual for music to comprise 40 percent of worship [meaning the whole church service] in paradigm communities.[25]

(B) BODY LANGUAGE

In new apostolic churches, worshipers do not all do the same things at the same time. They have the freedom to sit or to kneel, to stand or to walk around, to lie prostrate or to dance or any combination of the above. At any given time, some may be clapping to the rhythm, some may be holding up their hands, some may have their eyes closed and some may be looking at the ceiling. No one seems to care what others around them are doing. Each person is enjoying the direct presence of God in the way that best suits individual worship styles.

I remember once when my wife, Doris, and I were having lunch with our pastor, Ted Haggard, and his wife, Gayle. Ted mentioned a woman's name whom Gayle did not seem to recognize. By way of identification, he said, "You know who she is—the cartwheel lady!" Of course! She was the one who occasionally did cartwheels across the front of the church when the worship became particularly intense. I did see a man do a literal back flip during worship in a new apostolic church in Canada. Somehow, when he did it, his feet left his shoes and his shoes remained on the spot where he had been standing! I had never seen anything like that in my Congregational church.

I couldn't help but contrast the traditional body language of Southern Baptists with this scene. Awhile ago, I was meeting with 27 of the music directors of the nation's largest Southern Baptist churches. To begin their meeting, they naturally had a time of worship. During worship I counted 20 of them who had their hands in their pockets, 5 had their hands slightly above their waists, and 2 waved a hand briefly, but only up to their shoulders. In new apostolic churches, more body language than that is used even in their funerals!

(C) APPLAUSE

Applause is much more prominent in new apostolic churches than in traditional churches. It is used not so much to show appreciation for a quality performance as to honor God. It is the kind of applause we might expect if Jesus entered the sanctuary in person and walked to the front of our church. Frequently, the audience will break out in applause at the end of a worship song or at the end of a prayer. Loud clapping is another way of saying, "Amen! We like what is happening and we want more of it."

(D) FLOW

If quiet, as Tim Wright would say, is intimidating or uncomfortable to those of the younger generations, the flow of the worship service then becomes very important. There is no stopping between the end of one song and the beginning of the next. The most skillful worship leaders will have the congregation singing the next song before many of them realize they have finished the previous one. The transition is often made by prayer, sometimes by the worship leader alone accompanied by background music, or sometimes by leading the congregation in concert prayer and everyone praying individual prayers out loud at the same time.

A skill that not all the new apostolic churches have yet developed is the unbroken transition from the worship section of the service to the sermon. Some describe it as "from worship to the word." In most cases, there is a time of applause followed by a statement from the pastor coming into the pulpit such as, "Let's all praise the Lord," or "Please turn around and greet those around you." This maintains the flow, but not as smoothly as other pastors who come on the platform, take the microphone from the worship leader, lead the congregation during the last two or three minutes of worship and then move right into prayer and the word. My friend Jim Marocco of Maui First Assembly of God in Hawaii is the best I have ever seen at maintaining the flow from worship to the word.

I found the following suggestion from William Easum and Thomas Bandy revealing and informative: "The best way to determine if your worship is on the experiential track is to videotape your worship service and play it on a VCR side-by-side with a television tuned to MTV. The more similarity there is, the more likely it is that your worship is able to share the gospel with people, especially those born after 1965."[26]

6. FROM AWE OF GOD TO INTIMACY WITH GOD

Another one of Tim Wright's well-honed phrases is the following:

> Liturgical worship services and classical music inspire awe, moving us with the majesty and power of God.

They make us aware of God's universality and grandeur. Contemporary services, on the other hand, make worship more personal. Contemporary music and worship speak the language of the heart; consequently, they move worshippers toward intimacy. It is much easier for contemporary music to move people toward awe than for classical music and liturgical worship to move them toward intimacy.[27]

Emotion is usually not something to be avoided, but rather it is encouraged in most new apostolic churches. I recall one large church in which a box of tissues was strategically placed under every two or three chairs throughout the worship center. One of the ways worship leaders are aware that the Holy Spirit is truly present at certain points in the song service is by the number of people wiping their eyes and blowing their noses.

It also goes beyond that, however. Ron Kenoly, worship leader of Jubilee Christian Center in San Jose, California, says the following about worship leaders:

The function of a worship leader is to bring other people into God's presence. I'm often asked how I know when I have accomplished my job. The truth is that it's not something I see with the natural eye. I do not have a written formula. Sometimes I know I'm finished when I can feel the presence of the Lord in the room so strong that I know the only thing left for me to do is to get out of God's way. Many times it is not appropriate for me to say or do anything.[28]

7. FROM LITURGY TO LIBERTY

Liturgical worship services are highly predictable. The pastor reads the order of service from a book, and Sunday after Sunday it is the same. The liturgy can be memorized, and it often is. Even churches that do not have a prescribed liturgy often get into a rut so that the same things happen, in the same order, every week. New apostolic churches assiduously try to avoid developing a new form of liturgy. Granted, across the board there is much more liberty in new apostolic churches than, say, in a Greek Orthodox, a Lutheran or an Episcopal service. But "letting the Spirit take over" is a lofty ideal that tends to be fulfilled in varying degrees. Not all do it well or consistently.

LaMar Boschman says, "Although most new-paradigm churches place importance in a well-planned service, they also highly value the spontaneous. The worship leader may insert a song that wasn't planned or move into a time of ministry at the prompting of the Spirit. Some congregations are led in 'singing in the Spirit,' a free flow of spontaneous song without set lyrics or melody. Worship is expressed as each believer begins to sing his or her own song to the Lord."[29] Such spontaneous singing is a learned behavior, and some new apostolic churches are much better at it than others.

In general, however, liberty prevails in new apostolic worship. Lyle Schaller says, "The Contemporary Christian Movement consists of several strands. The first is a change from a European heritage, in terms of the form of worship, to a much more American form—less formal, less predictable, more spontaneity, and a greater emphasis on visual communication."[30] There is no doubt that this American form has been exported, much like Coca-Cola, McDonald's and Levis. It can clearly be seen in many other parts of the world, although this is not to deny that various cultures contextualize it in different ways.

KOREA IS DIFFERENT

The exception to this is South Korea. Because of a high degree of ingrained traditionalism in Korean culture, change seems to come extremely slowly. The New Apostolic Reformation is probably more retarded in Korea than in any other nation having a significant Christian population. This, undoubtedly, is one of the factors that has caused a stagnation of Korean national church growth in the 1990s. At this writing, however, new reports are coming in to indicate that things might be changing, and it will bode well for the salvation of the younger generation of Koreans if things are changing.

One of my favorite new apostolic churches is Grace Korean Church of Anaheim, California, of which I have spoken earlier. Pastor David Kim wrote an excellent chapter in my book *The New Apostolic Churches* (Regal Books). Although it is a new apostolic church, a great deal of formalism is found in its liturgy. The congregations sings a few songs following words on an overhead projector, but the worship service is mainly built around the Apostles' Creed, the Lord's Prayer, the Doxology and an anthem sung by a robed choir.

8. FROM MEDITATION TO MISSION

Years ago, Pastor Walt Kallestad of Community Church of Joy in Phoenix, Arizona, enrolled in one of my doctor of ministry courses at Fuller Theological Seminary. One of the assignments was to write an article for publication, so he wrote about "Entertainment Evangelism" and published it in *The Lutheran*, the official magazine of the Evangelical Lutheran Church of America.

Kallestad's article, which advocated tailoring the outreach of the church to contemporary culture, drew many times more letters to the editor than any article the magazine had ever published. Most of the respondents were furious. One pastor, the Sunday after he had read the article, mounted his elevated Lutheran pulpit, spent most of his sermon denouncing Kallestad and, as a climax, irately hurled his copy of the magazine from the pulpit down to the floor of the sanctuary!

More recently, Kallestad has expanded his article into a book titled *Entertainment Evangelism* (Abingdon Press). The fact that this philosophy of ministry has opened the way for his church to grow to more than 7,000 members has helped the message penetrate the thinking of many Lutheran leaders who want better things for their denomination. There is far less criticism of such contextualization than there used to be.

WHO DO YOU WANT TO IMPRESS?

A pioneer of focusing on the *mission* of the church to the surrounding world is Robert H. Schuller, founder of the Crystal Cathedral of Garden Grove, California. In the early 1970s, Schuller was lecturing on applying "seven principles of retailing" to local church growth. In his book *Your Church Has a Fantastic Future*, Robert Schuller expounds on these principles of retailing, basing them on his primary focus of reaching the unchurched in the community. He relates how his architect, Richard Neutra (a Jew), talked him out of stained-glass windows in his first sanctuary. Neutra's question, which helped change Schuller's thinking, was: "Who is it you really want to impress?"

Schuller explains his response:

> "Well," I thought, "I don't really want to impress believers; they've already accepted the message." So I had to transform a decision to be secular into an architectural statement. *We would be a mission first and a church second.* This meant giving up stained-glass windows all over the place, with their lambs and bunches of grapes and the whole colored array of holy symbols. To be a mission first meant a building that was comfortable for the uninitiated, understandable, yet beautiful too....We did not say, "You come to meet me at my level; I'm not going to meet you at your level."[31]

MARKETING THE CHURCH

This raises the subject of "marketing the church," an approach for which Robert Schuller was, and still is, a strong advocate. Twenty-five years ago, Schuller said the following about marketing:

Early in my ministry I said that the Church of the future must not think of itself as just a worship center, but it must be a "shopping center" for Jesus Christ. It must think of itself as meeting all the needs of a community that are not being met by any other institution. Now I rue the day I used that term because it keeps popping up all over, as if my motivation were commercial.[32]

Tim Wright, Walt Kallestad's worship leader, agrees:

Not all the values that guests bring to worship are compatible with Christianity; nor are such values confined solely to the irreligious. Believers also embrace some of these same values as they shop for a church home. However, in order to effectively reach new people, congregations must find ways to attract their attention. By creatively responding to consumer values, without compromising integrity, churches can impact people with the gospel.[33]

Let me remind you that our focus in this section is on *mission*, and that most new apostolic churches give mission very high priority.

Several influential authors have recently made strong statements against any notions that churches should be "marketed" to unbelievers. They think this compromises the purity of the Church. I am referring to books such as Douglas Webster's *Selling Jesus* (InterVarsity Press), Os Guinness's *Dining with the Devil* (Baker Book House), John MacArthur's *Ashamed of the Gospel* (Crossway) and others. Two of those who have most irritated John MacArthur are George Barna and I. One of Barna's books is titled *Marketing the Church*. In it he says, "I believe that developing a marketing orientation is precisely what the Church needs to do if we are to make a difference in the spiritual health of this nation for the remainder of this century."[34]

Check the libraries of new apostolic leaders and, needless to say, you will likely find George Barna's book there, but not the others.

CAN WORSHIP ATTRACT UNBELIEVERS?

Bill Hybels, new apostolic pastor of Willow Creek Community Church, Barrington, Illinois, and a longtime friend of Robert Schuller, agrees that pastors have the responsibility of determining the purpose of each corporate gathering. He has come to the radical conclusion that the Saturday and Sunday services should be programmed primarily for unbelievers, and not just for believers. Hybels's church is known as a "seeker-driven" church, and he explains his philosophy of ministry well in his chapter in my book *The New Apostolic Churches* (Regal Books). Does this approach work? Currently, the weekend attendance at Willow Creek is estimated at around 17,000!

The Willow Creek Association, which Hybels has formed, has helped hundreds of pastors develop either seeker-driven or the more moderate seeker-sensitive approach to their communities, and accomplishing outstanding results. One of the features of these churches is that they usually include very little worship, as we have been describing it in this chapter, in their weekend services designed primarily to communicate to unbelievers. On Wednesday nights they hold "believers' meetings" at which worship is featured.

At the same time, many, if not most, of the larger, growing new apostolic churches, particularly of the charismatic variety (Willow Creek is noncharismatic), would not be considered seeker-sensitive. Their worship services might be depicted as "wild" by many traditional church leaders. Nevertheless, many of these worship-centered churches are also growing. It is true that some have large percentages of transfer growth, but many are also experiencing substantial conversion growth coming through high praise and worship.

Sally Morgenthaler's book *Worship Evangelism* provides a thorough treatment of this phenomenon. She says, "I disagree with Willow Creek's contention that seekers and worship do not mix. If we truly understand what worship is, we will appreciate why worship services are an essential part of God's strategy for building the kingdom and drawing others into it."[35] More of Sally Morganthaler's helpful contributions will be discussed in the chapter about outreach.

WHAT MAKES THE DIFFERENCE?

Because both seeker-driven and worship-centered churches are growing in the United States, what makes the difference? It would require considerable research and another book to fully answer this important question. Meanwhile, I will offer a hypothesis that one of the variables could be the spiritual orientation of the unbelievers before they come to church. If their orientation is secular, having little or no operative sensitivity to the supernatural forces of the invisible world, they would be more likely to find God in a seeker-driven church.

However, if the unbelievers have had previous contact with the occult, believe in horoscopes, have dabbled in the New Age, have been into heavy metal music and, thereby, do have a sensitivity to the invisible world, the spiritual power of high worship and praise will likely make sense to them and they will perceive a power encounter. When they learn that God has more power than the "forces" or the "energy" or the "channeling" or the "spirits," they will gratefully accept Jesus as their Lord and Savior. This is more likely to happen in a charismatic than in a noncharismatic church, although both might be of the new apostolic variety.

Notes

1. George G. Hunter III, "The Rationale for a Culturally Relevant Worship Service," *Journal of the American Society for Church Growth* 7 (1996), p. 131.

2. Barry Liesch, *The New Worship* (Grand Rapids: Baker Book House, 1996), p. 13.

3. LaMar Boschman, *A Heart of Worship* (Orlando, Fla.: Creation House, 1994), p. 22.

4. Sally Morgenthaler, *Worship Evangelism* (Grand Rapids: Zondervan Publishing House, 1995), p. 47.

5. Bruce Leafblad, *Music, Worship and the Ministry of the Church* (Portland, Oreg.: Western Conservative Baptist Seminary, 1978), p. 21.

6. Donald Hustad, *Jubilate!* (Carol Stream, Ill.: Hope Publishing Co., n.d.), p. 64.

7. Hunter, "The Rationale for a Culturally Relevant Worship Service," pp. 132, 133.

8. Ibid., p. 133.

9. Tim Wright, *A Community of Joy* (Nashville: Abingdon Press, 1994), pp. 16, 17.

10. LaMar Boschman (paraphrased from an address to the National Symposium on the Postdemoninational Church at Fuller Seminary, Pasadena, California, May 21-23, 1996).

11. Gary McIntosh, "Worship and Church Growth," *Journal of the American Society of Church Growth* 7 (1996), p. 1.

12. Donald E. Miller, *Reinventing American Protestantism* (Berkeley, Calif.: University of California Press, 1997), p. 81.

13. See, for example, *Putting an End to Worship Wars* by Elmer Towns (Nashville: Broadman & Holman Publishers, 1997).

14. William M. Easum and Thomas G. Bandy, *Growing Spiritual Redwoods* (Nashville: Abingdon Press, 1997), p. 62.

15. Ibid., p. 69.

16. LaMar Boschman, "Worship Distinctives in New-Paradigm Churches," *Ministry Advantage* (July-August 1996), p. 6.

17. Liesch, *The New Worship*, p. 123.

18. Easum and Bandy, *Growing Spiritual Redwoods*, p. 70.

19. Wright, *A Community of Joy*, p. 68.

20. Liesch, *The New Worship*, p. 21.

21. William M. Easum, *Dancing with Dinosaurs* (Nashville: Abingdon Press, 1993), p. 88.

22. Ibid., p. 87.

23. Wright, *A Community of Joy*, p. 60.

24. Ibid., p. 73.

25. Easum, *Dancing with Dinosaurs*, p. 85.

26. Easum and Bandy, *Growing Spiritual Redwoods*, p. 96.

27. Wright, *A Community of Joy*, p. 61.

28. Ron Kenoly and Dick Bernal, *Lifting Him Up* (Orlando, Fla.: Creation House, 1995), p. 23.

29. Boschman, "Worship Distinctives in New-Paradigm Churches," p. 7.

30. Lyle E. Schaller, interview in *Worship Leader* (1995), n.p.

31. Robert H. Schuller, *Your Church Has a Fantastic Future* (Ventura, Calif.: Regal Books, 1986), p. 97.

32. Ibid., p. 99.

33. Wright, *A Community of Joy*, p. 23.

34. George Barna, *Marketing the Church* (Colorado Springs: NavPress, 1988), p. 12.

35. Sally Morgenthaler, *Worship Evangelism*, p. 46.

CHAPTER EIGHT

Outreach in
Overdrive

For those who have church growth eyes, it is no mystery why new apostolic churches constitute the fastest growing segment of Christianity today. Aggressive outreach is part of the new apostolic DNA. New apostolic churches want to grow and they are willing to pay the price for growth. Their outreach is intentionally focused on four central tasks: (1) expanding the local church, (2) planting new churches, (3) mercy ministries in the surrounding community and (4) cross-cultural missions. Let's study these four.

1. LOCAL CHURCH EXPANSION:
SPONTANEOUS COMBUSTION!

I think of two current book titles as examples. The subtitle of Ted Haggard's *Primary Purpose* (Creation House) is *Making It Hard to Go to Hell from Your Church*. Mike Berg and Paul Pretiz's book about the explosive growth of new apostolic churches in Latin America is titled *Spontaneous Combustion* (William Carey Library).

Rick Warren planted Saddleback Valley Community Church in Southern California in 1980. In his first sermon, he cast the vision of the church through his "seven dreams." Among other things, Warren said, "It is the dream of welcoming 20,000 members into the fellowship of our church family—loving, learning, laughing, and living in harmony together."[1]

Within 20 years, more than 20,000 people were attending his church on Easter weekends and more than 12,000 the other weeks of the year. There was no thought in his mind that his new church would do anything but grow.

My friend Joseph C. Wongsak started the Hope of God movement in Thailand in 1981 when Thailand was a spiritual desert as far as Christianity was concerned. Up till that time, 47 Christian mission agencies had worked in Thailand for 150 years, and the net result was 150 churches averaging about 100 members each. Wongsak's stated goal at that time was to establish 685 churches in Thailand by the year 2000.

At this writing, well before 2000, more than 700 Hope of God churches have been planted in Thailand. One of these had 6,000 members at the time of this writing. Wongsak's criterion for evaluating the quality of an individual's Christian life is the following: "Every church member should personally participate in planting at least one new church before they die."[2] His more recent goal is to have established 80,000 churches in Thailand by 2015.

LIVING ORGANISMS GROW

Rick Warren believes he doesn't have to stress church growth. He stresses church *life*, and it happens. Here is how he views it:

> All living things grow—you don't have to *make* them grow. It's the natural thing for living organisms to do if they are healthy. For example, I don't have to *command* my three children to grow. They naturally grow. In the same way, since the church is a living organism, it is natural for it to grow if it is healthy. The church is a body, not a business. It is an organism, not an organization. It is alive. If a church is not growing, it is dying.[3]

Mike Berg and Paul Pretiz have found that new apostolic churches are inherently "expansionist." They say, "It is only to be expected that new preaching points and new local churches are continually being planted by the major [grassroots] movements."[4] There is no apology whatsoever for an aggressive drive toward growth.

THE OLD AND THE NEW

Many traditional churches post a sign: Visitors welcome! The fact is that if a visitor ever came it would be a shock. Most new apostolic churches turn that phrase around. Their word is: Welcome, visitors! The shock would come if *no* visitors showed up on a Sunday!

Remarkably, a mind-set has implanted itself among many traditional church leaders that it is better *not* to grow than to grow. Kirk Hadaway and David Roozen have found the following:

> The liberal mainstream subculture, for instance, is not particularly friendly to growing congregations. In mainstream denominations, growing churches and their leaders are often considered "suspect." The pastor of a large, growing United Church of Christ congregation in Connecticut even suggested that other mainstream pastors think his church must have "sold out" in order to grow—resorting to questionable marketing techniques and other "gimmicks."[5]

If this were limited to the "liberal mainstream," it would be one thing. The prevailing soteriology there is not particularly conversionist and eternal salvation or damnation is not generally perceived to be at stake. However, even evangelical churches, which profess biblical soteriology and teach that "you must be born again," seem to be falling into a similar mind-set. Here is what John and Sylvia Ronsvalle's research has shown:

> This tendency for congregations to focus upon themselves—their own life and activities—while showing less commitment to the larger mission of the church

appears to be common across theological lines. Data for evangelical as well as mainline Protestant churches suggest that congregations are turning inward, and decreasing their support for denominational structures and the programs they provide.[6]

BAD NEWS AND GOOD NEWS

This brings both bad news and good news. The bad news, as we have seen, is that in many denominational systems, from top to bottom, little or no overt outreach is happening. The good news is that in many cases individual congregations, frustrated by the unenthusiastic and relatively inconsequential outreach vision of their denomination, have been exploring ways of doing end runs around their entrenched systems. Lyle Schaller says this:

> A consequence that troubles many church leaders is the reduction in dollars sent to denominational headquarters. As the laity become more involved in strategizing for mission and in doing ministry, it is not surprising that the financing of these new local outreach ministries takes precedence over sending money to others to enable them to do missions.[7]

The new paradigm arising in the more apostolically inclined denominational churches is that the *congregation* initiates outreach rather than supporting denominationally initiated programs. George G. Hunter III considers four major differences between these churches and the more traditional, status-quo churches:

- ♦ First, apostolic churches are reaching significant numbers of the unchurched, non-Christian, secular people in America's mission fields. (Indeed, that is their main business.)
- ♦ Second, they employ the language, music, and so on

of the people they are called to reach, rather than their tradition's language, music, and so on.

♦ Third, they are on the edge of their denomination (or they have no denominational attachment at all).

♦ Fourth, both the conservative and the liberal Protestant establishments are anxious about the new apostolic congregations; they are often quick to criticize, yet they envy their capacity to reach unchurched pre-Christian people.[8]

PRAGMATISM PREVAILS

Although, as Hunter says, traditional leaders are inclined to criticize the new apostolic churches, the reverse also applies. Churches that have a vision to reach the lost are fed up with traditional methods. Why? Because they haven't worked! Among new apostolic church leaders, whether denominational or otherwise, there is little aversion to pragmatism. They say, "If God has given us a job to do—let's get it done! If a methodology works, use it; if it doesn't work, scrap it!" This is not a statement of carnality; it is a statement of driving commitment. God's work must be done in God's way, true. However, throughout history, God's ways have changed and changed again. God's way of doing something yesterday is frequently not God's way of doing it today.

New apostolic church leaders constantly seek ways to update and contextualize their outreach ministries. Donald Miller says,

> Evangelism occupies a central place with new paradigm churches, but with a twist. The emphasis is not on converting people to a set of cultural values. Rather, the goal is a transformed life. Christianity has nothing to do with wearing polyester suits, singing 18th-century hymns, or worshipping in an architectural space that is surrounded by historic icons of the Christian tradition. One can be a Christian and wear

multiple earrings, love hard-rock rhythms, and surf on Sunday morning.[9]

That reminds me of one of the most radical examples of this philosophy: the New Wine Church of Fullerton, California. Its mission is to "reach out to people who the world has thrown away." It is a church of ex-witches, ex-convicts, ex-addicts and heavily tattooed bikers. Pastor Robert Nixon has served more time in jail cells than in theological seminary classrooms. Few other churches in the United States would thrive on New Wine's dress code, street language, rap dancing, pop theology or laid-back scheduling. New apostolic church leaders affirm New Wine, though, because its outreach *works* for evangelizing a target audience few others are reaching.

GEARING TO THE UNCHURCHED

Churches that have broken with the traditional outreach methods tend to fall into a typology of three philosophies of ministry, each of which has certain strengths:

♦ SEEKER-DRIVEN CHURCHES. The whole philosophy of the ministry of the church is prioritized around the felt needs of the unchurched. Architecture, dress, scheduling, music, sermons, church activities and ministries are all designed to communicate to unbelievers. Believers are also taken care of by the church, but the ultimate success of the church is measured by its effectiveness in converting unbelievers rather than nurturing believers. Willow Creek Community Church is an outstanding example of a seeker-driven church.

♦ SEEKER-SENSITIVE CHURCHES. This is a modified version of the seeker-driven churches in which believers and their needs are given, in most cases, a similar priority to reaching out to the unchurched. In all the activities of the church, however, a concerted effort is made to eliminate or greatly reduce elements of church life known to irritate or turn off the unchurched.

♦ POWER-ORIENTED CHURCHES. In these churches, the magnetism of supernatural power, both in worship and in public ministry, located in nontraditional church settings, appeals to the unchurched. The more charismatically inclined new apostolic churches fit this category. In seeker-driven churches, for example, the kind of high-energy, sustained and heavily participatory worship we described in the last chapter would not be appropriate, but it is in the power-oriented churches.

As I also mentioned in the last chapter, unchurched Americans can be viewed as two types: secular and spiritual. The seeker-oriented philosophies of ministries generally will attract the more secular unchurched, according to my hypothesis. The power-oriented churches tend to attract the more spiritually tuned unchurched.

The notion that all or most of the fastest growing churches are seeker oriented is not correct. Some are, but as Sally Morgenthaler argues in her superb book *Worship Evangelism*, churches that feature expressive worship, essentially geared to believers, are also among the fastest growing churches. In fact, outside the United States, a large majority of growing churches are of the power-oriented philosophy of ministry, far from being "seeker driven."

One testimony Sally Morgenthaler cites is especially instructive. A church leader says,

> The seeker event we were offering wasn't cutting it for some of the seekers who were coming. They said they were looking for something with more of a "spiritual" feel to it. So, we decided to provide a different kind of service, a celebrative time that both energizes believers and enlightens seekers. We wanted it to be kind of like the 1 Corinthians 14:22 worship where the unbeliever

looks around and says, "Hey, God's here!" a time where we invite God to "invade our space" and actually engage people with Him.[10]

2. CHURCH PLANTING

Mainline churches began declining in 1965. Ten years later, they began to ask: "Why?" It took them another decade to find some of the answers, and when they did, the alternatives in most cases were not acceptable to the church leaders. Planting new churches was one of the more unacceptable solutions.

To illustrate, a problem that accompanied denominational decline was a growing surplus of clergy. Churches were closing right and left, but seminaries were continuing to grind out graduates who expected to pastor churches. Jackson Carroll and Robert Wilson conducted a study about the clergy job market and published their findings in a book called *Too Many Pastors?* (The Pilgrim Press).

In their book, Carroll and Wilson described the plight of churchless pastors, and then summarized their suggestions for a solution to the problem in a chapter called "Survival Tactics for Clergy." There they listed eight suggestions about what could be done in the future to alleviate the problem. Surprisingly, not a single one of the suggestions was to plant new churches! Apparently the idea never occurred either to the authors or to those they interviewed. If it did, it was rejected as a major opportunity to utilize pastors who had no parish.

I know that many new apostolic pastors will chuckle in disbelief when they read about that study. With few exceptions, new apostolic pastors agree with what I have called "The Wagner Theorem," which states: *The most effective evangelistic methodology under heaven is planting new churches!*

Some raise the question: Why plant new churches when our community already has too many empty existing churches? Why not spend the time and money on renewing them? The answer is that it will waste both time and money that could be directed toward reaching the unchurched. We have few examples of how efforts to renew existing churches have effectively increased evangelistic effectiveness. What could be called "The Wagner Corollary" states: *It is easier to have babies than to raise the dead!*

New church plants are, by nature, younger
and smaller than most churches.
New wine still needs new wineskins.

Research shows that young churches grow faster than old churches and that small churches grow faster than large churches. That is why multiplying new churches is such a dynamic growth principle. New church plants are, by nature, younger and smaller than most churches. New wine still needs new wineskins.

ARE WE REACHING THE UNCHURCHED?
Almost all new apostolic church leaders will affirm that their church planting ministry is designed to reach the unchurched. They will strongly proclaim that they do not welcome *transfer growth*, but that they want their new churches to grow by *conversion growth*. They will agree with Robert Schuller, who says, "Other than our commission from Christ, *the challenge of the unchurched people—more than anything else—sets the goals in our church*. And if that should ever change, you will see the Crystal Cathedral begin to die."[11]

Although this may be the desire, often a bothersome gap exists between the desire and the reality. I have an inherent suspicion of insider-generated statistics about conversion growth. Some might be accurate, but I remember one that stated: "Our conversion growth is high—we have baptized 70 percent of our members." Further investigation suggested that this might say as much about their views of baptism as their evangelistic effectiveness. A born-again Presbyterian who had been sprinkled as an infant and then immersed would be included in the 70 percent. A retired Quaker missionary who had never been baptized in water would be required to be baptized before joining the church and also counted as "conversion" growth.

One of the more reliable research projects about conversion growth was done in the University of Southern California study of Calvary Chapel, Hope Chapel and Vineyard, led by Donald Miller. Three questions were asked: How old are you? At what age were you born again? How long have you been attending this church? The study found the following:

- ♦ Calvary Chapel, 44% conversion growth
- ♦ Hope Chapel, 39% conversion growth
- ♦ Vineyard, 18% conversion growth[12]

Most new apostolic pastors will agree that this is an area in which we hope to see substantial improvement in the years to come.

HOW NEW CHURCHES START

There are a variety of good ways to plant churches. I list and describe 12 of them in my book *Church Planting for a Greater Harvest* (Regal Books). However, new apostolic churches, at least in the United States, have established a prevailing, although not an exclusive, pattern:

1. The base for planting a new church is ordinarily an existing local congregation. The assumption is that if we are a biblical church, we must reproduce and plant new churches.
2. The church planter and the team surface within the congregation of the parent church. James Feeney says, "The local congregation [is] a church planting center. The single most significant person in that regard...is

the one individual uniquely called by the Lord Jesus to pioneer and pastor that new church."[13]

3. The senior pastor recognizes and commissions the church planter. In some apostolic networks, the overseeing apostle is called in. In others, the autonomy of the local church precludes that.

4. They agree on a target site. This kind of an agreement is ordinarily reached in several ways:

   a. Through prophecy;

   b. Through God's specific call to the church planter;

   c. Through applying sound principles of site selection:

   + Where churches are currently growing;
   + Where new people are moving in;
   + Where the culture matches the church planter;
   + Where the target audience lives or will live.

5. They relocate on the site. Sometimes this is just the church planter's family. Sometimes it involves a team.

6. They begin Bible studies in their home. As this grows, they move into rented facilities such as a school, a shopping mall, a hotel conference room or the like. If the church continues to grow, they buy land and build a building.

7. They continue relating to the parent church. In some cases it is a satellite relationship; in others the new church is totally autonomous from the beginning. In almost all cases, the new church pastor remains under the spiritual authority and covering of the parent church pastor and/or the apostle.

8. They receive on-the-job training, which can take many different forms and which is expected to continue indefinitely.

A ONE-WAY TRAIN TICKET

The previous description of starting churches is the most common method of church planting in the United States. However, in other parts of the world things can be different. For example, this report comes from China:

> Committed to evangelism and missions, Chinese Christians train the young people in their late teens and early twenties to become missionaries for several years. These evangelists purchase a one-way train ticket to wherever they feel the Lord is calling them; usually within three to six months they establish a church. In this way, evangelism and church planting are crisscrossing China, and the gospel is being spread like wildfire.[14]

STARTING NEW APOSTOLIC NETWORKS

In chapter 6, I explained how multiplying apostolic networks is necessary to prevent the routinization of charisma. Here I want to mention it again as a radical extension of evangelizing a region by planting churches. In the Body of Christ, diversity is a positive quality. Each individual church member is different from the others and has different spiritual gifts. In a family of churches, each local church is different and is known by its individual characteristics. In the kingdom of God, there are many different families of churches, each with their unique qualities. In my opinion, the more individual Christians we have the better; the more local churches we have the better; and the more apostolic networks we have the better.

How do new networks start? Plan A is to design them, spin them off and encourage them to relate constructively to one another. These are friendly starts. However, throughout history we also see many unfriendly, but nevertheless successful, starts. Most of us are glad, for example, that we now have Lutheran churches even if Catholics initially were unfriendly. In like manner, Anglicans were not friendly to Methodists, Methodists were not friendly to Nazarenes, and Calvary Chapel was not friendly to Vineyard, just to choose some random examples out of many. Most would agree, though, that the kingdom of God is better off having these new families of churches than it would have been without them.

3. MERCY MINISTRIES

By "mercy ministries" I am referring to the deeply ingrained desire on the part of new apostolic church leaders to reach out with compassion to the poor, the needy, the homeless and the oppressed of their communities. This is social service. If I were writing in a more theological vein, which I have occasionally done, I would address this dimension of outreach as the "cultural mandate" as opposed to the "evangelistic mandate."

Although others may disagree, I continue to argue that prioritizing the cultural mandate over the evangelistic mandate was, in all probability, *the* major cause of the decline of mainline denominations during the past 30 years, beginning in 1965. In chapter 1, I addressed this under the section "The Plight of the Denominations."

My understanding of the Scriptures is that Christian social responsibility is, indeed, mandatory, not optional, for churches.

My understanding of the Scriptures is that Christian social responsibility is, indeed, mandatory, not optional, for churches. If the evangelistic mandate is kept as the first priority, social service can be maximized. However, if the cultural mandate is given equal or greater priority, both will suffer. Prior to 1965, for example, the National Council of Churches was the most socially influential Protestant body in America. When priorities were changed, it began to lose strength until today it is a mere shadow of its former self. The one mainline denomination that did not switch priorities is the Southern Baptists, and they have been the major exception to the overall decline.

THE CAUSE OF SOCIAL PROBLEMS? SIN!

Enough of theory. How does this work out in practice? Donald Miller, who identifies himself as "a lifelong Democrat and a theological liberal," says that he was somewhat surprised when he uncovered the philosophy underlying the social ministries of the new apostolic (he calls them "new paradigm") churches he studied. Miller says,

> New paradigm members and their pastors see human selfishness—or, to use the old-fashioned term, *sin*—as the core cause of all social problems. They do not think that a few more social programs will make the streets safe, remove the menace of drugs from public schools, or reverse the breakdown of the American family. A much more fundamental change is needed, one that tackles the problem at its roots—namely, that people need to shift from serving *self* to serving *God*, and hence be "born again."[15]

Because new apostolic churches put a high value on being *biblical* churches, they, for the most part, engage in mercy ministries as a part of the normal routine of church life. I cannot remember ever hearing a debate in a new apostolic church about whether we should feed the hungry, minister to the homeless, tutor the illiterate, assist single moms, warn against the consequences of abortion or take a firm stand against racism. In most cases, the major limitation is budget. Churches that have large budgets can do more than churches that have small budgets.

RELATING MERCY MINISTRIES TO EVANGELISM

Is social service a means toward an end (the end being evangelism, for example), or can social service be an end in itself?

The more liberal traditional churches have said that social service should never be a means of evangelism. They argue that if it is a means, it then is nothing more than a bait and switch tactic. Some contend that doing good to others is the gospel. Evangelism, by this definition, is showing the love of Jesus by *serving* people, not *converting* them.

New apostolic churches take a different view. One of the best-known spokespersons is Steve Sjogren of the Vineyard Community Church of Cincinnati, Ohio. His books on the subject, *Conspiracy of Kindness* and *Servant Warfare* (Servant Publications), have been widely read and appreciated. Sjogren advocates "servant evangelism." This phrase clearly establishes the relationship between the two ministries: "evangelism" is the noun and "servant" is the adjective.

Steve Sjogren uses "kindness" and "niceness" as technical terms. He argues that only Christians can be *kind*. Other human beings can be *nice*. His idea of kindness originates from Romans 2:4 (see *NIV*): The kindness of God leads us to repentance. Sjogren says, "The Bible seems to distinguish between the divine quality of kindness and the human quality of niceness. In short, if kindness originates in the heart of God, then only Christians have the ability to be kind in the biblical sense of the word."[16]

Showing how this applies in real life, Sjogren relates that the producer of Oprah Winfrey's talk show once invited him to be a guest on a program featuring "random acts of kindness." Steve says, "I explained that what we do isn't based on our desire to be nice, but to show the kindness and love of God. 'We are filled with God's Spirit and do acts of kindness in order to show people the reality of God and hopefully bring them to Christ. As we are kind in the name of Jesus Christ, those we serve open their hearts to a relationship with God.' The producer's response? 'Interesting...we'll get back to you on that.'"[17] Needless to say, that was the end of the invitation.

In one way, the act of kindness itself can legitimately be seen as an end. It meets the need of the person and it has no strings attached. If the person is helped, it counts. However, the long-range purpose of the act is eternal, not temporal. One of the things Steve Sjogren's people do is to feed overdue parking meters with coins as an act of kindness. What do they pray for as they are doing it? They do not pray that the delinquent drivers will be spared a ticket. That is secondary. They pray that God will be glorified and that the driver, if an unbeliever, will be saved. They understand that the evangelistic mandate takes priority over the cultural mandate.

JUSTICE AND THE KINGDOM OF GOD

John Wimber roots mercy ministries in his theology of the kingdom of God. He says,

> If we are in fellowship with God and if we are living under his kingdom, we will seek justice for all those around us. Social justice isn't a new gospel (the so-called "social gospel" of early twentieth century Protestantism); it flows directly from the gospel of forgiveness and new life in Christ. Seeking justice in society has gone hand in hand with past revivals; great leaders in the history of the church have understood the relationship between the gospel and justice.[18]

New apostolic mercy ministries are most often ministries of social *service* rather than social *action*, if "social action" implies overt sociopolitical involvement designed to change social structures. Several apostolic networks advocate forms of what some call "dominion theology," meaning that Christians are expected to infiltrate social structures at all levels and, once there, use their influence to inculcate biblical values throughout their society. Christians, for example, are encouraged to run for public office, and when they are elected, do what they can to promote biblical morality and social justice. By and large, however, new apostolic leaders do not promote politically motivated public demonstrations such as Operation Rescue, although some do. Most prefer apolitical Marches for Jesus or Promise Keepers rallies.

FOOD DISTRIBUTION

In 1979, Pastor Kenny Foreman of Cathedral of Faith in San Jose, California, set up a food closet in his church. This has developed into a nonprofit ministry called Reaching Out, Inc. The ministry now boasts a $1 million, 15,800 square-foot warehouse equipped with freezer and cold storage facilities, forklifts, trucks and everything else needed for food distribution. It is run by a husband and wife team who are paid by the church and aided by a ministry team of 60 volunteers. As many as 100,000 people are fed each year, which calculates to between 200 and 300 each day. Each Christmas more than 2,000 food boxes are distributed, including a turkey in each box. Reaching Out, Inc. continues to be one of the largest sources of emergency food in Northern California.

A subsidiary ministry of the Anaheim Vineyard Christian Fellowship, founded by John Wimber, is called Compassion Ministries. For one thing, the ministry distributes 31 tons of food a month to 10,000 people. On a recent Christmas, a special offering for the poor totaled more than $700,000. In one year, the organization distributes $1.6 million worth of food, clothing and other essential items. It is hard for me to resist noting that few local churches that have paraded their theology of prioritizing the cultural mandate over the evangelistic mandate have ever helped as many poor people year after year as Cathedral of Faith or Anaheim Vineyard or many other new apostolic churches.

A CHRISTMAS PARTY FOR THE POOR

The Jubilee Christian Centre of Calgary, Alberta, serves the poor of its city in a different way. The last Sunday before Christmas every year, Pastor Phil Nordin invites the poor to a massive Christmas party. He makes free tickets available in food banks, hostels, drop-in centers and wherever poor people might be found. The party is funded by local corporations and businesses. Last year, 400 volunteer servers were on hand, drawn from politicians, oil company executives, businesspeople, their employees and church members. Sixteen hundred people came and received hot, full-course meals, 55,000 articles of used clothing were distributed and between 200 and 300 children each received a wrapped Christmas gift, for some the only gift they would have received that Christmas. A Christian superstar public figure delivered a 10-minute message at the event, and several valuable door prizes were given at the end so people would be sure to stay for the message.

What is the prayer of the church? That many of the poor of the city will find new life in Jesus Christ.

ROCK CONCERTS FOR SLUM DWELLERS

I recently visited Goiania, Brazil, where I met Pastor Cesar Augusto of the Comunidad Crista Church. At the time, he had 12,000 members and an average attendance of 8,000. His worship center accommodated 4,000 and he had built an additional 14 church buildings around the city seating 350 each so they could reach the unchurched in their neighborhoods.

The church sponsors regular Christian rock concerts in the city sports arena, which are attended by 11,000 to 12,000 youth each time. The admission? One kilo (two pounds) of food for the poor. At each concert they collect 15 tons of food, which they deliver to the people of the slums of the city.

On top of this, church families have legally adopted 33 street children to give them the love and protection of a Christian home. The church also has a fully equipped dental office, staffed by volunteers, and services are available at no charge to the poor of the city.

4. CROSS-CULTURAL MISSIONS

One of the principal nuances of "apostolic" in the New *Apostolic* Reformation is the root of the Greek *apóstolos*—one sent with a commission. Although, technically speaking, "apostle" is not a synonym for "missionary," they are inseparably linked in the popular mind. Therefore, no church would consider itself truly "apostolic" if it were not sending cross-cultural missionaries.

Churches that correctly understand this can avoid the "bless-me syndrome," which is an ongoing temptation, especially for churches that have been influenced by certain "revival" manifestations. It is all too easy to prioritize the blessings of God for Christian individuals, families and churches over God's desire to save the lost. Most new apostolic churches know this and try to keep the focus on outreach to the unchurched. One of my favorite songs, which I frequently hear in new apostolic churches, goes like this:

> *Let Your glory fall in this room;*
> *Let it go forth from here to the nations!*

CRACKS IN THE OLD MISSIONARY WINESKINS

The modern missionary movement began when William Carey went to India in 1792. For the next 200 years, the kingdom of God advanced throughout the earth like nothing that had ever been seen before. The "new wineskins" that carried this phenomenal movement were mission agencies, both denominational and interdenominational.

Two important changes have now entered the picture:

- The missionary movement was largely Western until the 1990s. Now the majority of missionaries are from the Third World, and that percentage will continue to increase.
- In the Western world, what were once new wineskins are now old wineskins, and they are deteriorating.

For 25 years, the number of missionaries sent by Western agencies has been declining. The older mainline denominations (excluding Southern Baptists) listed 8,471 career missionaries in 1968 and 3,235 in 1992.[19]

As an example of this, John Leith's study of Presbyterians has found the following:

> The decline in missionaries from 1,738 career missionaries in 1960 to around 400 (long-term, compen-

sated personnel) in 1996 is a crucial indication of the [Presbyterian] church's problem. Whenever the leadership of the church and seminaries passionately believe that Jesus Christ is the word made flesh, that in Jesus God has wrought the salvation of all people, that God raised Jesus from the dead, then the sending of evangelistic missionaries to proclaim the gospel and build churches becomes a high priority.[20]

Unfortunately, Presbyterians have seen fit to give such a thing a low priority, if any at all. The old wineskin is badly cracked.

The evangelical mission agencies, affiliated with the I.F.M.A. and E.F.M.A. (Evangelical Fellowship of Mission Agencies), grew from 12,393 career missionaries in 1968 to 14,473 in 1992. However, they peaked in 1988, so the current trend is downward. Pentecostals and charismatics had 3,838 missionaries in 1988, down to just more than 2,000 in 1992.[21]

THIRD WORLD WINESKINS

The missionary movement from Third World churches began picking up steam only about 20 years ago. Nevertheless, the number of missionaries sent out has already surpassed missionaries from Western churches. They are surging ahead because they are doing things differently and using new wineskins. For example:

- There is less bureaucratic structure and more entrepreneurship.
- There is more trust in individual missionaries rather than in boards or field committees.
- They are learning from current experience rather than from theory rooted in the past.
- The cost is much less. For example, in 1993 the cost for each United Methodist missionary was $31,541 a year. The Third World churches cannot afford those kinds of budgets.

A "HOUSE CHURCH" OF 20,000!

My friend David Wang recently visited a Chinese "house church" in a city of 6.5 million people. There are 4,200 churches (of the new apostolic variety) in the city and 1.2 million believers (20 percent of the population). Wang had been invited to speak at the dedication of a new church building that accommodated 5,000 people. Interestingly enough, the building looked very much like a Russian Orthodox church because the architect, whom the Chinese government furnished for the church, had studied architecture in Moscow. The congregation numbers 20,000!

While there, David interviewed the senior pastor, who had no Bible school training and whose wife was illiterate, about their missionary outreach. He found that they had sent six missionary teams to plant churches in Tibet, Malaysia, Thailand, Burma and two teams to Vietnam.

David asked, "Do they have passports?"

"No."

"Do they have visas?"

"No."

"Do they have traveler's checks?"

"No."

"What do they have?"

"They have their feet, and they just walk across the borders. They know how to take care of themselves."

David Wang's mission, Asian Outreach, which is based in Hong Kong, trains these kinds of missionaries. Among many other things, they hold an annual two-week training program in a place near Tibet. There are three entrance requirements: (1) Students must have the oversight of 5,000 to 10,000 believers. (2) They must find their own transportation. (3) They must bring enough food for two weeks. The school is ordinarily packed.

Stories such as these, which could be multiplied in the Third World nation after nation, leave little doubt that the future of Christian missions will be characterized by new wineskins.

WESTERN NEW APOSTOLIC WINESKINS

Aware to a good degree of what is happening in the Third World, new apostolic church leaders in the United States and other Western nations are ready to do missionary work in new ways. For example, John Eckhardt of Crusaders Ministries in inner-city Chicago, is trying to break the "import mentality" of many believers and replace it with an "export mentality." He says,

> Third-World cultures often have had a colonial mindset, believing that other cultures are more capable of sending. But God is breaking the old thinking...and replacing an *import* mindset with an apostolic *export* mentality to take the message of redemption globally...Third-World churches now send more missionaries than all Western nations combined. We need to establish networks across cultures to help facilitate this expansion. This cannot and will not be done without these apostolic churches.[22]

John Kelly agrees that building personal relationships and networking with the apostolic leadership God has already established in the Third World is a viable way to do foreign missionary work. He tells of his own experience in which Antioch Churches and Ministries sent three missionary church planting couples to Mexico, along with several single people who helped them. In three years, they had built a church consisting of 300 people.

During the same period of time, he looked for three "apostolic-type" Mexicans whom he would mentor. John Kelly says,

> We went on several short-term trips to Mexico, meeting with these three men in houses, not doing big meetings, spending hours upon hours training them. Each one already had a church of about 1,000 each with four to six other churches relating to them. That

was a total of about 20 churches to begin with. Today, we can count about 680 churches that have emerged from that missionary work.[23]

John Kelly calculates that the more traditional church-planting model costs about $150,000 a year, and the apostolic model costs about $30,000 a year. His price tag per church was $450,000 by using the church-planting model versus $132 by using the apostolic model!

PASSPORT SUNDAY

To help break the "import mentality" of his African-American church in Chicago, John Eckhardt organized a "Passport Sunday." He says,

> I began to preach about going to the nations, and that was something unheard of in our church. Before that, we had never had a class on missions. Nobody had preached on missions. Our mindset was to build a church in our community and minister to our community. But the Spirit of God began to deal with us about going to the nations.[24]

This began to work. The old mind-set began to change. John Eckhardt then says,

> To stir our members to go to the nations, I encouraged every member of Crusaders Church to obtain a passport. We then had a "Passport Sunday" when all the members brought their passports to receive prayer for the Lord to open the way for them to go to the nations! As a result, many of our members have taken prayer journeys to nations of the 10/40 Window and have joined teams for other mission trips.[25]

This is outreach in overdrive!

Notes

1. Rick Warren, *The Purpose Driven Church* (Grand Rapids: Zondervan Publishing House, 1995), p. 43.
2. Notes from a sermon preached by Joseph C. Wongsak in April 1996.
3. Warren, *The Purpose Driven Church*, p. 16.
4. Mike Berg and Paul Pretiz, *Spontaneous Combustion: Grass-Roots Christianity, Latin America Style* (Pasadena, Calif.: William Carey Library, 1996), pp. 63, 64.
5. C. Kirk Hadaway and David A. Roozen, *Rerouting the Protestant Mainstream* (Nashville: Abingdon Press, 1995), p. 61.
6. John and Sylvia Ronsvalle, "The End of Benevolence: Alarming Trends in Church Giving," *Christian Century* (October 23, 1996), p. 1010.
7. Lyle E. Schaller, "The Call to Mission," *The Parish Paper* (April 1996), p. 2.
8. George G. Hunter III, *Church for the Unchurched* (Nashville: Abingdon Press, 1996), p. 1.
9. Donald E. Miller, "Evangelism Within New-Paradigm Churches," *Ministry Advantage* (September-October 1996), p. 8.
10. Sally Morgenthaler, *Worship Evangelism* (Grand Rapids: Zondervan Publishing House, 1995), p. 78.
11. Robert H. Schuller, *Your Church Has a Fantastic Future* (Ventura, Calif.: Regal Books, 1986), p. 72.
12. *Journal for the Scientific Study of Religion* 36, no. 1 (1997).
13. James H. Feeney, *Church Planting by the Team Method* (Anchorage, Alaska: Abbott Loop Christian Center, 1988), p. 97.
14. Jonathan Chao, "China's Cross," *Christianity Today* (November 13, 1995), p. 49.
15. Donald E. Miller, *Reinventing American Protestantism* (Berkeley, Calif.: University of California Press, 1997), p. 109.
16. Steve Sjogren, *Servant Warfare* (Ann Arbor, Mich.: Servant Publications, 1996), p. 82, 83.
17. Ibid., pp. 83, 84.
18. John Wimber, "The Kingdom of God and Social Justice," *Equipping the Saints* (4th Quarter 1995-1st Quarter 1996), p. 5.
19. Robert T. Coote, "Good News, Bad News: North American Protestant Overseas Personnel Statistics in Twenty-Five-Year Perspective," *International Bulletin of Missionary Research* (January 1995), p. 11.
20. John Leith, *Crisis in the Church* (Louisville, Ky.: Westminster John Knox, 1997), pp. 3, 4.
21. Coote, "Good News, Bad News," pp. 11, 12
22. John Eckhardt, "An Apostolic Movement Across Cultures," *Ministry Advantage* (July-August 1996), p. 8.
23. John Kelly (address at the National Symposium on the Post-denominational Church, Fuller Seminary, Pasadena, Calif., May 21-23, 1996).

24. John Eckhardt (address at the National Symposium on the Postdenominational Church, Fuller Seminary, Pasadena, Calif., May 21-23, 1996).

25. John Eckhardt, "Crusaders Church and International Ministries of Prophetic and Apostolic Churches," *The New Apostolic Churches*, C. Peter Wagner, ed. (Ventura, Calif.: Regal Books, 1998), p. 54.

CHAPTER NINE

Multiplying
Ministers

John Maxwell's best-known quote is the following: *"Everything rises or falls on leadership!"*

It has become a modern-day proverb, just a few degrees shy of divine inspiration.

Organizations, therefore, do not grow in any significant measure without multiplying leaders. Consequently, it should go without saying that the New Apostolic Reformation could never have become the fastest growing segment of contemporary Protestantism without an efficient system of selecting and training leaders. The leaders are designated as "ministers," so an essential key to new apostolic church growth is multiplying ministers.

THE CONGREGATION IS THE INCUBATOR

How are ministers multiplied in new apostolic churches? It all starts when one first becomes a member of a new apostolic church. Membership is not a legal contract; rather, it is a spiritual covenant. To be regarded as a member in good standing, active participation is demanded in at least three areas:

- Worship;
- Receiving ministry;
- Ministering to others.

Although, admittedly, few churches reach it, nevertheless, the ideal is that every single church member function as a minister. New apostolic leaders take their roles as apostles, prophets, evangelists, pastors and teachers, as found in Ephesians 4:11, very seriously. Their primary task is detailed in the next verse: "For the equipping of the saints for the work of ministry" (Eph. 4:12). When this happens well, the congregation then becomes the primary incubator for ministers, both lay ministers and staff ministers.

Lyle Schaller observes how this has been happening across the United States to a greater and greater degree. He says, "Congregations, not academic institutions, once again are becoming the primary place for training program staff members for large congregations. This is consistent and compatible, but farther advanced, than a parallel trend: that is for large churches to replace theological seminaries as the primary source for clergy."[1]

LEVERAGING MINISTRY

New apostolic pastors have long since recognized that to the degree they themselves attempt to do all or most of the ministry of the church they clasp an impenetrable lid on the growth of their congregation. Therefore, they make it a point to train others to minister. Reggie McNeal says, "Church leaders today know that the strategic way to leverage their ministry efforts is to empower others to minister. They assist believers in discovering and developing ministry role opportunities."[2] McNeal's word "empower" is very important. Laypeople have to be both trained and empowered for ministry if the church is ever to become anything other than a small, static church.

When I first visited Jubilee Christian Centre in Calgary, Alberta, I was surprised. Here was a vibrant, growing church passing 600, and having an incredible influence on the community. I would have expected a staff of about six or seven, as well as backup personnel. What did I find? Senior Pastor Phil Nordin had an assistant pastor, a youth pastor and an administrator, and two part-time secretaries. The rest were lay volunteers! This is what Reggie McNeal means by "leveraging" the ministry of the senior pastor.

PART 1: LAY MINISTRY

This is not confined to Calgary. One of the first things traditional church leaders begin to notice when they first visit new apostolic churches is the abundance of volunteers. Whenever I am invited to a new apostolic church, I cannot help but marvel at the personal attention I receive. Volunteers will meet me, drive me wherever and whenever I want to go and make sure my hotel room is comfortable. They also provide an attractive fruit basket, give me their home phone number, escort me into and out of the church and bring me coffee or water or whatever I ask for. They see that the sound system is adjusted if I don't like it, make appointments for me and are at my beck and call for anything else I could possibly need.

Where do they recruit all these volunteers?

THE APOSTOLIC THEOLOGY OF LAY MINISTRY

The apostolic theology of lay ministry is a fairly recent discovery in church history—namely, a discovery of the past 25 or 30 years. We do not find this in Martin Luther or John Calvin or John Wesley or other classic theologians, either Protestant or Catholic. There was some of this in the British Plymouth Brethren Movement and some in the U.S. Restoration Movement led by Alexander Campbell and Barton Stone and some in fringe movements here and there. However, it did not mainstream into the Body of Christ, at least in the United States, until the publication of Ray Stedman's book *Body Life* (Regal Books) in 1972. This was the first widely recognized and accepted biblical theology of lay ministry, although written in a popular style.

The concept caught on. Now we have an abundant bibliography about lay ministry. Some of my favorite recent books on the subject are Greg Ogden's *The New Reformation* (Zondervan), Jim Rutz's *The Open Church* (The Seed Sowers) and Melvin Steinbron's *The Lay-Driven Church* (Regal). For example, Jim Rutz details 10 chronic church problems, and then makes this statement: "I'm claiming that all of these maladies, and more, are caused by one master malady: the closed church, in which laymen tend to be passive observers while ministers tend to be overworked insiders."[3] Most new apostolic pastors would agree with him.

EVERY CHURCH MEMBER IS A MINISTER

The assumption that every church member is a minister comes from the Bible. The apostle Peter writes, "As each one has received a gift, *minister* it to one another, as good stewards of the manifold grace of God" (1 Pet. 4:10, emphasis added). Peter is writing this letter to believers in general, so the "each one" means all of us. First Corinthians 12 is one of the major New Testament passages about spiritual gifts. In it, Paul says, "But one and the same Spirit works all these things, distributing [spiritual gifts] to *each one* individually as He wills" (v. 11, emphasis added). We all have one or more spiritual gifts and these are given for us to minister.

How, then, are we supposed to minister? We do it as part of a Body: "For as the body is one and has many members, but all members of that one body, being many, are one body, so also is Christ" (1 Cor. 12:12). Jesus Christ is the head of the Body, so we minister according to what the head tells us to do. I remember once hearing Greg Ogden say: "The head does not tell the hand to tell the foot what to do. The head tells the foot."

RECONSIDERING "CLERGY" VERSUS "LAITY"

New apostolic church leaders take "body life" literally. As soon as they do, however, it forces them to reconsider the traditional church distinction between "clergy" and "laity." Greg Ogden, borrowing from Paul Stevens's *Liberating the Laity* (InterVarsity Press), describes the traditional mind-set like this:

> Ministers are those who go into "the ministry." How many of us talk about "the ministry" that we are in? If we are in "the ministry," what is left for everyone else? Priests are confessors. Clergy are representatives of the institution of the church. Laity are spiritual amateurs who cannot be entrusted with real ministry. That's the way we use the language today.[4]

Admittedly, this puts us all into a bit of a dilemma. The words "clergy" and "laity" are there whether we like them or not. It may require a couple of generations to change them, even though I would be in favor of speeding it up as much as possible. So, meanwhile, if we use the words (which I continue to do), it is important to add the necessary disclaimers and explanations. Eventually we will have better vocabulary. One possible improvement I hear in many churches these days is "staff" and "volunteers." The idea is that everyone ministers, but some happen to get paid for it and they are put on staff.

THE STRATEGIC DESIGN

A few years ago, I wrote a whole book, *Leading Your Church to Growth* (Regal Books), about this subject of lay ministry. In it, I tried to help pastors understand their primary role as opposed to the primary role of the laypeople in their churches. I remember once hearing Rick Warren say, "What are the things you will have to give up if you want your church to grow? As a starter, pastors will have to give up their *ministry*, and laypeople will have to give up their *leadership*." This cuts directly to the heart of the issue. The traditional concept is that the congregation owns the church and that they hire the pastor to do their ministry for them. New apostolic churches, like Rick Warren's, turn this around 180 degrees, as he explains in his best-seller, *The Purpose Driven Church* (Zondervan).

I have found it helpful to use a pair of diagrams to clarify this concept. At the left-hand side of this first diagram, the pastor is doing most of the leading, but as we move toward the right, the congregation does more and more of the leading. Research shows that the more we can keep toward the left, the greater the church growth potential.

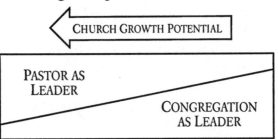

At the left-hand side of the second diagram, the pastor is doing most of the ministry of the church. On the right-hand side, the congregation is doing most of the ministry. This time, the further we can get toward the right, the greater the church growth potential.

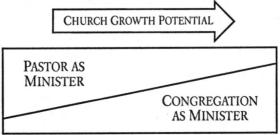

The Pastor as "Coach"

Several new apostolic leaders are advocating "coach" as a helpful role designation for the pastor. Bill Hamon says, "The position that is now called the 'pastor' of a church will be redefined. Those who fill that position will function more like the coach of a sports team rather than the owner."[5]

Greg Ogden agrees: "I think perhaps the best modern day idiom for pastor is 'coach.' If you come into my office today, you would find the sign that says, 'Greg Ogden—Coach. On this team everyone plays.'"[6]

What does the coach do? The coach sets the game plan and deploys all available personnel for executing it and winning the game.

If everyone plays on the team, what positions do they play? Functionally, this is determined by the spiritual gifts God has given to each believer. It is up to the pastor or the coach to help each one discover what gift or gifts they have, develop them, and then use them to the fullest extent possible for ministry.

THE SPIRITUAL GIFTS ISSUE

Although virtually every new apostolic church leader would agree with what I have just said, not all of them seem to grasp its full implications. One of my personal disappointments in my association with many (not all) new apostolic pastors has been their relatively underdeveloped understanding of the biblical teaching about spiritual gifts. Spiritual gifts, however, are frequently mentioned in new apostolic preaching and teaching.

Many times I have asked myself, "What is going on here? How could it be that so many new apostolic leaders end up on the shallow side of a doctrine they profess to believe in?" The best answer I have been able to come up with is that we may be seeing a hangover from classical Pentecostalism in which many of these leaders have their spiritual roots. Classical Pentecostals have done a great service to the kingdom of God by taking spiritual gifts out of the closet at the beginning of the twentieth century and spreading the concept by word and deed so powerfully that ministry through spiritual gifts is now widely accepted across the board. However, there are two notable weaknesses in the classical Pentecostal view of spiritual gifts:

1. For many classical Pentecostals, the list of "spiritual gifts" is restricted to the nine gifts mentioned in 1 Corinthians 12:8-10. They do not give equal emphasis or attention to at least 16 other New Testament spiritual gifts. It produces an awkward situation not dissimilar to a coach going onto the field with a football team consisting of a backfield, but no line.

2. Some classical Pentecostals take the position that all believers have access to all the gifts whenever they are needed. This "situational view" of spiritual gifts was developed as a rationale to explain why all Christians should expect to speak in tongues at least once in their lives as an initial evidence of the baptism of the Holy Spirit. The more biblical view, in my opinion, is the "constitutional view" of spiritual gifts based on the analogy of members of the Body. My hand always functions as a hand, not sometimes as an ear or as a liver. To return to the coach idiom, the center of a football team would not be expected to function sometimes as an end or as a quarterback. I regard spiritual gifts as God-given attributes.

I believe this is not the place to elaborate greatly on the doctrine of spiritual gifts, except I do want to point out that the phenomenon that some believers who do not have the *gift* of tongues do speak in tongues or that some believers who do not have the *gift* of healing pray for the sick and see them healed and so on can biblically and rationally be understood by distinguishing between *spiritual gifts* and *Christian roles*. All this is explained in considerable detail in my book *Your Spiritual Gifts Can Help Your Church Grow* (Regal Books).

One of the best new apostolic models I have discovered for mobilizing the ministry of laypeople through spiritual gifts is Hillcrest Church in North Dallas, Texas, pastored by Dr. Morris Sheats. In 14 years, the church steadily grew from nothing to 5,000 members. New members must (1) commit to minister, (2) commit to tithe and (3) attend a 13-week new members class. They are then expected to enroll in an additional 13-week class, "Mobilization of Spiritual Gifts," to prepare to fulfill their commitment to minister.

Hillcrest is open to all the New Testament spiritual gifts, and it takes the "constitutional view," which gives them the freedom to help members concentrate on developing their specific gifts, and then find their God-ordained ministry slots long-term.

THE SECRET OF SUCCESS

In many traditional churches, if everyone started discovering spiritual gifts it would cause a problem because there wouldn't be enough ministries in the church to absorb those who wanted to minister. Such ministries couldn't be started rapidly because incorporating a new parish ministry ordinarily requires a long study process followed by successive reviews by permission-withholding boards and committees. New apostolic churches have discovered a more viable option.

Robert Schuller says, "The secret of success is to find a need and fill it."

Initiation of new apostolic ministry comes from the bottom up based on a free enterprise model. Robert Schuller's well-known saying is: "The secret of success is to find a need and fill it." No church can do everything. What, then, shall we do? How do we choose? The new apostolic answer is simple—do whatever works. If the new ministry is meeting a need, it will work. If not, it will fail.

Who initiates ministry? Not some committee or church board or denominational agency. *Anyone* can initiate a new ministry in most new apostolic churches. Each new ministry, of course, requires staff approval, but staff members, up through the senior pastor, are more inclined to respond, "Why not?" instead of "Why?" This has two important advantages:

1. It creates unlimited options first for meeting the felt needs of the congregation and the community and second for wide ranges of volunteer service.
2. It screens out what is not needed or what is poorly

led, because such ministries won't succeed. If they
don't, let's try something else!

Traditional churches usually have a certain set of ministries
that are assumed to continue every year whether they succeed
or not. At the beginning of each year, a "nominating committee" undertakes the responsibility of filling all the necessary
slots. The result of this is that too many lay positions in the
church are filled on the basis of *availability* rather than *giftedness*.

Having said this, I hasten to add that even in new apostolic
churches there are necessarily some fixed ministries that originate from the top and that must be supplied with volunteers
every year. Worship teams, choirs, ushers, greeters, nursery
attendants, Sunday School teachers and other like things are
examples. They are intentionally kept to a minimum, however,
and bottom-up ministries are maximized as much as possible.

THE TWO PRIMARY STRUCTURES FOR LAY MINISTRY
The two major structures for organizing lay ministry in new
apostolic churches are *ministry teams* and *small groups*. Some
churches major in one and some in the other. Some combine
the two. Some are transitioning from one to the other. For
example, Willow Creek Community Church at first put nearly
all its eggs in the ministry team basket, but later introduced a
dynamic small group ministry.

Although some ministry teams, such as those relating to
worship, are managed by church staff, many of them operate
on the free enterprise model. They are largely self-directed and
self-financed. Some focus inward, designed to meet the needs
of the congregation, and others focus outward toward the community.

I mentioned in the last chapter that Cathedral of Faith in
San Jose, California, sponsors a food distribution program that
now utilizes a $1 million facility. How did this start? A lay cou-
ple approached Pastor Kenny Foreman in 1979 and asked permission to start giving food to the poor. Foreman's response

was, predictably, "Why not?" Currently, along with a part-time staff couple, 60 volunteers are finding their ministry opportunities in that department.

Virtually every new apostolic church sponsors small groups of one sort or another. Yonggi Cho of Korea popularized the cell-based church in which all members are expected to belong to a home cell group. Ralph Neighbour's *Where Do We Go from Here?* (Touch Publications) is the standard text for "pure cell" churches. Carl George, in *Prepare Your Church for the Future*, advocates the "metachurch model." He strongly affirms home cell groups, but suggests that other small groups of variable sizes and functions also can serve the useful purpose of providing ministry opportunities for laypeople.

GIVING GROUP LEADERS A CARTE BLANCHE

Traditional churches have strict rules separating the functions of clergy from those of laity. Laypersons would never be permitted to perform certain so-called "sacerdotal functions." This distinction tends to vanish, however, in many new apostolic churches. To open the doors for maximum lay ministry, small-group leaders often receive a carte blanche: they baptize, serve communion, conduct worship, preach and teach, marry, bury and raise needed funds. Rick Warren was the first pastor I knew who allowed this freedom, but many others have followed suit.

Carl George says, "These clergy of the future have removed the OFF LIMITS signs from every level of pastoral care. They've restructured the training and organization of the entire church to enable every willing person to find a quality opportunity for life-changing ministry."[7]

PART 2: CHURCH STAFF

When laypeople are ministering throughout the congregation, this provides the primary incubator for new staff leaders. Most new apostolic churches are characterized by homegrown staff.

For the most part, staff members continue ministering as they did previously, the difference being they are now paid for it so they can minister full-time.

This is in contrast to the traditional model where laypeople assuming staff positions is the exception rather than the rule. New staff members usually come from outside the church. They are located, screened and presented to the congregation by a "search committee." In many cases, the senior pastor is not even a member of the search committee. More than once the search committee has selected candidates who would not be the pastor's first choice "in order to keep balance in our staff." Even the thought of such a thing would produce a combination of horror and disbelief in the minds of a typical new apostolic senior pastor.

ADVANTAGES OF HOMEGROWN STAFF

Recruiting new staff from within the congregation has five tremendous advantages over bringing in someone from the outside:

1. The new staff members already agree with the vision of the pastor and the way it is being implemented in the church. If they didn't, they would have left the church long ago.
2. They are loyal to the pastor. This is important because in most new apostolic churches the senior pastor does the hiring and firing.
3. They are motivated to do what they can to implement the pastor's vision. Otherwise, they wouldn't have responded positively to the initial overtures to consider a staff position.
4. They know how the church's philosophy of ministry operates, both formally and informally.
5. They have proven that they have the spiritual gifts necessary for their jobs by their previous track record in lay ministry.

Note that in traditional churches, all these five are relatively unknown factors when a new staff person comes in from outside. Only time tells if they apply, and sometimes when they don't, it is too late to prevent damage.

ORDINATION

Can these laypeople who come on staff be ordained? It all depends on your understanding of what ordination really is. Here is my definition:

> *Ordination is the public recognition by qualified spiritual leaders that a believer has spiritual gifts for the ministry to which he or she feels called, and the authorization by the church to use them in an appropriate office.*

The traditional requirements for ordination include meeting certain academic standards, recommendation by one or more ordained persons and examination by a committee of ordained individuals. The agenda of most ordination examination committees centers on theological orthodoxy, biblical knowledge, a personal testimony of salvation and call to the ministry, and agreement with the polity (rules and regulations) of the denomination.

Although there is some overlap, most new apostolic ordination requirements usually do not begin with academic qualifications. For example, John Eckhardt says about ordination,

> The relationship between ordination to ministry and academic achievement is not on the same level in new apostolic churches as in more traditional churches. In other words, we believe in academic achievement, but we do not believe it is the major qualification for ordination. We tend to look more closely at such things as anointing, calling, gifting, character, and practical knowledge of the Word of God. The acceptance for ordination is based mostly on whether a person fills those particular requirements.[8]

I was impressed when I first read Bill Hamon's requirements for "true ministers." For one thing, no statement of theological sophistication or academic credentials appears on the list. He states his criteria under 10 words all beginning with *M*: "manhood [implying both genders], ministry, message, maturity, marriage, methods, manners, money, morality, and motive."[9]

THE NEW REALITY

The new apostolic paradigm of homegrown staff carries with it a series of new realities. The rules of the game of training for and ordination to professional ministry are changing.

The ordination process is more often than not initiated by the pastor of the congregation, not by the candidate. Previously, a young person would feel called to ministry, the pastor and the church would examine the person and approve, and the ordinand would then enroll in the appropriate Bible school or seminary. After receiving the required academic training, ordination would be scheduled. Now, in many cases, the major decision is not whether the church will accept the candidate's overtures, but whether the candidate will accept the pastor's overtures.

One of the outcomes is that individuals who are ordained in new apostolic churches tend to have a considerably higher age profile than in traditional churches. The church member who has demonstrated outstanding spiritual gifts as a layperson is frequently well into a secular career. Mid-career changes into full-time Christian ministry are now becoming commonplace. These individuals do not first attain ordination and then send out resumes and wonder where they might eventually be located. Their job offer comes before, not after, ordination.

BYPASSING SEMINARIES

Picture a new staff member in his mid-forties who has 20 years of experience as a structural engineer in a leading construction corporation. He has lived in his present home with his wife and three children for the last eight years. He has a sizable mortgage, his kids are deeply involved in school activities and his oldest is ready to enter college. If packing up and spending three years in a theological seminary were a prerequisite to his ordination, he wouldn't even be able to consider a mid-career change into the ministry. It is not that such things never have happened in the past, but when they have, the person involved was rightly regarded as a heroic figure, and such heroes were few and far between.

Seminaries previously functioned like dental schools or police academies. The job market is closed to those who haven't been to the approved schools. When this was the case, seminaries had an established constituency and they could function almost indefinitely. No longer. Training remains important for staff-level church ministry, but the training preferably comes *after*, rather than *before*, ordination, and it takes several new forms.

This is a special challenge to traditional seminaries. Their product, namely, quality training for ministry, remains in demand, but if it is going to be utilized to any significant extent in the future it requires radical repackaging and a reengineered delivery system. Otherwise, theological seminaries, as Donald Miller says, are in danger of being "viewed as anachronisms of an earlier age."[10] In his view, it may now be too late to change.

Apprenticeship has been a chief form of training pastors in Third World churches for some time, and it is now gaining much more of a place in the Western world. Working under the mentorship of a successful pastor and learning from experience is a procedure that is now producing an increasing number of church staff leaders. To supplement that, nonformal training experiences such as seminars and pastors conferences, as opposed to accredited courses and degree programs, are the choice of many. For example, John Wimber led the Association of Vineyard Churches to more than 500 congregations by using Vineyard pastors conferences as his primary training format.

This can pose some problems for those unaccustomed to the new ways. Ralph Moore, whose Hope Chapel movement is a part of the International Church of the Foursquare Gospel, tells this revealing story:

I recently received a call from a friend. He was involved in a headquarters discussion about licensing pastors for Foursquare churches. It seems an influential businessman in one of our churches had complained that his child was attending LIFE Bible College (at dad's expense) to get a pastor's license. A staff pastor in his home church held license by virtue of his responsibility. The man was frustrated that the staffer held license without expending the time or money required by this businessman and his offspring. He saw us giving away "free licenses."[11]

WHY SEMINARIES ARE SOMETIMES CALLED "CEMETERIES"

In seminary environments, where I have spent 40 of my adult years, the occasional intentionally facetious slip of the tongue in calling a seminary a "cemetery," is met with a polite chuckle, as if to say, "I know you didn't really mean it!" Well, maybe not always when spoken in the company of seminary professors like me. Behind our backs, though? Many, in fact, really do mean it. I think it is time we who have had vested interests in seminaries begin to stop fooling ourselves and to face realities.

Reggie McNeal says,

> Where will the training for apostolic leadership take place? Traditional credentialing processes will, for the most part, find it extraordinarily difficult to rise to this challenge. Typically, in the prevailing church culture, Bible colleges, seminaries, and denominational program support have served as the training grounds. But only the most dynamic and innovative of these old training institutions will maintain viability as credible sources of ministry preparation.[12]

SEVEN TOMBSTONE MARKERS

Seminaries have at least seven common characteristics, as we have known them, that in all probability will prevent them from becoming the "dynamic and innovative" institutions of which Reggie McNeal speaks. Seminaries that somehow break these molds will flourish. Those that don't, unless they are heavily endowed, face a bleak future. Let's call these seven characteristics "tombstone markers."

TOMBSTONE MARKER 1: ACADEMIC ACHIEVEMENT IS CONSIDERED MORE IMPORTANT THAN MINISTRY SKILLS.

Traditional seminaries have chosen to cultivate the public image that their product, so to speak, is "theological education." Their curriculum, accordingly, has evolved to include around 80 percent theory and 20 percent practice. On the other hand, new apostolic schools want to be seen as offering "ministerial training." Their curriculum is 20 percent theory and 80 percent practice.

To illustrate, the faculty publications that invariably receive the highest peer acclaim in seminary communities are those that dialogue with fellow scholars of present and past generations. Their writings:

- Are peppered with long and detailed footnotes;
- Use frequent quotes in German, Latin, Greek and Hebrew;
- Are based on library research;
- Exhibit philosophical underpinnings;
- Go through one or two printings;
- Find their way into academic libraries;
- Are reviewed by academic journals.

Relevance to ministry is usually a secondary consideration.

On the other hand, faculty publications that are written in the following manner are all but ignored by faculty peers. They:

- Are written in a popular style;

+ Are focused on effectiveness in ministry at all levels;
+ Are peppered with anecdotes;
+ Try to simplify complex theological issues;
+ Are based on field research;
+ Go into multiple printings;
+ Find their way into pastors' libraries and Christian bookstores;
+ Are reviewed in popular magazines.

One seminary president, while addressing his faculty, scornfully referred to such books as "potboilers," implying that he considered it beneath the dignity of his faculty to indulge in such debased literary pursuits.

A tongue-in-cheek comment among professors: "Seminary would be a great place to work if it only weren't for the students!"

TOMBSTONE MARKER 2: THE HIGHEST PRIORITY IS OFTEN TO IMPRESS ACADEMIC PEERS, NOT TO TRAIN STUDENTS.
Many seminary professors love to teach students, but as a rule, they find themselves in the minority. Professors, quite frequently, regard teaching classes as an inescapable nuisance that detracts them from the more weighty pursuit of scholarly research and producing papers for academic communities. An in-house tongue-in-cheek comment among professors is: "Seminary would be a great place to work if it only weren't for the students!"

In large segments of the traditional church, the relentless drive for academic one-upmanship and political correctness has helped pave the road to liberalism. John Leith describes the situation in mainline seminaries as well as anyone:

> The seminaries face a crisis of belief. Many basic Christian doctrines are at risk on seminary campuses

today. Furthermore, there is little evidence of any passionate proclamation of the foundational convictions of Christian faith or of the Christian gospel of what God has done for the salvation of human beings. Passionate convictions do exist on seminary campuses, but they frequently find their most vigorous expression in the advocacy of causes such as the agenda of the feminist movement, or the black caucus, or left-wing political organizations. There is little evidence that seminary faculties have a similar passion for proclaiming the foundational doctrines of Christian faith in a secular age. They censor chapel speakers as to the political correctness of their language, but not as to the orthodoxy or integrity of their theology.[13]

In evangelical seminaries, where a residue of theological conviction persists, this attitude can be reflected in other ways. One evangelical seminary, for example, vetoed a proposed invitation to noted theologian J. I. Packer to do a special lectureship on campus because he was known to question the ordination of women, an item not found in the seminary's statement of faith, but nevertheless elevated to a nonnegotiable level by the faculty.

Where can this lead? John Leith says, "The consequence is that theological seminaries are no longer seen as primarily institutions for the training of pastors, but as institutes for the discussion and study of religion."[14] That danger cuts across theological traditions of all kinds.

TOMBSTONE MARKER 3: THE ACADEMY IRRESISTIBLY TENDS TO ENTRENCH IRRELEVANCE THROUGH FACULTY TENURE AND REQUIRED COURSES.

The academic game, as I have watched it being played for decades, is fascinating. The goal for faculty is to rise to the top of their given field.

One way to succeed in this is to narrow a field as much as possible, a technique that is strongly engrained in the Ph.D.

process. If the field becomes narrow enough, the top is wide open. I recall, for example, that while I was doing my undergraduate work at Rutgers University, part of the standard public relations pitch stressed how proud the university was to have on its faculty the world expert—in oysters! A cursory reading of the article titles in *The Journal of Biblical Literature* will show how narrow fields and specializations in religion can become. I, personally, know that it works because my own field of church growth was narrow enough for me to make it to the top for a while. I had very little competition.

Once a professor arrives at or near the top, the way to stay there is to be awarded tenure, the ultimate in job security. Thomas Oden, a distinguished tenured faculty member himself, takes a penetrating look at the inside of the seminary system in his remarkable book *Requiem: A Lament in Three Movements*. In it, he includes a section called "The Structural Irreformability of Self-Cloning Faculties." On the subject of tenure, he says, "The tenure principle, which was designed to protect academic freedom, has become so exploited as now to protect academic license, absenteeism, incompetence, and at times moral turpitude. Once tenure is offered, it is virtually impossible to withdraw."[15]

FACULTY FEATHERBEDDING

Oden goes on to say, "Marriage has annulment, separation, and divorce, but there is no nullification and no easy procedure for dissociation from tenure once extended....There is no job security in our society so fixed in stone as academic tenure. Featherbedding has become a perfected art, not in teamster union halls, but in faculty clubs."[16]

How does this lead to irrelevance? First of all, the tenured faculty members determine curriculum. The tendency is to project their personal priorities on the students.

Because scholarship is a high value to the faculty members, the assumption is that it should also be a requisite for practicing pastors. Somehow an axiom has crept in that if pastors can read the Old Testament in Hebrew and the New Testament in Greek, their effectiveness in ministry will increase. Survey data shows that most seminary graduates never again read the Bible in the original languages after graduation, but that does not seem to change the faculty mind-set. They are not significantly impressed with the fact that few megachurch pastors, who are leading the churches that are having the greatest influence in their communities, ever engage themselves in Greek or Hebrew exegesis.

The upshot is that, as I have pointed out, curriculum becomes something like 80 percent theory and 20 percent practice. Much of the theory is especially irrelevant because of required courses. The traditional model for seminary curriculum assumes that students are youngsters who are laying a foundation for future ministry. Therefore, students are not expected to have the wisdom necessary to decide which courses would be most relevant for ministry, so the presumably wiser faculty must decide on their behalf. Because faculty members are academics, the theoretical content would naturally be quite high. As well, because some are so specialized that virtually no one would *elect* to take their course, they have the power to *require* the course for graduation. Irrelevance easily becomes entrenched.

Because only so many courses can fit into a three-year seminary program, change and innovation are difficult to achieve. Tenured faculty members understandably do not want their courses replaced. Kenneth Meyer, then president of Trinity Evangelical Divinity School in Deerfield, Illinois, participated in Murdock Charitable Trust study of seminaries a few years ago. In his report, he stated: "The curriculum for the M.Div. in most of our schools has had little change in twenty years. At Trinity, we changed two courses between 1975 and 1990. Yet think of the changes that took place in the church during the same period."[17]

Because the tenured faculty are the ones who have the final say in inviting new faculty members to their institution, a tendency for "self cloning," as Thomas Oden would say, can persist

from generation to generation. Only an act of God could produce meaningful change in many existing seminaries.

TOMBSTONE MARKER 4: SEMINARY FACULTY MEMBERS RARELY ARE
OR HAVE BEEN PASTORS THEMSELVES, AND ALMOST NONE HAVE
BEEN SUCCESSFUL PASTORS.

Experience in the local church is not considered a particularly
desirable quality for recruiting new seminary faculty. Even
active *membership* in a local church is not always considered
important and the subject often does not constitute a significant part of the job interview process. Kenneth Meyer addresses
this by saying,

> The curriculum has called for professionals of the
> academy rather than professionals of the church. The
> truth is, students will model their professors. In our
> shop some 75% of faculty have never pastored a
> church longer than an internship during graduate
> studies. Is it any wonder that graduates come out
> "heady" and lacking ministry skills? The "profession-
> als of the church" need to be deeply involved in teach-
> ing and changing curriculum.[18]

From what we have seen, however, such a scenario seems
highly unlikely in our old wineskin seminaries.

TOMBSTONE MARKER 5: SEMINARIES ARE ACCOUNTABLE TO
ACCREDITING ASSOCIATIONS, NOT TO THE CHURCHES FOR WHICH
THEY ARE PRESUMABLY TRAINING PASTORS.

Accrediting associations, like tenure, began for highly com-
mendable reasons. The educational level of church members
was rising with the escalation of schooling in our society, and
seminaries were meeting the demand of denominations to
maintain an established academic level for ordinands. The
assumption was that clergy needed to keep up with parish-
ioners educationally if they were to minister well. Like-minded

seminaries therefore banded together to form associations that would hold them accountable to maintain mutually agreed upon minimum standards of quality control.

As seminaries began to move more from *ministerial training* to *theological education*, the accrediting associations did likewise. As time went by, the accrediting associations, as institutions in general tend to do, began to take on a life of their own. Rather than controlling the accrediting associations, the individual seminaries found themselves controlled by the accrediting associations. They became subject to an abstract manual of standards that they had little or no voice in establishing and that, in many cases, were contrary to the best interests of a particular seminary. By then, however, there were few alternatives for individual members of the association except to drop accreditation. Most would decide to conform, at the price of agreeing not to introduce certain creative innovations that would have been considered by the accrediting agency as coloring outside the lines.

One professor of an ATS (Association of Theological Schools)-accredited seminary told me that for a nine-month period he was not able to do original research or upgrade his courses or write for publication. This was the case because virtually all his time outside of classroom was taken by mandatory committee meetings and writing reports for the accrediting association's approaching on-site visit.

ACADEMIC ATTAINMENT AND EFFECTIVENESS IN MINISTRY

Notice that accrediting associations have never developed a way of testing member schools for the effectiveness in ministry of their graduates. Therefore, they rely on testing for academic attainment as if the question of how ministers are actually being trained to do effective parish work were a secondary matter.

Nor would I imagine that most accrediting agencies would even *want* to conduct such tests. For years I have had a lingering, and perhaps a bit pernicious, desire to engage in a research project that would test the relationship between academic attainment and effectiveness in ministry. Using the available tools of social scientific research, such a project would be eminently doable. I doubt that other interests would ever allow that item to rise to the top of my personal agenda, but I have a strong hunch that evidence would show an *inverse* correlation. For example, a friend of mine who pastors a 6,000-member Presbyterian (U.S.A.) megachurch once told me that he rarely hires seminary graduates as staff members. When I asked why, he replied, "Because they are useless!"

Robert Patterson, analyzing the crisis in evangelical seminaries in *Christianity Today* magazine, says,

> Ironically, at the very moment evangelical theological education appears to have come of age, some influential parachurch and megachurch leaders are questioning the whole idea of theological education. The observation is made that if men who never spent a day in seminary can build successful ministries like Prison Fellowship, Focus on the Family, and Willow Creek Community Church, why have seminaries at all? In fact, a seminary degree will actually disqualify a candidate from a staff position at some megachurches.[19]

TOMBSTONE MARKER 6: THE NATURE OF ACADEMIA IS TO PRODUCE A CRITICAL SPIRIT THROUGHOUT THE COMMUNITY.

In academia, displaying a "critical mind" is considered a badge of distinction. In my seminary, an evaluation form is completed by each student at the close of each course. One of the items on which the professor is to be rated reads, "Students were encouraged to think critically." The higher the score, the more highly ranked is the professor.

I consistently score low on that item because I would rather help my students think positively and creatively than critically. I dislike reading book reviews in journals in which the reviewer has a compulsion to end the review criticizing the author. The underlying message is, "If only the author were as smart as I am, the book could have been much better than it is." Journals whose editorial policy I have been able to influence through the years prohibit this kind of academic one-upmanship, driven by the notion that it is better to be astutely critical than to be naively affirming. Ted Haggard, a new apostolic pastor, would characterize this mind-set as emerging from a "tree of the knowledge of good and evil" perspective rather than from a "tree of life" perspective.[20]

The following is prevalent in most seminaries today:

♦ Skepticism is valued over belief (which is seen as "gullibility");

♦ Pessimism is valued over optimism (which is seen as "unrealistic");

♦ Losing is valued over winning (which is seen as "triumphalism");

♦ Complexity is valued over simplicity (which is seen as "naiveté");

♦ Committees are trusted over individuals (who are suspected of "arrogance");

♦ Bureaucrats are valued over entrepreneurs (who are seen as "empire builders").

None of this should be interpreted to mean that I am advocating anti-intellectualism. The Body of Christ needs the finest and best-trained minds in its leadership. I am not addressing the quality of the intellect, but rather the personal attitudes that govern the application of that intellect to matters involving fellow humans. Mental brilliance needs to be subsumed to spiritual character.

TOMBSTONE MARKER 7: SEMINARY TRAINING IS PRICING ITSELF OUT OF THE MARKET.

I began to notice the disproportionate escalation in tuition when, year after year, our seminary raised tuition by 10 percent, but professors' salaries by only 3 percent. Something other than training, apparently, was costing a lot of money. Many new apostolic leaders have concluded that the time and money invested in seminary training produces scant dividends.

More now than previously, students are questioning whether the product they are buying, namely, an academic degree, is worth the endless years of paying off student loans. It probably is worth it as a union card for graduate-level teaching positions, for training ministers in Asia and for ministries that are targeting college-level campus audiences. As a vehicle for credentialing a person for ordinary grass-roots parish ministry, however, the value of a seminary degree is clearly not what it used to be.

As an example, my son-in-law, who is a graduate of a prestigious seminary and now on staff at a new apostolic church, once said: "I paid $8,000 to learn Greek and Hebrew, and, now that I am in ministry I consider it a waste of money. I have never found a use for what I was taught."

As they were doing field research about money concerns in the church, John and Sylvia Ronsvalle discovered a considerable gap between seminary curricula and today's churches. Among other things, they report:

> Dan Conway observed, "The person going into ministry feels the dichotomy, and everything in seminary reinforces that. In the seminary curriculum, management, money, human resources are all incidental things you have to pick up. They're electives, not the substance of Christianity. Patristics, Scripture are the important things. Nobody says, 'how do you integrate God's word with balancing the checkbook?'" In Conway's opinion, the future pastor ought to be given the...general knowledge that the executive of any comparably sized voluntary organization has.[21]

THE NEW APOSTOLIC SCHOOLS

Church leaders and educators in the New Apostolic Reformation are well aware of the current maladies of theological seminaries.

This is one reason ordination-track training is returning to the local church. Homegrown staff, trained in conferences, are increasingly staff members of choice. Almost each apostolic network also has its own schools, but they are innovative and radically different from what we have known in the past.

Hardly any two new apostolic training schools are the same. In the first assembly of new apostolic educators, held in June 1998, the 65 base schools represented ran the spectrum from networks targeting college students, which, therefore, needed accredited graduate-level courses for their workers, to one that said they often have to read the exams to their students because they are training illiterates! Although they are remarkably different, almost all these schools have six fairly common characteristics. Every one of the characteristics can be viewed as an antidote to the "tombstone markers" of traditional seminaries.

SEVEN WAYS TO AVOID TOMBSTONE MARKERS

1. NO ACADEMIA. New apostolic churches do not allow degrees to become prerequisites for ordination. In most apostolic networks, having a degree or desiring one is not a disqualification for ministry. Degrees are clearly optional. Exceptions are networks such as Morningstar International whose target audience is undergraduate and graduate college students.

2. A NEW BREED OF FACULTY IS SURFACING.

    ♦ Historians are replaced by visionaries.
    ♦ Biblical exegetes are replaced by cultural exegetes.
    ♦ Theologians are replaced by entrepreneurs.
    ♦ Critics are replaced by cheerleaders.
    ♦ Distinguished scholars are replaced by dynamic pastors.

Professors are favored who have the ability to impart life and vision and anointing to the students. When I am invited to teach in a new apostolic school, I ask the dean what they want me to teach. They often reply, "You can teach anything you want!" The message behind that statement is, obviously, that they are asking me to come to provide impartation, not information. The information will be there, of course, but it is not primary.

3. CURRICULUM IS BROAD AND PRACTICAL

- History of dogma is now history of revivals.
- Greek is now Bible software including *Strong's Concordance*.
- Homiletics is now preaching.
- Exegesis of certain books is now English New Testament survey.
- Epistemology is now prophetic intercession.

I recently perused catalogs of new apostolic training institutions and found many course titles I would never expect to see listed in traditional seminary catalogs. Most established faculty members would have no idea what might be the possible content of such courses. Some examples:

- Demonology Exposed; Destiny and Leadership; Perils of Pastoring (Eagles Nest Training Institute, Gary Greenwald).
- Nurture of Prophetic Ministry; Missions and Church Planting Vision; Intercession for Revival (Grace Training Center, Mike Bickle).
- Roots of Character; Understanding the Anointing I and II; Building a Strong Spirit; Diplomacy, Protocol and Tact (Spirit Life Bible College, Roberts Liardon).
- Vision; City-Taking Strategies; Apostles and Apostolic Ministry; Communion with God (Impact School of Ministry, David Cannistraci).

♦ The Theology of Praise; Becoming Who You Are; Money and the Christian (Christian Life School of Theology, Ron Cottle).

♦ Understanding and Receiving Anointing; Living by the Word of God; Goal Setting and Assessment of Achievement (Kingdom Faith Bible College, Colin Urquhart).

4. DELIVERY SYSTEMS ARE DESIGNED FOR STUDENT CONVENIENCE. The old wineskin of young precareer students gathering to live for three or four years in an academic community directed by resident scholars who have a complete theological library is becoming a thing of the past. New apostolic students are more than likely older individuals who are already employed in full-time ministry or who are in secular careers. Class schedules are, therefore, designed not for the convenience of faculty and staff, but for the convenience of the students.

The length of courses can vary from 6 to 8 contact hours to 15 or 20 or more. A common format for a course is Thursday and Friday nights plus Saturday. All day Saturday and Sunday afternoon works for some. Almost any schedule is flexible, and it can be adapted, for example, to the availability of a professor who may be making a short visit to town.

5. PRIMARY ACCOUNTABILITY IS TO THE LOCAL CHURCH OR TO THE APOSTOLIC NETWORK. Each training institution is set up for the express purpose of training leaders, both staff-level and lay-level leaders, who will contribute to the particular vision or mission statement or philosophy of ministry of the local church or network of churches. Its success or failure is gauged by how well the graduates are doing the ministry to which they have been called, not by a manual of standards developed by an outside accrediting association.

I recall talking to Roberts Liardon two years after the first class had graduated from his Spirit Life Bible College. He was very proud of his students. Why? Because in two years the students from that class had planted 30 new churches! I wouldn't be surprised that some traditional seminaries of a similar size could not count 30 new churches from their past *10* graduating classes.

6. SECONDARY ACCOUNTABILITY IS TO EACH OTHER. The directors, presidents or deans of new apostolic training schools have a strong desire for peer accountability. They do not want to be hanging out there alone, doing their own thing, without reference to what the Spirit may be saying to fellow educators in other apostolic networks. They are well aware of the shortcomings of the institutionalized accrediting associations I just described. As are all new apostolic leaders, these educators are much more highly motivated and driven by personal relationships than by organizational affiliations.

To explore options for meeting this need, a large number of new apostolic educators met in June 1998 and formed the Apostolic Council for Educational Accountability (ACEA). This has taken shape, not as another accrediting association, but rather as a functional substitute for accreditation in general. Personal peer-level relationships, the basis for apostolic accountability, are established and nurtured in the annual meetings of ACEA, as well as in many ad hoc meetings and faculty interchanges throughout the year.

Membership in ACEA is maintained by an annual institutional self-study that describes and evaluates how well the institution has accomplished *its own stated purposes* throughout the past year. I stress "its own stated purposes" because each institution has the liberty to establish its own standards of excellence according to the way it feels God is leading, rather than being evaluated by adherence to standards established by an external accrediting association. Each self-study is read and commented on by two other members of ACEA and returned to the institution. On-site visits by educational consultants approved by ACEA leadership are available by invitation of the institution that desires their services.

Some ACEA member institutions also seek and receive accreditation at their discretion because their primary target audience requires it. However, this does not make them first-class citizens as contrasted to other AECA members who do not need or desire accreditation. One would never characterize the other as a "diploma mill," because all members mutually respect the integrity of the apostles who head up the networks and their ability to hear clearly from God about what their ministry thrust and accompanying training program should look like.

7. GRADUATES ARE EXPECTED TO BE LEADERS. Whereas traditional curricula minor in or even omit leadership training, probably because most pastors are assumed to be employees of the churches they will serve, rather than their leaders, new apostolic curricula major in leadership development. Faculty role models are more than likely successful megachurch pastors rather than scholars. It is more important to them to learn how to lead a church council than to understand the nuances of the Council of Nicea. Interestingly enough, academic and scholarly achievement is not ordinarily a characteristic of leaders in general. I recall reading a survey that indicated that most leaders of Fortune 500 corporations were *B* and *C* students in college.

CONCLUSION

New apostolic networks are, indeed, multiplying ministers. Leadership training is taking new and different forms, as would be expected in a movement characterized by new wineskins. Those who are still training pastors and other church leaders in old wineskin institutions would do well to take notice. It may not be too late to make the adjustments necessary to continue serving the churches of the new millennium.

Notes

1. Lyle E. Schaller, *The Senior Minister* (Nashville: Abingdon Press, 1988), p. 84.

2. Reggie McNeal, "Apostolic Leadership: An Emerging Paradigm," *Ministry Advantage* 6, no. 6 (n.d.), p. 4.

3. Jim Rutz, *The Open Church* (Auburn, Maine: The Seed Sowers, 1992), p. 2.

4. Greg Ogden (from an address to the National Symposium on the Postdenominational Church held at Fuller Seminary, Pasadena, California, May 21-23, 1996).

5. Bill Hamon, *Apostles, Prophets, and the Coming Moves of God* (Shippensburg, Pa.: Destiny Image, 1997), p. 12.

6. Ogden (Postdenominational Symposium).

7. Carl F. George, *Prepare Your Church for the Future* (Grand Rapids: Fleming H. Revell, 1991), p. 155.

8. John Eckhardt in personal correspondence with the author, March 1996.

9. Bill Hamon, "Determining True Ministers by the 10 M's," a conference handout, n.d.

10. Donald E. Miller, "Postdenominational Christianity in the Twenty-First Century," *The Annals of the American Academy of Political and Social Science* (July 1998), p. 197.

11. Ralph Moore, "Equipping Ministry in Search of a Model," *What Shape Tomorrow?* Ralph Moore, ed. (Kaneohe, Hawaii: Straight Tree Publications, 1995), p. 155.

12. McNeal, "Apostolic Leadership," p. 4.

13. John H. Leith, *Crisis in the Church: The Plight of Theological Education* (Louisville, Ky.: Westminster John Knox, 1997), p. 10.

14. Ibid.

15. Thomas C. Oden, *Requiem: A Lament in Three Movements* (Nashville: Abingdon Press, 1995), p. 37.

16. Ibid.

17. Kenneth M. Meyer, "The M. J. Murdock Charitable Trust Review of Graduate Theological Education in the Pacific Northwest," *Faculty Dialogue* (Spring-Summer 1994), p. 179.

18. Ibid.

19. Robert W. Patterson, "Why Evangelicals Have the Biggest Seminaries: And Why They Are in Crisis," *Christianity Today* (January 12, 1998), p. 50.

20. See Ted Haggard, *Primary Purpose* (Orlando, Fla.: Creation House, 1995), pp. 105-118.

21. John and Sylvia Ronsvalle, *Behind the Stained Glass Windows* (Grand Rapids: Baker Books, 1996), p. 156.

CHAPTER TEN

Money?
No Problem!

Cognizant of the risk in starting a chapter about money with a rather mercenary anecdote, I will, nevertheless, begin by talking about honoraria for visiting speakers. Why this is almost a taboo subject, I am not quite sure, but it seems to be. Virtually all my peers speak at places where they expect to receive an honorarium for their ministry. Perhaps the fear of being characterized as mercenary, as opposed to spiritual, keeps many from mentioning it. Or perhaps it can be attributed to the simple fact that, at least for Americans, personal finances are considered to be just about the most private area of our lives.

Although it is not a regular part of my schedule, from time to time I do accept invitations to minister to local congregations in their weekend services. When I began to speak in new apostolic churches not too long ago, I soon discerned a pattern: New apostolic honoraria were considerably higher than honoraria from traditional churches!

For example, a short time ago I spoke in a traditional church one weekend, and then a couple of weeks later I spoke at a new apostolic church. In the traditional church, which had around 5,000 members, I spoke at their Saturday night and two Sunday morning services. As I left, I was handed an honorarium of $300. The new apostolic church, which has about 1,000 members, also had a Saturday night and two Sunday morning services. There I was handed an honorarium of $2,500. So I took out my calculator. At the traditional church I received $100 per service, or less than 1 cent per member. At the new apostolic church,

I received $830 per service, or about $2.50 per member.

Because I wasn't used to this, I said to the new apostolic pastor, "This is too much!"

His reply? "No, it isn't—we want to bless you!"

CHRONIC MONEY PROBLEMS

My first 35 years of ordained ministry were spent in the environment of churches that seemed to have chronic money problems. Out of that grew an assumption that no church has enough money to do what it believes it really ought to be doing. During the past few years, however, I have discovered that there are, in fact, many churches that have relatively few money problems and that seem to be able to do just about everything they want to do.

By this I do not mean that new apostolic churches never experience financial ups and downs. They all do. What I *am* saying is that the downs are comparatively few compared to those found in traditional churches.

For example, John and Sylvia Ronsvalle of Empty Tomb, Inc., published a "State of Church Giving" report in 1995. In it, they reported the results of a survey of 29 traditional denominations and found the following:

+ In 1968 the members gave 3.14% of their income to the church.
+ In 1993 the members gave 2.52% of their income to the church.[1]

Another Empty Tomb report revealed that in the mainline denominations, giving to missions has suffered a much more severe loss than church membership loss. During the period from 1972-1996:

+ The Evangelical Lutheran Church of America lost 1% of their members, but they lost 43.5% of their missions giving.

- The Presbyterian Church (U.S.A.) lost 27% of their members, but they lost 43% of their missions giving.
- The United Methodist Church lost 14% of their members, but they lost 40% of their missions giving.[2]

CHURCHES THAT CAN DO IT

In contrast, let's look at two new apostolic churches that seem to have the money they need to accomplish whatever they perceive God is calling them to do.

CRENSHAW CHRISTIAN CENTER is an African-American church in the inner city of Los Angeles, pastored by Fred Price. When they outgrew their building on Crenshaw Avenue, they purchased the old Pepperdine University campus and built the Faithdome, a worship center that has 10,146 theater seats. The total cost was $26 million, $14 million for the land and $12 million for the building.

I was honored to be invited as a speaker at the three-hour gala dedication service. The grand finale was Fred Price taking the microphone and pulling a letter out of his coat pocket. The letter was from the Security Pacific Bank, and it read "Paid in full"!

LAKEWOOD CHURCH in Houston, Texas, pastored by John Osteen, is a multiethnic church also located in a huge metropolis. It began in 1959 having 234 people and conducted building programs in 1973, 1975, 1977 and 1979 to accommodate the growing congregation. In 1979 they more than doubled the seating capacity. When they outgrew that in 1986, they had 5,000 members. They had thought about moving to a more affluent part of the city, but God told them to build right where they were in a deteriorating community in northeast Houston.

In 1986, Houston was in the middle of a deep recession. The oil crisis had erupted and the city entered a period of economic collapse. When businesses and individuals were going bankrupt, and just two months after Pastor Osteen had undergone open-heart surgery, God spoke to him and said: "Tell the congregation this morning that you are going to build a new sanctuary seating 8,000 and that it will be paid for debt-free in one year. You will know that it is Me and not you!" In one year they moved into their new building debt-free!

Then in 1992, the Lord spoke again to John Osteen to build a $6 million Family Life Center and office building. The Lord said: "Tell the people two things: (1) to be faithful to tithe their income, and (2) obey Me when I tell them to give, and the building will be built debt-free in one year without taking a single offering." It was finished in one year, and paid for in cash without taking one special offering!

John Osteen, who says, "The church is a good investment of your money," teaches that generous givers ordinarily rise on the economic scale.

The result? The church now has more than 15,000 members and has planted new churches all around the Houston area. Their most recent annual budget at the time of this writing is $14.5 million, of which more than $4.5 million goes to missions! John Osteen teaches his people: "The church is a good investment of your money! Don't put your money into dry ground—give it to live works!"

ALSO IN LATIN AMERICA

Similar stories are being told by new apostolic churches in other parts of the world. My wife, Doris, and I were missionaries to Bolivia for 16 years at the beginning of our ministry. The people we worked with were very poor, and we thought that if their churches were going to grow they would need subsidies from North America. Under that policy, which was the general mode of missionary thinking in those days, churches grew very slowly.

Now things are different. The people are still relatively poor, but they are able to meet the money needs for church growth. When Mike Berg and Paul Pretiz did their research on what they call Latin American "grassroots churches" they reported some of their findings on money by using this dialogue:

"'Look at the grassroots churches,' we said. 'Somehow they have captured the enthusiasm of the people so that they really sacrifice for the Lord. Some of them have built enormous buildings, and they are filled with people.'

"'I really can't believe,' replied the Central American pastor of a traditional Protestant group, 'that the poor in these countries are raising the money to construct those churches. They must be getting money from abroad.'"[3]

That Central American pastor is not the only one who has trouble understanding how the New Apostolic Reformation is so well financed.

THE FOUR AXIOMS OF
NEW APOSTOLIC FINANCING

Predictably, the first question that is asked when the funding differences between traditional churches and new apostolic churches surfaces is: How does this happen? Where is all this money coming from? In other words, What are new apostolic churches doing that the rest of us have not been doing? The answer lies in what I call "the four axioms of new apostolic financing."

The first two of the axioms are taught—this is *indoctrination*. The second two axioms are imparted—this is *anointing*. I will use the balance of the chapter to explain these axioms in as much detail as possible.

- ◆ AXIOM 1: Giving Is Expected
- ◆ AXIOM 2: Giving Is Profitable
- ◆ AXIOM 3: Giving Responds to a Vision
- ◆ AXIOM 4: Giving Is Cheerful

AXIOM 1: GIVING IS EXPECTED

Members of new apostolic churches are taught that all good Christians tithe their income. Certainly some Christians are extraordinary, but even just plain ordinary Christians are expected to exhibit certain behavior patterns, including, among others:

+ They attend church regularly;
+ They confess their sins;
+ They are faithful to their spouses;
+ They pray;
+ They tithe their income.

The general principle taught in new apostolic churches is that the first 10 percent of income goes to the local church. Over and above that, *offerings* go either to the local church or to parachurch organizations of choice.

A chief biblical text for this teaching is Malachi 3. I like the way Sam Taylor of Eternal Light Ministries in Bangalore, India, understands giving. Taylor is an apostle heading a network of 3,000 churches. At present, he has 1,900 graduates of his Word of Light Bible School planting churches throughout the resistant areas of North India, Nepal and Bhutan. His goal is to plant 50,000 churches!

ROBBING GOD

In his excellent booklet *Biblical Finances*, Taylor says,

> A precise teaching is found on the subject [of tithes and offerings] in Malachi 3:8-12. Verse eight mentions two types of robbery—robbery of the tithe and robbery of the offering. Verse nine says that there is a curse attached to these two robberies! Is it any wonder that many people suffer because they do not know this truth?
>
> "What are 'tithes' and what are 'offerings'?"

God is so generous that ninety percent of our money is ours, and only ten percent does not belong to us. A tithe is ten percent of the money or salary that we earn. The tithe belongs to the Lord. He receives it from us. We have no hold over it. There is always something in our lives that does not belong to us. This is a spiritual principle. So this leaves us with a remaining ninety percent, which is ours. From this we can determine how much we can give as an offering.[4]

This kind of teaching is rarely heard in traditional churches. As a result, few mainline church members even come close to tithing their income to the church. In 1993, Michael J. Donahue, Patrick McNamara, Charles Zech and Dean Hoge studied the giving patterns of 625 congregations. Among other things, they found:

- The average Catholic household gives $386 per year. If this were a tithe, their annual household income would be $3,860.
- The average Evangelical Lutheran Church of America household gives $746 per year. If this were a tithe, their annual household income would be $7,460.
- The average Presbyterian (U.S.A.) household gives $1,085 per year. If this were a tithe, their annual household income would be $10,850.

Interestingly enough, even some of the more conservative denominations are under par. For example:

- The average Southern Baptist household gives $1,154 per year. If this were a tithe, their annual household income would be $11,540.
- The average Assemblies of God household gives $1,696 per year. If this were a tithe, their annual household income would be $16,960.[5]

Dean Hoge, in analyzing the results of this research, says, "[The study] suggests that both the Catholic and Protestant approaches to stewardship are succeeding at the basic goal of paying the bills and maintaining the operations of the congregation....In my judgment, there are many Christians who think in terms of keeping the place open."[6] By having this mind-set, funds for outreach in the immediate community or for foreign missions or for expansion of any kind are perennially scarce.

THE ANTI-TITHE PHILOSOPHY

Some traditional pastors actually teach *against* the tithe. In their study of mainline and evangelical churches, John and Sylvia Ronsvalle discovered, "There is by no means a clear consensus on the tithe as an accepted standard of stewardship or as an aspect of discipleship." Only 27 percent of the laity and 20 percent of the clergy consider the tithe a minimum standard.

The Ronsvalles go on: "One Baptist leader worried that the tithe was increasingly being promoted through legalism rather than calling people to a grace-filled response." Some contend that stressing duty, obligation, responsibility or discipline does not make sense to our present culture. So they avoid preaching about the tithe.[7]

As I read this, it occurred to me that these same people think nothing of paying sales tax when they make a purchase. Some might respond that this is simply obeying the civil law. True, but they also leave a 10 percent to a 15 percent tip when they eat in a restaurant, and no law says they must. Most of them would feel as if they were robbing the server if they did not tip, and rightly so. Curiously, though, they have no parallel feeling about robbing God.

GOOD STEWARDSHIP

This kind of reasoning is not found among new apostolic pastors or laypeople. They would agree that if you fail to give your tithe, you should confess it as a sin! They are very conscious of the need to be good stewards. Stewardship is a lifestyle, and it involves much more than money. Still, 95 percent of the times "stewardship" is mentioned in churches, it refers specifically to stewardship of money.

George Barna says,

> Clearly, there is a tangible benefit to emphasizing the biblical teachings about money, stewardship and church responsibilities. There is also a benefit to concentrated doses of wisdom about stewardship: Preaching a stewardship series has a much greater and more predictable effect than does preaching unrelated, time-remote stewardship messages throughout the year.[8]

Pastor Bob Russell of the new apostolic-type Southeast Christian Church of Louisville, Kentucky, found that he needed to examine his own attitudes toward preaching stewardship. He went public by writing an article titled "Why I No Longer Back Away from Preaching About Money." He admitted that he shied away from preaching about money, because he did not want to offend influential people in the congregation. In his own words, "The reason I wasn't preaching on stewardship was cowardly; I wanted to please people more than I wanted to please God." After he repented and began doing it, he says, "People really do want to hear what the Bible says about money, because it's a matter close to the heart and such a divisive issue for families."[9]

Russell would agree with George Barna that it is best to do a series. He says, "For the last three or four years, I've used the month of January to teach sermon series on money—giving, earning, spending, and saving it. By consistently speaking to the inescapable way money affects our lives, I am less likely to come across as a fund-raiser."[10]

Has this change paid off? In 1998, Southeast Christian Church had more than 10,000 people in attendance and moved into a brand new 9,100-seat worship center on 108 acres. The package cost $80 million! This seems like an enviable track record for a non-fund-raiser!

PASTORS SET THE EXAMPLE

New apostolic pastors not only teach strongly about generous giving, but they and their families also usually model it. Most of them follow Dan Reiland's advice:

> This may seem basic, but you cannot expect God to bless your efforts to lead your congregation in financial commitment if you and your core leaders are not dedicated tithers. The leadership's personal commitment to tithing and giving will serve as a model to your people, and allow you to share God's truth with integrity.[11]

This is usually not done in secret. In all due humility, many new apostolic pastors have found that they need to communicate their personal giving patterns to the congregation both in word and in deed.

Gerry Giddings of Antioch Churches and Ministries says, "Share that you are giving personally and do it. Pastors lead by example. If it is not important enough for you to give, it will not be important enough for your congregation to give."[12]

George Barna agrees: "The church typically benefits by intentionally providing for the congregation clear indications that their spiritual leaders *believe* in stewardship and *practice* the very principles they teach the congregation."[13]

There is no set rule about how specific a pastor should be about disclosing the details of personal giving habits. King David was detailed when he gave to the construction of the Temple: "Moreover, because I have set my affection on the house of my God, I have given to the house of my God, over and above all that I have prepared for the holy house, my own special treasure of gold and silver: three thousand talents of gold, of the gold of Ophir, and seven thousand talents of refined silver, to overlay the walls of the houses" (1 Chron. 29:3,4). The margin of my Bible says this was worth $3.28 billion! The people followed David's example and they also gave generously (see v. 6).

THE GRADUATED TITHE

I personally became deeply grateful to Ray Ortlund during the time when he was my pastor in Lake Avenue Congregational Church in Pasadena, California. In a memorable sermon in 1976, he said, "I've never done this before, but I sense that God wants me to tell you how much my family gives. Anne and I give 25 percent off the top of all the income we receive!" This changed my life.

Ever since the day we were married, my wife, Doris, and I had faithfully tithed our income. Before Ray Ortlund preached, I was feeling pretty good that we were usually up to 10.8 or 11 percent a year. When Ortlund said *25 percent*, the Lord immediately spoke to us clearly about the graduated tithe. Since then, every year that our income has gone up, we have raised the *percentage*. I don't feel the Lord telling me to disclose the percentage we are now giving, but I will say that we have left the 25 percent behind. In fact, we no longer can deduct from our income tax all that we give because we have passed the IRS limit. Has this hurt? No—we have more discretionary money now than we ever thought we would have or that we feel we deserve!

AXIOM 2: GIVING IS PROFITABLE

Awhile ago I quoted John Osteen as saying, "The church is a good investment of your money." By saying this, he had several things in mind, one of which was that investing your money in God's work will not only be profitable for the kingdom of God, but it will also be profitable for you and your family. He teaches that generous givers ordinarily rise on the economic scale.

This kind of teaching raises red flags in the minds of many Christian leaders because it can open the door for people to give for the wrong motive. The wrong motive is frequently stated: "You give in order to get." As a way of putting this into the proper perspective, Axiom 1 must *precede* Axiom 2. In other words, the primary motive for giving is to obey the will of the Lord. Once we agree to do that, God comes back with some rather astounding promises.

A common teaching in new apostolic churches is that you cannot outgive God. Jesus' teaching in Luke 6:38 is taken literally: "Give, and it will be given to you: good measure, pressed down, shaken together, and running over will be put into your bosom. For with the same measure you use, it will be measured back to you."

Samuel Taylor elaborates on this:

> When Jesus says "give" in Luke 6:38, it means we give from our ninety percent. The ten percent tithe is already the Lord's. We cannot "give" from something that does not belong to us! This "giving" from our ninety percent activates a supernatural power that will bring a return. From this we can again "give" and thereby perpetuate a cycle of "giving" and "receiving." The less we use on ourselves, the more will be available to give! The more we give the more we will receive. Giving will then become a lifestyle.[14]

WHAT ABOUT "PROSPERITY THEOLOGY"?

Some may dismiss Samuel Taylor's teaching by labeling it "prosperity theology." In the minds of some Christian leaders, prosperity theology is supposed to be on the list of dangerous heresies. I believe this came about because some early advocates of prosperity theology, particularly from the Word of Faith Movement, tended to model "prosperity" as *opulence* in a rather distasteful way. Some high-visibility preachers, many of them raised in households far below the median income, began practicing Luke 6:38, and choosing to display their resultant prosperity by public status symbols such as Lincoln automobiles,

Rolex watches, silk tailor-made suits, extravagantly furnished offices, luxury suites in hotels and other similar things.

In my view, the Word of Faith Movement has done a service to the kingdom of God by calling our attention to the dynamic role of faith in the everyday Christian life. It was needed because many of us had fallen into the rut of a watered-down and relatively powerless view of faith. Some of the early advocates, however, tended to go to extremes such as declaring that driving a Rolls Royce was a theological statement.

Going to extremes while reemphasizing a half-forgotten Christian truth is not unusual. Early Calvinists went to extremes with the sovereignty of God, arguing for double predestination, which threatened to develop into a Christian dualism. Early faith healers went to extremes such as choosing not to take medicine or go to the doctor. Early holiness advocates went to extremes and taught complete eradication theology. In all these streams, later generations invariably gravitated toward a more moderate and more biblical position. When all is said and done, we are now grateful for more emphasis than there used to be on God's sovereignty, on praying for the sick and on personal holiness.

A similar thing is happening with later generations of Word of Faith advocates. For example, Samuel Taylor acknowledges that one of his mentors is Kenneth Copeland, a first-generation Word of Faith leader. Here is how Taylor defines prosperity:

> To me, prosperity simply means having more than what I require for myself. Too often we have heard this saying: "I am content in life, I just need enough for my basic needs, and my family needs, nothing more, nothing less." I think this is a selfish statement! It is like saying, "I am not concerned about the needs of others as long as I have enough for myself." If we have only enough for ourselves, then we will never have enough money for God's kingdom or for other people.[15]

Reciprocity with God

The researchers Dean Hoge, Charles Zech, Patrick McNamara and Michael Donahue found that members of churches that taught what they call "reciprocity with God" (a.k.a. "prosperity theology") did, in fact, exhibit a higher level of giving than those from other churches. They also found that traditional church leaders had developed strong theological convictions against such a thing. They say,

> The theological issue of reciprocity with God is both crucial and sensitive. Pastors and theologians of all types have strong feelings about it. *From our research we concluded that churchpeople who believe that God will reciprocate for their monetary gifts tend to give more to their churches.* Hence it is a keen temptation for church leaders in need of financial support to preach about how God rewards givers, even though it flies in the face of long-held theological prohibitions in many denominations (emphasis mine).[16]

Although some new apostolic leaders are bolder in this matter than others, very few would consider it a "keen temptation" to preach a literal interpretation of Luke 6:38 and to declare to their people that generous givers can expect financial rewards from God. This axiom, that giving is profitable, explains to a quite significant extent the answer to the question: Where does all this money in new apostolic churches come from?

Antioch Stewardship Council

I will conclude this section by providing a concrete example from one of our more prominent apostolic networks, Antioch Churches and Ministries. Apostle John Kelly is a strong believer in God's desire to increase the wealth of Christian people and Christian churches. He says,

> To maintain our financial integrity and assist our churches in financial matters, we have created the

Antioch Stewardship Council (ASC). ASC provides individuals with financial services in the following areas: accounting, budgets, taxes, mutual funds, financial planning, mortgages, trusts, pensions, IRAs, CDs, and insurance.[17]

To illustrate, here are some quotes from the Antioch Stewardship Council brochure:

♦ You may be like many who live pay check to pay check with no plan and no financial activity other than just trying to get by.
♦ God wants you to be financially free so you can put Him first in your life and be sensitive to His voice, ready to follow Him whenever—and wherever—He leads. If this is God's plan, why do many Christians live in financial bondage?
♦ Financial freedom means having enough to provide adequately for your household and to give generously and joyfully to God's work.
♦ Like planting good seed in fertile ground, your task as a steward is to seek the greatest possible return for the sake of God's kingdom. You do not appraise good stewardship by the amount of your gifts, but by how wisely you invest your resources.
♦ Have you ever had the feeling that you seem to be on a financial treadmill? You are working harder, yet getting farther behind. Your checking account seems to have sprung a leak.
♦ At ASC we would love to offer you a blueprint for investments that will most likely make you money.
♦ We provide consistent Bible-based stewardship principles of tithes, offerings, and good financial concepts reinforced through informational seminars, pulpit ministry, and practical individual plans.[18]

AXIOM 3: GIVING RESPONDS TO A VISION

As a reminder, Axioms 1 and 2 are taught. Axioms 3 and 4, on the other hand, are *imparted*, not *indoctrinated*. When I say that "giving responds to a vision," it is the vision of the senior pastor imparted to the congregation that produces the abundant funding.

THE PLIGHT OF DENOMINATIONAL PROGRAMS

The traditional alternative to giving as people's response to a vision is giving to support a program. Especially among baby boomers, giving to denominational programs such as a "benevolence program" or a "missions program" is losing appeal.

John and Sylvia Ronsvalle studied the giving patterns of 29 mainline and evangelical denominations during the period 1968-1993. They report, "Trends of giving as a percentage of income in both evangelical and mainline Protestant churches are in a downward direction, although evangelicals continue to give at a higher rate than mainline denominations."[19]

The Ronsvalles found that in all denominations almost all the available income is used for maintenance of the current operations, not for advance. They add:

> Although many evangelical churches have continued to add members since the late 1960s, should that rate of membership growth stall, indications are that evangelicals would be facing denominational funding crises similar to those that have been highly publicized among mainline denominations.[20]

This traditional denominational funding crisis relates directly to the matter of vision or lack of it. The Ronsvalles say,

> There seems to be little doubt that churches today do not have a strong vision around which to rally their financial giving. In the Stewardship Project survey, 81 percent of the pastors and 94 percent of the regional

officials agreed, "Congregations do not have a clear overarching vision with which to challenge their members to improve their stewardship."[21]

THE STRONG APPEAL OF LOCAL CHURCH VISION

Why is it that many traditional churches lack this overarching vision? A principal reason is that they insist on using democratic principles to govern their churches. In analyzing the leadership style of new apostolic pastors in chapter 4, I inserted a section "What Happened to Democracy?" The answer is that, in this day and age, democracy, strictly applied, can turn out to be a dysfunctional form of church government for aggressive growth and expansion. It may work well for maintenance, but for little else.

The study about church giving conducted by Dean Hoge, Charles Zech, Patrick McNamara and Michael Donahue included Assemblies of God, Southern Baptists, Evangelical Lutheran Church of America and Roman Catholics. Four of their initial working hypotheses were unsupported by subsequent research, one of which had to do with democratic procedures. They say,

> At the outset we believed that democratic procedures encouraged giving. This premise was based on the fact that Catholic parishes are less democratic and have a lower level of giving. Some Catholic writers have argued that adopting more democratic processes in parish governance would encourage higher giving. Our study found governance to be only a secondary factor, however. What is crucial is trust in leadership, in whoever actually has the power in the congregation, whether clergy or lay leaders.[22]

The researchers' major example came from the observation that giving levels in Assemblies of God churches was notably higher than in the other three. They then said,

Assemblies of God congregations are not very democratic. Even though some have pro forma elections of
lay officers, the clergy greatly influence the selection
of candidates for office. The ministers run the
churches, and everyone accepts this situation as proper.
Yet the level of giving is high.[23]

What is the problem with democracy? The problem is that
dynamic vision casting is replaced by Pablum, plain-vanilla,
least-common-denominator programs for the church. Among
the parishoners, especially baby boomers, motivation for giving
to support such programs is virtually nil. What motivation
remains for giving largely emerges from a sense of obligation to
provide minimal, status-quo maintenance of the institution.

THE CRUCIAL ROLE OF THE PASTOR

In new apostolic churches, as I have said again and again, a high
level of trust is placed in the leadership of the senior pastor.
The expected role of the pastor is to cast the vision for the
church and take personal responsibility for the finances to
implement the vision. The financial responsibility is not delegated to a finance committee or a business manager, as is frequently the case in traditional churches. One traditional pastor
I know makes a practice of having all platform reports and
appeals for finances done by laypeople while he remains in the
background. The church, predictably, suffers chronic financial
shortages.

One of the strongest appeals for vision to promote giving
comes from George Barna. He says,

People gravitate to a compelling vision of tomorrow.
One reason many churches struggle to raise money is
that their leaders fail to effectively cast vision for the
future. Robert Schuller of the Crystal Cathedral in
Garden Grove planted his church in Southern
California and guided it from zero to huge. He then

became the most-watched television preacher in America. He conceived the glass cathedral in which his church worships. During the course of his four-decade ministry, he has raised more than $500 million. The secret? "In order to raise money, you have to have a bold vision. It has to be dramatic and exciting. No one has a money problem—only an idea problem."[24]

An important part of the training programs for new apostolic pastors, as contrasted to traditional seminaries, is whole courses in their schools of ministry about how to cast vision. It is not left to chance. Although George Barna does not specify new apostolic churches, he reflects their mind-set accurately when he says,

> Vision motivates people to action. The people who develop an unwavering sense of commitment to a ministry are most often those who have been exposed to God's vision for the ministry of the church. When the church's leaders are vision driven, they minister with an unusually high degree of spiritual depth and strength of conviction. Such focus and intensity is attractive to most donors.[25]

Gerry Giddings, a new apostolic pastor, gives this advice to colleagues who want to maximize their offering: "Share the vision behind the offering. How will this offering help to fulfill the vision and the mission of the church or network? If there is no vision and mission statement in your church—get one! Get it from God and write it down and run with it."[26]

THE PASTOR KNOWS THE SHEEP

Most traditional pastors make it an explicit policy never to look at the giving records of their people. They argue that if they knew the giving records, they might be tempted, even inadvertently, to show favoritism to the most generous givers. They like to quote Jesus' story of the widow's mite to reinforce their position. In their minds, sometimes those who give the least might be the most faithful in God's eyes.

Here is the concern as John and Sylvia Ronsvalle uncovered it in their research:

> Although more than three-quarters of the pastors and regional officials responding to the Stewardship Project survey agreed that "the pastor's knowledge of what individual members give to the church can be a helpful assessment tool of individual members' spiritual health," more than three-quarters of them also agreed that "most church members do not want the pastor to know how much individual members contribute to the church." Knowledge of giving may be a helpful spiritual tool, but it is not one readily available to most pastors.[27]

New apostolic pastors generally do not think that way. I was trained in the traditional mind-set in seminary, and I assumed it was correct until my friend John Wimber broke the mold. I was talking to John soon after he had founded the Anaheim Vineyard Christian Fellowship, which was well on its way to becoming a megachurch.

John said, "If someone in my church comes to me with a suggestion as to the direction of the church, the first thing I do is to look up their giving records."

I said, "Why?"

He replied, "It is very important to me to know where their *heart* is before I know how much weight to attach to their suggestion. How can I tell where their heart is? Jesus said that where your *treasure* is, there your heart is also!"

John Wimber is joined by most other new apostolic pastors in concluding that giving to a cause is a biblical measuring scale for commitment to that cause. In their minds, the amount, of course, is proportionate to the income level of their church members. How do they know the income level? It is simple. A good pastor knows the sheep.

A LITMUS TEST FOR LEADERSHIP

Recently, I was having breakfast with three new apostolic megachurch pastors from various parts of the country. I asked about accessing their church members' giving records, and all three of them did. They looked at me as if to say, "Why are you asking such an obvious question?" I then went on and asked them how they used the information.

- ◆ Two of the three receive printouts each Monday of those who gave generously the day before. One asks for a list of those who gave $1,000 or more and the other of those who gave $2,500 or more. These individuals receive special attention.
- ◆ One uses it for counseling. If the records seem to indicate that an individual or a family is not tithing, the pastor calls them in and talks to them about it. When I asked, "Why?" the pastor said, "Because they are under a curse [referring to Malachi 3:9], and my job as a pastor is to help break any curse my people might be under."
- ◆ All of them use it as a litmus test for lay leadership in the church. Individuals who are not generous in tithes and offerings are disqualified for leadership roles. Each of them said that all other new apostolic pastors they are aware of would agree on this point.
- ◆ One uses it to recognize and honor large donors. Every year the church hosts a special banquet for their "Gideon's Army," meaning their 300 largest donors.

CONTRIBUTING TO PARACHURCH MINISTRIES

This last item—recognition of large donors—is a reminder of the important matter of donations to parachurch organizations. I heard one traditional megachurch pastor strongly scold his church members for being generous to parachurch ministries while they were being stingy to their local church. This was one of those churches that did not allow the pastor to inspect the giving records.

Why is it that many church members are more generous to parachurch ministries than to their own church? There are two major reasons:

1. *Parachurch ministries have a focused vision on a specific vital task.* George Barna says, "The distribution of funds among these kinds of ministries often indicates the areas of ministry these donors believe are inadequately addressed in their church. Many of these parachurch donors would give their money to their church if they believed their church was doing a good job in a similar ministry."[28]

2. *Parachurch leaders recognize and honor their most significant financial partners in ministry.* For years, I have been leading a parachurch ministry. I see a photocopy of every check that comes in to support the work, and I pray blessings on each donor, large and small. However, I pay special attention to the large donors. I flag them and they receive a personal telephone call. We say, "How can we pray for you?" The upshot is that each one of them is assured that I, as president, know their names and appreciate the crucial role they have in our ministry. I do not take them for granted. I have heard that the couple who founded one of our large parachurch ministries in the United States personally spends a week a year in a luxury resort hosting its million-dollar donors!

The problem is that very few pastors pay this kind of attention to their donors. This surfaced in George Barna's research, and he says,

> In the local church [our high-touch culture] is translated in the hearts of donors knowing they count as

individuals, not just as faceless sources of money facilitating the conduct of worthwhile ministry activity. Most church donors desire accessibility to the thrones of power within the church—starting with, but not limited to, the senior pastor. Having the ability to converse with key decision makers and ministry leaders...is a major plus in the eyes of the donor.[29]

HOW PRIVATE SHOULD GIVING BE?

Just as a concluding thought, why should giving be more private than other aspects of life? Almost every experienced pastor has counseled church members about substance abuse, lust, homosexuality, lying or other personal concerns. John and Sylvia Ronsvalle cut to the very heart of the matter in a convincing way:

> The issue of the pastor knowing or not knowing what people give is controversial, both at the lay and the ministerial levels. Some pastors resist knowing because, they say, they are afraid it will influence their treatment of parishoners. In one Stewardship Project workshop, a pastor challenged his colleague on this point. "Do you feel that you can treat parishoners fairly when some share personal moral aberrations with you? Why, then, would information about their giving practices have an inordinate influence over you?"[30]

AXIOM 4: GIVING IS CHEERFUL

Almost all preachers I know, both traditional and new apostolic, frequently quote Paul's remark, "God loves a cheerful giver" (2 Cor. 9:7). Few, however, can go on to claim that in their churches giving is fun. In most churches, giving is about as exciting as brushing your teeth in the morning or enduring stop-and-go traffic on the freeway.

This axiom is another impartation. If the pastor loves to give and displays that characteristic to the people in whatever way, it becomes contagious. One of my memorable experiences in church was the first time I had attended a Sunday service at Portland Bible Temple in Portland, Oregon, now called City Bible Church. Things were going well. I thought the service was exciting and uplifting.

Then it came time for Pastor Frank Damazio to say, in an upbeat voice, "Folks, it's time for us to give our tithes and offerings to the Lord!" I could not believe the cheering, yelling, clapping and whistling that broke out in the congregation when he said that. Everybody was ecstatic that they could now give some money! It was the highest point of the meeting up till then. Predictably, when the noise had finally died down and the offering had been taken, the offering plates were heaped to overflowing!

This was a first for me, but the same thing, apparently, is happening in many other churches as well. LaMar Boschman has seen it enough to consider it a trend. He says, "I have really enjoyed a trend I've seen in several churches recently. When the offering is announced, the congregation breaks into applause, symbolizing their joy in worshipping the Lord through giving."[31]

Dan Reiland tells of an unusual experience in a church service in Africa where he had been invited to preach. He says,

> When the time came for the offering, I discovered that the most important part of their service wasn't the American guest speaker, but the celebration of giving gifts to God. The offering lasted nearly a full hour. Throughout this festival of worship and giving, ushers stayed up front and counted money as it came in. Not enough yet? They just passed the plates again, until they had what they needed![32]

The Power of Personal Testimonies

Many new apostolic churches have discovered that a good way to increase cheerfulness in giving is to feature testimonies of givers who have good reasons to be cheerful. Bob Russell does so in his 10,000-member Southeast Christian Church in Louisville, Kentucky, and he says, "Advertisers know that nothing is as powerful as the personal testimony. We use them as often as possible."[33]

My favorite book discussing the new apostolic perspective about giving is Morris Cerullo's *Giving and Receiving*. His concluding chapter, "Givers Today," contains 25 personal testimonies of cheerful givers. I want to share the one by Mr. and Mrs. Donald Wilsie:

> We first met Dr. Cerullo nearly thirty years ago in Casper, Wyoming, where we pastored a church before Donald was injured in a car wreck and disabled. Morris asked us to give $300 and Donald pledged to do this. In the following months and years we lost contact with the ministry of Dr. Cerullo and for thirty years we did not fulfill the pledge. Two months before the Chicago Partners' Seminar in 1992, some dear friends sent us information about Dr. Cerullo.
>
> Our financial situation was terrible. We had no money, but God provided finances for us to go to the seminar—and we took with us $300 finally to fulfill our pledge. We were giving all we had.
>
> Incredibly, our small business began to grow rapidly. We had been at zero balance, but in seven weeks we showed a $200,000 balance.
>
> Donald was also healed of diabetes. He had been taking medication for years, but was able to quit the medication. Donald knew that God had healed him.
>
> Three months after the Chicago meeting, we put $17,000 in the offering. We had gone from barely being able to give a twenty-eight year old $300 pledge to being able to contribute $17,000...God has blessed us with both a brand new van and a truck. We also

bought a new home—even though the offer we made to the sellers was ridiculous.[34]

"IT'S OFFERING TIME—HALLELUJAH!"

I wish you could have been with me a few months ago when I attended a service in Kingdom Faith Church in Horsham, England. My previous experiences in England had been in churches that seemed to be characterized by a gloomy attitude toward finances. Poverty seemed to be equated with piety in some of them. Now I was in one of England's highest-profile new apostolic churches where 1,500 members would congregate weekly in a newly renovated warehouse building.

The worship was upbeat. It was truly "plugged-in worship," as I have described it earlier. High praise had invited the presence of the Holy Spirit, and He had accepted the invitation. Then came the time for Pastor Colin Urquhart to announce the offering.

The congregation was on its feet. The words flashed across the screen in the front of the church, and 1,500 people read them in unison, the volume and pitch increasing with just about each line. Here is what we shouted at almost the top of our lungs:

As we give today's offering, we are believing the Lord for:
Jobs or better jobs
Raises and bonuses
Benefits
Sales and commissions
Settlements
Estates and inheritances
Interest and income
Rebates and returns
Checks in the mail
Gifts and surprises
Finding money
Bills paid off
Debts demolished
Royalties received
It's offering time—hallelujah!!

By the time we had finished, you would think the British soccer team had won the World Cup. The congregation was cheering and applauding as if they were out of control. The offering was amazing!

It is understandable why in Kingdom Faith Church they say, "Money? No problem!"

Notes

1. *Los Angeles Times*, 9 March 1996, sec. B, p. 4.
2. *Charisma* (March 1997), p. 25.
3. Mike Berg and Paul Pretiz, *Spontaneous Combustion: Grass-Roots Christianity, Latin American Style* (Pasadena, Calif.: William Carey Library, 1996), p. 187.
4. Samuel A. Taylor, *Biblical Finances* (Bangalore, India: Eternal Light Ministries, 1994), pp. 30, 31.
5. *Los Angeles Times*, 9 March 1996, sec. B, p. 4.
6. Ibid.
7. John and Sylvia Ronsvalle, *Behind the Stained Glass Windows: Money Dynamics in the Church* (Grand Rapids: Baker Books, 1996), pp. 188, 189.
8. George Barna, *How to Increase Giving in Your Church* (Ventura, Calif.: Regal Books, 1997), p. 93.
9. Bob Russell, "Taming Money Fears: Why I No Longer Back Away from Preaching About Money," *Leadership* (Spring 1996), pp. 95, 96.
10. Ibid., p. 96.
11. Dan Reiland, "Four Steps to Increasing Your Tithes and Offerings," *The Pastor's Coach*, Injoy (May 1996), p. 1.
12. Gerry Giddings, "Maximizing the Offering," *The Networker* (April 1997), p. 10.
13. Barna, *How to Increase Giving in Your Church*, p. 152.
14. Taylor, *Biblical Finances*, p. 33.
15. Ibid., p. 9.
16. Dean R. Hoge, Charles E. Zech, Patrick McNamara and Michael J. Donahue, "Who Gives to the Church and Why," *Christian Century* (December 4, 1996), p. 1196.
17. John Kelly, "Antioch Churches and Ministries," *The New Apostolic Churches*, C. Peter Wagner, ed. (Ventura, Calif.: Regal Books, 1998), p. 38.
18. Antioch Stewardship Council, 7018 Baker Blvd., Richland Hills, TX 76118; Fax 817-595-8884.
19. Ronsvalle, *Behind the Stained Glass Windows*, p. 52.
20. Ibid., pp. 52, 53.
21. Ibid., p. 53.
22. Hoge, et. al., "Who Gives to the Church and Why," p. 1194.
23. Ibid.
24. Barna, *How to Increase Giving in Your Church*, p. 110.

25. Ibid., pp. 110, 111.

26. Giddings, "Maximizing the Offering," p. 10.

27. Ronsvalle, *Behind the Stained Glass Windows*, p. 133.

28. Barna, *How to Increase Giving in Your Church*, p. 115.

29. Ibid., p. 34.

30. Ronsvalle, *Behind the Stained Glass Windows*, pp. 133, 134.

31. LaMar Boschman, *A Heart of Worship* (Orlando, Fla.: Creation House, 1994), p. 50.

32. Reiland, "Four Steps to Increasing Your Tithes and Offerings," p. 1.

33. Russell, "Taming Money Fears," p. 96.

34. Morris Cerullo, *Giving and Receiving* (Robertsbridge, England: Battle Books, 1995), pp. 166, 167.